STUDIES IN SOVIET HISTORY AND SOCIETY
General Editor: R.W. Davies

The series consists of works by members or associates of the interdisciplinary Centre for Russian and East European Studies of the University of Birmingham, England. Special interests of the Centre include Soviet economic and social history, contemporary Soviet economics and planning, science and technology, sociology and education.

Series Standing Order

If you would like to receive future titles in this series as they
are published, you can make use of our standing order
facility. To place a standing order please contact your
bookseller or, in case of difficulty, write to us at the address
below with your name and address and the name of the
series. Please state with which title you wish to begin your
standing order. (If you live outside the UK we may not have
the rights for your area, in which case we will forward your
order to the publisher concerned.)

Standing Order Service, Macmillan Distribution Ltd,
Houndmills, Basingstoke, Hampshire, RG21 2XS, England.

The Rise and Fall of the Soviet Rural Communist Party, 1927–39

Daniel Thorniley

M

MACMILLAN
PRESS

in association with the
CENTRE FOR RUSSIAN AND
EAST EUROPEAN STUDIES
UNIVERSITY OF BIRMINGHAM

First published 1988

Published by
THE MACMILLAN PRESS LTD
Houndmills, Basingstoke, Hampshire RG21 2XS
and London
Companies and representatives
throughout the world

Filmsetting by Vantage Photosetting Co. Ltd
Eastleigh and London

British Library Cataloguing in Publication Data
Thorniley, Daniel
The rise and fall of the Soviet rural
Commmunist Party, 1927–39.—(Studies in
Soviet history and society)
1. Kommunisticheskaia partiia Sovetskogo
Souiza—History 2. Soviet Union—Politics
and government—1917–1936 3. Soviet Union—
Politics and government—1936–1953
I. Title II. University of Birmingham *Centre for
Russian and East European Studies* III. Series
324.247'075 JN6598.K7
ISBN 0–333–385144–4

To Maureen with love

Contents

List of Tables

x

List of Figures

List of Appendices

Acknowledgements

My most important acknowledgement for assistance in completing this book is to my editor and colleague Professor Bob Davies, Centre for Russian and East European Studies (CREES), University of Birmingham, who has also nursed this work through the earlier stage of a doctoral thesis. I owe him thanks for his many constructive and incisive criticisms, his frequent helpful advice and especially for his unstinting and meticulous care and attention throughout the long preparatory stages. Dr Steve Wheatcroft, also of CREES, made helpful comments on a number of draft chapters for which I am grateful. It goes without saying that any remaining faults or omissions are mine entirely. I would also like to express my thanks to Jenny Brine, librarian of CREES, for her numerous commissions on my behalf and to the staff of the Bodleian Library, Oxford. A longstanding debt is also owed to my parents and to Mr William Pearson, an early mentor, for having given me a helpful hand on the road to academic study. My final debt of gratitude is to my wife Maureen who has been a constant source of support and happiness over many years and has shown so much understanding and forbearance during my work.

DANIEL THORNILEY

Introduction

This study seeks to assist our understanding of the Soviet communist party, the most crucial institution in the Soviet political system, by examining the party in the countryside during the inter-war years, with special reference to its size, membership, organisation and functional role.[1] Our work concentrates on the lower, grass-roots level of the party, in particular on the district committee (*raikom*) and cell, although the affairs of superior party bodies – the regional party committees (*kraikoms/obkoms*) and Central Committee (C.C.) – are not entirely neglected and discussed when relevant. The reason for this emphasis is that there already exist some adequate studies of party organisation at the centre during the 1930s.[2] More importantly it is also the case that the fulfilment of organisational reforms was more straightforward in the political centres, whereas this was less so at the grass-roots where cadres were invariably less reliable and control less secure: here the gap between organisational theory and practice was wider, the achievement of any sort of praxis more problematic.

Major themes of this study include: (1) the Soviet rural communist party was in large part an organisation with an urban background and ideology superimposed upon the rural scene; (2) the rural communist party was not properly prepared for collectivisation which resulted in severe complications, stresses and strains later; (3) the rural party membership and structure were greatly transformed as this weak, ill-prepared body sought to adapt to the demands and rigours made upon it; (4) a major trauma for the rural population and the rural party membership was the failed grain procurement campaigns of 1931–32 and the ensuing famine; (5) the rural party 'rose' during the years of the first Five Year Plan period, 1929–32, and it 'declined' during the years of the second Five Year Plan, 1933–37, a feature which can be explained in part by some of the preceding points. When these themes are fully elucidated they support to a large degree the hypothesis that the Soviet (rural) communist party was not an efficient, monolithic, totalitarian machine capable of manipulating the rural population at will.

The rural party, and by this we mean communists in cells and groups located in rural production centres, villages, rural settlements and rural *raion* centres, was an organisation, designed over a period of time, to facilitate and achieve social, political and economic change and improvement.[3] It was a body that developed through several stages and

1

we take trouble to clarify what the various stages were in its evolution and what were its goals, dictated by the political centre, at each of these stages. In simplified diagrammatic form this development may be depicted as in Table I.1.

It is the object of this study to analyse and to explain the foregoing shifts in the rural party that accompanied the trends and events in society. To assist in this end the work is divided into three major chronological sections: the first dealing with the period up to 1929 is presented as background to enable the reader to make the necessary comparisons with ensuing periods (Chapter 1); the second, encompassing the years 1929–32, represents the core of the study and brings together most of the work's central themes (Chapters 2–6); the third part portrays the decline of the rural party, suggests reasons why this happened, cites reasons why the authorities were able to dispense with the services of the rural party and states what institutions took over the party's role (Chapters 7–12).

In terms of chapters, we embark upon our project in the following manner. Chapter 1 provides some selective background material on the Soviet countryside in the 1920s, and examines the rural party membership and organisation prior to mass collectivisation. It argues that the party in the countryside was little involved in production questions, and

Table I.1   Stages in the development, membership, organisation and objectives of the Soviet rural communist party, 1917–41

Chronological period (some overlapping)	Trends in size of membership	Level of sophistication of party organisation	Objective
1917–21	growth	non-existent/ very basic	*modus vivendi*
1921–24	decline/ stagnation	basic-simple	*modus vivendi*
1924–27	rapid growth	simple-developing	*modus vivendi*
1927–29	stagnation	simple-developing	change and rupture
1929–32	rapid growth	very complex	societal transformation
1932–38	huge decline	simplified	consolidation/ *modus vivendi* (modified)
1938–41	renewed growth	developing	*modus vivendi* (modified)

poorly prepared in terms of size, organisational sophistication and psychology to assist greatly, or as much as the authorities wished, in societal transformation. It is suggested that the 1928 grain crisis acted as a turning point in the way the local authorities and rural communists behaved. It is felt that this introductory chapter is essential for comparative purposes to highlight future changes in the rural party during the 1930s.

Chapter 2 is a brief selective introduction to the core of the study. It is concerned predominantly with placing the rural communist party in the context of some of the most important, relevant, political, social and especially economic trends and developments. Chapter 3 examines in some depth the rural party membership during the first Five Year Plan. Emphasis is placed on the effects of the 1929–30 purge, the recruitment policies implemented and the resultant effects for rural party membership size and composition. A case study is made of the rural communists' entry into the collective farms, where it is argued that communists acted as a vanguard to the peasantry, for reasons which are adumbrated. Following this is an analysis of how communists were employed in the countryside and of the campaigns to direct them to involvement in production processes. A major question which now arises is how well the authorities were able to keep in control of the expanding membership in the sense of processing, training and directing it to desired goals. This question is treated explicitly and implicitly continuously throughout. Chapter 4 highlights the crucial position and important role of the rural party district committee (*raikom*). This chapter begins by placing the *raikom* in the organisational framework, a point to which it returns later with a discussion of the *raikom* superiors: the *obkoms* and *kraikoms*. The *raikoms'* development in 1928–29 into becoming the key middle-level party link is traced briefly. Another case study is made of the problematic, if not failed transfer of party and non-party personnel from the abolished *okrug* administrative units to the *raions*, a transfer designed to strengthen considerably the latter. This serves as one of several examples of how recalcitrance at the local levels by party members could undermine or defeat the authorities' objectives. As with other chapters devoted to organisational aspects, included here is an examination of the relevant party personnel: the *raikom* secretaries, heads of *raikom* departments and the size of the *raikom* apparatus in different regions at different times. Chapter 5 deals with the rural party cells, their numbers, deployment, internal organisation and personnel. Major topics include: the turn to production of the cells, from being based predominantly in villages and Soviets to centring themselves on the production units of *kolkhozy* (collective farms), *sovkhozy* (state farms) and MTS (machine tractor stations); the increased sophistication in internal cell structure, as some cells expanded in size and took on more responsibilities, and relevant to this the debate about the intermediary link between *raikom* and cell, which is taken up with a detailed consideration of the cell structure known as support points; attention is also focused on the sub-cell units of party groups and individual party organisers which proliferated in the latter half of the first Five Year Plan; once again, a section of this chapter examines party personnel working in this instance at the cell and sub-cell levels. Chapter 6 differs from the two preceding chapters concerned principally with organisation and personnel, and yet is a logical extension of them in that it depicts how the organisation was put to use in the operations of collectivisation, dekulakisation and the collections of agricultural produce; it also depicts other ordinary day-to-day activities of a mass cultural – political nature. Great attention is paid to the part of rural communists in the procurement campaigns of 1931 and 1932 and to how they were blamed in large part for the failures and singled out unfairly it seems for punishment. The extraordinary purges of 1932–33 in the southern regions are treated in this chapter, whereas later purges and the ramifications of these events are dealt with in subsequent chapters. The events of 1932 are singled out as the key turning point in the rural communist party's fortunes. A major preoccupation for us is how the rural communists responded to pressure in 1931 and 1932, and also in the late 1920s.

Chapter 7 is an introductory, linking chapter which provides relevant background material on the second Five Year Plan period. Chapter 8 discusses how the authorities responded to the 1932 rural economic crisis with emergency measures including the political departments in 1933–34. We examine their background, composition, activities and their at times difficult relations with the regular party network. Chapter 9 assesses the impact of the various purges and screenings of party members, expecially those of 1933 and 1934. Data are collated on the reasons given for expulsion and the traditional interpretation on this matter is questioned. The full extent of purge losses in the rural party compared with the party as a whole is brought out and the damage inflicted on the *kolkhoz* party membership and rural communists in the southern regions, where grain procurements had been particularly problematic in 1932, is highlighted. Much of this is related to and a consequence of the events depicted in Chapters 6 and 8. The rebuilding of the party membership in the post-1937 years is also looked at briefly.

Chapter 10 examines the developments in the rural party network during the second Five Year Plan: the major reorganisation beginning in June 1933 and the problems that arise in explaining its rationale; the consequences of the purges for the rural cell network; the breakdown in cell size with the consequent sharp rise in the number of single communists (those not attached to any party cell); and the increase in cell numbers in the years immediately prior to the war. In Chapter 11 we return to an examination of the *raikom*, how it changed in size and composition as the political department staff were incorporated into the regular party network at the beginning of 1935, and how the *raikoms* adapted to the different environment of the second Five Year Plan compared with the more turbulent first Five Year Plan period. Chapter 12 considers how the rural party operational role changed during 1934–39 from that of the first Five Year Plan and looks at this role in perspective from the 1920s until the outbreak of the war. By looking briefly at the rural party in the 1920s in an earlier chapter and by making brief references to the post-1939 period in the final chapters, we are able to see the rural communist party in perspective during the inter-war years and to make meaningful comparisons with the main chronological period of our work, 1927–39.

In trying to reinterpret some important issues and to emphasise problems rather than solutions, many negative aspects of Soviet programmes in the countryside are revealed; this is not to say that we are unaware of some of the successes in fulfilling the authorities' plans, and we have taken several opportunities, where appropriate, to mention and stress successes so as to counter-balance the underlying thread of much of our argument. In seeking to reassess issues, there nearly always arises this danger of overemphasising one's principal hypotheses. Our study also raises another difficult question: how did the Soviet regime function without an efficient, pervasive, dominant vanguard communist party in the majority of the country's geographical area and among the mass of its population? Such a question raises issues in the sphere of the role and purpose of political parties generally, particularly in Marxist regimes and developing countries. We have touched upon this issue, and discussed why the authorities relinquished even the attempt to do something about this in the years 1934–37, but further empirical study of the Soviet communist party in other spheres of life, urban and rural, is required, as well as an examination of other organisations and institutions, in isolation and in their relation to the party: these would include the *komsomol*, the Soviets, the trade unions, the grain procurement and law enforcement agencies among others.

1 The 1920s: The Soviet Communist Party and the Rural Scene

BACKGROUND

The Bolsheviks at the time of the 1917 revolutions were an urban party whose ideology was founded on Marxism and who came to power in the proletarian centre of Petrograd: Russia in 1917 was predominantly a peasant country. The peasant's outer limits were traditionally the commune and village, which he regarded as his own world: Moscow and the state appeared remote and alien.[1] By the time of the revolution this alienation had abated somewhat. With the rise of Russian industry in the 1890s, peasants increasingly undertook seasonal work in the towns (*otkhodniki*), were often employed in construction work and increasingly engaged in trade, and during the world war and the civil war many of them served in the tsarist and Red armies.

The Bolsheviks were faced with the problem of backwardness in peasant Russia. For Trotsky the effects of social and economic backwardness and an economic development in Russia distorted from the standard Marxist model were integral to his theory of Permanent Revolution. If backwardness could be a positive factor in the permanency of the revolution, then Trotsky and other Bolshevik leaders realised that after the successful proletarian revolution this backwardness could only retard and even endanger the future development of Soviet society along socialist lines: 'The agrarian problem in Russia is a heavy burden to capitalism: it is an aid to the revolutionary party and at the same time its greatest challenge'.[2] The party could not envisage any way of avoiding the consequences of backwardness without the revolution becoming international. But this was not to be, and the Soviet Union developed uncertainly for some ten years before drastic measures were adopted to square the peasant circle.

The Bolsheviks appreciated that without peasant support, or at least neutrality, it was improbable that the regime would be able to surmount the economic difficulties which were a legacy of war, German invasion and international isolation. Bolshevik legislation in the form of the

6

Decree on Land of 26 October 1917 and the Law of the Socialisation of the Land dated 19 February 1918 allowed for the survival of the agrarian commune (*mir*)[3] and promulgated the principle of equal rights to the land and its distribution according to consumer standards (that is according to the size of households and number of mouths to feed). It would have been political suicide for the Bolsheviks to have gone against peasant wishes at this stage, presented with a fait accompli by a peasantry which had already seized much land. By 1920, after the upheaval and carnage of the Civil War, the Bolsheviks were still less in a position to bring about a radical transformation in the political–economic relationships in the countryside. The party and the country were exhausted. The widespread disorders of 1920 were expressions of peasant discontent with the expropriation of agricultural surpluses (*prodrazverstka*) employed during War Communism. These emergency measures, once the Civil War reached its end, were in obvious need of replacement by some medium-term economic strategy.

On 21 March 1921, Lenin's proposals to this end were adopted. Requisitioning was replaced by a grain tax and cultivators were permitted to dispose of their after-tax surplus in local exchange.[4] During the next few years, when social differentiation was increasing but stood at a level lower than before the revolution, the New Economic Policy (NEP) was consolidated, expanded and refined. The mid-1920s have been rightly described as 'High NEP'.[5] This policy was promoted by Bukharin and Stalin in the course of their arguments with the Left and Leningrad Oppositions. The high water mark of the pro-peasant policy came in the legislation of the fourteenth party conference of April 1925 with decrees which reduced taxation on rural producers and eased limitations on the leasing of land and the hiring of labour.[6] In 1925 the leadership seemed to be relying on NEP to act automatically as a consequence of the concessions made to wealthy peasants. Whether NEP in this interpretation represented an advance to or a retreat from socialism remained a keen debating point within the party throughout the 1920s. It would be incorrect to attempt to explain the various events of the 1920s as elements of a consistent Soviet development strategy. The policy makers failed to resolve the essential problems and responded on an *ad hoc* basis to events and trends occurring in the countryside. In the 1920s the countryside was little advanced on the road to socialisation and hardly prepared for collectivisation.

A factor which cast doubt on the advisability of current policies was the difficulties experienced in obtaining the requisite amount of collections at state designated prices from the 1924–25 harvests. In the

1924 collections the state had to raise its maximum prices.[7] Developments in the grain purchasing from the 1925 harvest were more disconcerting for the regime. The 1925 harvest was comparatively good at 72.5 million tons (a mere 51 million in 1924), but grain deliveries were held up as peasants refused to respond to the lower official prices at a time of consumer goods shortages. The authorities were doubtful of the success of insisting on low prices and were unprepared to resort to administrative measures. Instead plans for other sectors were cut back: grain exports were abandoned and plans to import equipment reduced. Problems with prices and collections were to recur with the 1927 harvest, but the conclusions drawn then were fundamentally different from those of 1925. The need to cut back on industrial expansion came at a most inappropriate moment when so recently the ground plans had been laid at the fourteenth party congress of December 1925. This launching of industrial expansion raised fundamental problems of the relation between the regime and the peasants. A policy of conciliating the well-to-do peasantry, and indeed one that supported the small-producer system, gradually began to appear incompatible with that of intensive industrialisation.

The change in the policy to the countryside was gradual but persistent until the catalyst effect of the 1928 grain procurement crisis. As early as April 1926 modifications to taxation were introduced which represented the beginning of tax pressure on the well-to-do element in the peasantry. An amendment to the criminal code adopted in 1926 'envisaged imprisonment for up to three years with total or partial confiscation of property for those guilty of malicious increases in prices of commodities through purchase, hoarding or non-placing on the market'; this became known as article 107 and was used on a wide scale in 1928–29 to force produce onto the market.[8]

The 1927–28 grain crisis ushered in new ways of thinking which brought an end to NEP. The background and causes of the crisis are well-known and related elsewhere.[9] In response to a hold up in grain deliveries at the turn of the year 1927–28, the party leadership, that is Stalin and his supporters, embarked upon a campaign of 'extraordinary measures'. At the beginning of 1928 grain was seized by invoking article 107 of the criminal code; in some places local sales of grain were prohibited, and free markets closed; fines of five times above the quota amounts not supplied were imposed; *skhod* meetings were pressurised to impose delivery quotas upon the *mir* with disproportionately heavy amounts falling on the *kulaks*; party forces were mobilised to support the grain collection agencies and to supervise many *skhod* meetings. All this represented a physical and psychological leap in the regime's approach to the countryside: 'This was the beginning of the end of NEP'.[10] With the defeat of the Right opposition towards the end of 1928, another variant of the 'extraordinary measures' was employed in the collections from the 1928 harvest.

Further legislation followed in the wake of the grain procurement crisis. The contract system was modified so as to pressurise prosperous peasants to deliver their produce at planned prices. Towards the end of 1928, the attack came from another angle: the Land Code of December 1928 virtually eliminated the legal basis of the peasant's right to land in perpetuity; preferential treatment was promised to *kolkhozy* and important responsibilities transferred from the *mir* to the Soviet. As the authorities were actively undermining the small-producer system, collectivisation gathered momentum in 1929 with the final decision for an all-out drive taken at the November 1929 C.C. plenum. But on reflection the interlude between the emergence of the grain difficulties early in 1928 and the expansion of collectivisation in mid-1929 was largely one of lost opportunities. Little thought was given to any preparation of an alternative policy or of creating 'strategic positions'[11] in the countryside. This intervening period, in particular 1928, has rightly been termed a 'year of drift'.[12]

The dilemmas of party policy were revealed particularly clearly in relation to the collective sector. A prominent characteristic of the regime's approach to the countryside was the absence of a consistent, coherent policy towards agriculture and towards the collective sector in particular. As Moshe Lewin has pointed out, the promotion of the small-producer system in agriculture contrasts with the neglect of the collective sector: 'the leadership had almost completely abandoned the state and collective sectors in the countryside'.[13] When the slow advance of the *kolkhozy* resumed, most of the growth in *kolkhoz* numbers was due to an increase in the *'toz'* (Association for the joint cultivation of land), the least socialised form of collective agriculture.[14] A C.C. resolution of 30 December 1926 listed the shortcomings of the *kolkhozy* as low productivity, poor internal organisation, small size and high turnover of peasant membership, but central policies were not blamed for these failings.[15] The marketing co-operatives were favoured rather than the producer *kolkhozy*. To reconcile these two branches of co-operativism was not easy as the agricultural and credit co-operatives, whose membership was by far the largest, were the bulwark of the well-to-do peasants. Even in the eyes of the co-operative authorities the prosperous peasant seemed a better investment than the poor one.[16] The peasantry in general only seemed interested in receiving state-provided funds as a benefit of co-operation and were reluctant to risk any of their own finances or resources: the traditional peasant individualism did not blend well with the supposed collective spirit of co-operation. Several commentators have pointed out that co-operation was not a springboard to collectivisation and instead served to bolster prosperous peasants, who in the future would be staunch enemies of collectivisation,[17] although it should not be forgotten that a more optimistic view of the potentialities of the co-operatives' role had been held by, amongst others, Bukharin.[18]

The weakness of the collective sector was highlighted by the continued vitality of the *mir* and peasant gathering (*skhod*).[19] On 1 January 1927, of 233 million hectares of peasant land in the RSFSR, 222 million were held in the *mir* system, two million in *khutors*, six million in *otrubs* and only two million in various forms of collective farms.[20] In order to circumvent the commune's authority, the state attempted to breathe life into the rural Soviet network. In theory, the Soviets were to supervise rural administration: in practice, the peasant gathering managed peasant affairs. With few rural Soviets having independent budgets, the peasantry was thrown back on to the gathering, which could meet the financial demands of economic, cultural and social needs through the process of self-taxation. In reality, instead of the Soviet infiltrating and taking over the *mir*, more often a converse process occurred, and the Soviet submitted to the gathering. Rural Soviets were often run solely by a chairman who, in his geographical isolation, was faced with the awesome task of overcoming the inertia or hostility of the local community.

Even after the campaign to revitalise rural Soviets in 1925, the proportion of communists among rural Soviet chairmen actually fell from 26.2 per cent in 1924 to 14.8 per cent in 1925.[21] Rural Soviets were hardly bastions of party and state interests in the countryside. The party layer in the Soviet system at the lower levels was not very significant, prosperous peasants tended to earn respect and election to responsible administrative posts, and Soviet chairmen and delegates very often tried to avoid conflict with the general peasant mood. To counteract the presence in the Soviets of what were seen as potential alien elements, the party saturated the upper echelons of the Soviet hierarchy. In 1927 the party layer among rural Soviet chairmen was 23.8 per cent, 90.1 per cent among chairmen of *volost* executive committees (the basic rural administrative unit) and even among ordinary members of *volost* executive committees it was a substantial 54.7 per cent.[22] But this party saturation of the Soviet hierarchy provided no guarantee that policy was enforced at the lower level.

With a more logical price policy, a better developed co-operative movement, a more adequately maintained state and collective farm sector, there would have been more chance to avoid the serious agricultural crisis which came about in 1928.

THE RURAL COMMUNIST PARTY BEFORE MASS COLLECTIVISATION

The rural party, like the Soviets, co-operatives and *kolkhozy*, was unprepared for the 'great break-through' of 1929, as an examination of its membership, organisation and activities will reveal.

In the development of rural party membership in the years 1921–28, three phases are discernible: 1) neglect and mistrust of the rural party from 1921 to 1923; 2) concern and interest for the size and composition of the rural element in 1924–26; and 3) interest peters out in 1926–28 as greater attention is focused on the proletarianisation of the party as a whole.

The rural wing of the primarily urban Bolsheviks had been traditionally weak; prior to 1917 there appear to have been only four Bolshevik party village cells.[23] At the end of 1919 rural party membership was not more than 60 000, but with subsequent recruitment and as a result of the demobilisation of the peasant army, this figure rose to nearly 200 000 by September 1920.[24] However, the authorities tended to neglect rural party members, did not encourage their party work, nor did they regard rural communists as particularly reliable. The 1921 purge hit the peasants as a class more heavily than any other with expulsions of some 40 per cent of members registered as peasants, as compared with only 16 per cent of workers and 33 per cent of white collar workers.[25] As a result of purging and voluntary withdrawals, the size of the rural party dropped from 200 000 in the autumn of 1920 to 137 000 in early 1924:[26] 'The Soviet regime was thus becoming more rather than less isolated from the peasants in the early 1920s'.[27]

The thirteenth party congress in May 1924 resolved to encourage peasant access to the party. The immediate result was that 23 000 peasants became candidate members in the latter half of 1924 compared with 12 000 in the first half.[28] As a result of further encouragement at the fourteenth party conference in April 1925, the proportion of peasants among new recruits rose from 11 per cent in 1924 to 30 per cent in 1925 and 39 per cent in 1926.[29] Such were the opportunities provided by NEP for the peasants to join the 'vanguard' at a time when worker recruitment was comparatively downgraded.

The attempt to develop the rural party following the 'scissors crisis' in economic relations between the regime and the peasants in the autumn of 1923 was made the more urgent by developments at the time of the 1924 harvest. From June 1924 the threat to the harvest as a result of drought in the Volga basin and south-eastern Russia focused the party's attention on rural matters. In the autumn of 1924 an uprising in Georgia emphasised to the party authorities the need for better supplies to rural areas and improved prices for the peasants' products, and also for stronger political influence in the countryside. An influx of urban party cadres was utilised to re-educate rural cadres and to control better the peasantry, and party members were intended to be used to assist in the difficult grain collections and to galvanise the state and co-operative agencies, although if the latter was an aim, it was not successfully achieved by party cadres at the lower levels, only by central reforms over a number of years. This attention to rural affairs and the role of the party was to continue and increase in intensity during the next decade.

The intensified peasant recruitment in the mid-1920s together with the Lenin enrolment of industrial workers early in 1924 substantially reeduced the average length of party membership. By early 1927, some 59.1 per cent of full party members and 96.8 per cent of candidate members had joined the party since 1924.[30] Of 137 443 rural party members in 1927, 42.5 per cent were recruited in the years 1925–26 and the first ten days of 1927, and of 126 612 candidates, 88.8 per cent were recruited in the same period.[31] This break-down of figures for the rural party does not include 1924, another year of high peasant intake, and so one can safely conclude that the large majority of rural party members and nearly all candidates were recruited in the years 1924–26. A few years later, this NEP generation of rural members was rising in the rural party local élite: at the beginning of 1928, of some 18 000 rural cells providing information, 58.4 per cent of members of rural cell bureaux and 56.9 per cent of rural cell secretaries were recruited in 1924 and after. This brief period of party membership, combined with the fact that most of those rural communists who engaged in agriculture worked their individual holdings within the *mir* system, supports the view that such recruits would favour the state's pro-peasant NEP line, at a height in 1925 in the midst of this recruitment.[32]

From the end of 1926 other priorities were of even greater importance, with the beginning of the industrialisation drive. Renewed proletarianisation of party ranks, a logical and essential objective if a strong party presence was to be maintained on the shop-floor of expanding industry, had two main effects on the rural party: firstly, the expansion in the rural party's size slowed as the proportion of new peasant recruits was greatly reduced; secondly, emphasis was placed on recruiting the representative of the proletariat in the countryside in the shape of the *'batrak'*.

The *batrak* worked in the countryside for some sort of wages in cash or in kind, usually the latter. They often possessed their own plot of land, but had no animals to work them, and were obliged to hire themselves out in exchange for the use of animals and machinery. *Batraks* were regarded together with the poor peasants as allies of the Soviet regime in the countryside. Between 1925 and 1929, the number of *batraks* in the party increased from 11 800 to 30 000, or from five to about ten per cent of the rural party.[33] This success was not as great as the authorities had hoped for. *Batrak* recruitment was resisted by many rural communists, some of whom belonged to the economically strong stratum. Budennyi complained to the fifth Union Congress of Soviets in May 1929 that the 'top level' of the party workers, who formed a 'cultural élite', showed themselves 'thick skinned and wholly insensitive' to the *batrak*.[34] Aspersions were cast on the *batraks* who were said to be drunkards, illiterate or lazy. A memorable phrase with biblical overtones was coined at the time: 'It is easier for a camel to pass through the eye of a needle, than for the batrak to join the party'.[35]

The problem of *batrak* recruitment to the party was part of a wider question of socio-economic differentiation within the rural party. Ideally from the authorities' point of view, there would be a larger proportion of poor peasants and *batraks* in the party than among non-party peasants, with comparatively fewer communists in the economic bracket owning 800–1600 rubles worth of means of production and still fewer communists in the wealthiest grouping (over 1600 rubles).[36] But in practice by the years 1926–27 the peasants of the rural party, like some of the non-party peasants, were able to consolidate their economic standing. Investigations conducted in 1926 showed that large proportions of rural communists were in the 'well-to-do' category: 21.7 per cent in the North Caucasus and 49 per cent in Siberia.[37] The findings of A. Gaister and A. Levin in the most comprehensive article on social differentiation among rural communists and non-party peasants testify that the rural party peasants were relatively more prosperous (see Table 1.1).

Table 1.1   Communists and non-party peasants according to value of means of production in 1927

Value of means of production	RSFSR		Ukraine	
	Communists	all peasants	Communists	all peasants
0–200 rubles	12.7%	28.3%	14.9%	17.0%
201–800	52.2%	62.9%	53.9%	56.6%
800–1600	26.7%	15.4%	23.9%	21.7%
over 1600	8.4%	3.4%	7.3%	4.7%

Source: A. Gaister and A. Levin, in *Bolshevik*, No. 9–10, 31 May 1929, pp. 75–90.

These figures display a more pronounced economic differentiation as measured in terms of means of production within the party in comparison with the non-party peasanty. They suggest that in 1927 not only was the party unable to restrain economic differentiation within its own ranks, but was in fact reflecting it in an extreme form as a consequence of its recruitment policies and pro-NEP line.

An advantage in the ownership of the means of production often entailed the opportunity of acquiring further economic and social benefits. Wealthier rural communists, like their fellow non-party peasants, rented out more means of production for longer periods of time in return for more money than their poorer colleagues. Rural communists in the RSFSR actually hired labourers more frequently and for longer periods than non-party peasants.[38] The wealthier rural communists sought to consolidate their economic position and to assert themselves in rural society. The economic advantages possessed by the wealthier peasants, party and non-party, facilitated their participation in social and political roles. It may be a sociological fact that poor peasants in most rural societies look up to their economic 'betters' and defer to them. It is also likely that whenever a poor peasant was in debt or beholding to a more prosperous neighbour, he would hesitate before opposing his political or social aspirations and advancement.[39] In this too, communists distinguished themselves from the peasant masses by being more involved in the administration of Soviets and co-operatives, and it was the well-to-do communists who participated on a greater scale. The dividing line between party and non-party was in danger of becoming blurred; the well-to-do, regardless of their party allegiance, were the advanced elements who led society.

Many rural communists did not distinguish themselves from the peasant masses by promoting socialist relationships in rural society. The problem was so general and deep-rooted that the party press warned rural communists lest they forgot who they were and 'hang up their party card with their coat on arriving home'.[40] It would seem from the evidence that, rather than being immune from the peasant 'infection' of entrepreneurial characteristics, rural communists were often unable to break away from or break down the traditional modes of life of their individualistic peasant milieu. Basically the rural party was too weak and overpowered by the peasant masses and the size of the country to mould peasant Russia, and frequently acted as a mere reflection of it by following similar economic, political and social paths, certainly until 1927 and in places even until 1929. This is one reason why mass collectivisation would be a psychological shock for the rural party members just as much as for the ordinary peasant.

But the rural party organisation in the 1920s also suffered from an even more fundamental deficiency. At the beginning of 1924 the rural party with its 14 630 party cells could still only provide one communist to every six rural Soviets and 250 peasants.[41] More than half the rural cells (8 000) in 1924 were located in settlements which acted as the *volost* administrative centres; this single cell at the *volost* centre was frequently the only party presence in the whole *volost*.[42] Generally these cells comprised the administrative élite, such as members of the *volost* executive committee, and of an average 12–15 communists, rarely more than two or three had any connection with agriculture. This alienated them further from the day-to-day cares of the ordinary peasants.[43] Rural party cells subordinate to the *volkoms* fared little better. They were expected to provide a lead for the non-party peasantry, but the prospects of success in this general goal were not good. A primary reason why the cells were unable to secure effective control of the rural areas, and from this vantage point propagandise the regime's values and goals, was that they were too few in number. With more than 8 000 out of about 14 000 rural cells in 1924 located in *volost* centres, barely 6 000 remained to cover the remaining population centres. This difficulty was compounded by other problems. The *volkoms* frequently neglected their cells, not bothering even to listen to their reports.[44] The cells' work was disrupted by the bane of party life throughout the years: incessant transfers of personnel. Many cells failed to hold regular meetings, although there was some justification for this latter failing. Outside the *volost* centres, it was rare for all the members of a cell to live in the same settlement; usually the cell, composed of five or six communists, was spread over three or four settlements at distances of five to ten miles. To attend frequent cell metings, especially during the harsh winter months, was not an enticing prospect for many rural communists, particularly those poor peasants who were poorly clad and horseless, obliged to tramp to and from party meetings.

Of a rural party membership in September 1924 of 152 993, only 12 000 were in *kolkhoz* or *sovkhoz* cells, the vast majority being organised on a territorial basis in settlements and villages.[45] That the rural cells were so deployed could not but affect their outlook and activities, and indeed it did. The rural cells tended to focus attention on the administrative, financial, social and educational aspects of rural life, a tendency which was further emphasised by the occupations of the party cadres. It is a most important point that, generally, rural cells at this time were little concerned with agricultural production.

Commencing in the summer of 1924,[46] the party authorities took steps on three fronts to eradicate some of the rural party's deficiencies. Firstly, as we have already noted, recruitment was greatly intensified; second, party workers from urban organisations and higher echelons were drafted into the local rural party apparatus; and third, a rationalisation of the party's structure was undertaken.

The sending of party members from urban areas and high party levels to the countryside for short and lengthy visits was to become a feature of long-term significance. At the beginning of 1925 the *Orgburo* decided to dispatch 35 leading workers of various institutions for a period of one-and-a-half months, and in April 1925 a special high-powered commisson on rural affairs sent out 300 senior party workers to the localities. The fourteenth party conference in the same month decided to send 3 000 propagandists to the countryside, as well as 1 000 party workers from the largest party organisations (invariably urban) to work at the rural *ukom* level.[47]

As a result of the interest in rural affairs at the thirteenth party congress of May 1924, a review of the rural party organisation led to the publication in April 1925 of a C.C. resolution which emphasised that party cells were to be organised on an administrative–territorial principle, most often at Soviets, or on a production basis where *kolkhozy* and *sovkhozy* existed.[48] Since so few *kolkhozy* and *sovkhozy* were in operation at this time, it followed that the vast majority of rural cells were based on the administrative–territorial principle.

In the following years the effects of the measures taken in 1924–25 began to filter through. By 1 January 1926, the number of rural party cells had risen to 15 819 from a figure of 13 897 a year before.[49] Because party recruitment had outpaced the rate of cell construction, the average number of communists in a rural cell increased from 11 to 15. Of the cells at the beginning of 1926, 14 918 (94.3 per cent) were situated in settlements, Soviets, *volost* executive committees and economic organisations; only 560 (3.5 per cent) were located in collective farms and 341 (2.2 per cent) in *sovkhozy*.[50] The number of rural party cells (and candidate groups) rose from 15 819 (1 502) in 1926 to 17 456 (3 422) in 1927 and 20 719 (3 393) in 1928.[51] This growth kept pace with expansion of urban and other party cells: the proportion of all cells was the same in 1928 at 45.1 per cent as it had been in 1925, with only minor variations in between.[52] Between 1925 and 1930, the average number of communists per rural cell, a figure always much smaller than that of urban cells, only rose from 11 to 12. Of importance was the fact that the deployment of rural cells in the period 1926 to 1928 did not change appreciably: during this time the proportion of collective farm cells actually fell from 3.5 per cent to 3.0 per cent, due perhaps to the collapse of *kolkhozy*, whilst territorial cells dropped only marginally from 94.3 per cent to 94.1 per cent and *sovkhoz* cells registered a small increase from 2.2 per cent to 2.9 per cent.[53] In absolute terms this meant that the number of *kolkhoz* party cells barely rose from 560 at the beginning of 1926 to 591 in mid-1928 and *sovkhoz* cells from 341 to 602.[54] This preponderance of territorially deployed rural party cells remained until the very beginnings of mass collectivisation; it meant that the party had few deep roots in the collective sector. Notwithstanding the rural party growth in numbers and cells, the rural party remained in 1928 inadequate numerically and qualitatively when faced with the geographical expanse of the Soviet Union, and unprepared for the exigencies soon to be made upon it. By August 1928 20 660 rural cells covered 546 747 population centres and 80 000 rural Soviets,[55] and even at the beginning of 1930, there was still only one rural cell for approximately three rural Soviets.[56]

The grain difficulties of 1928 uncovered numerous failings to the eyes of the authorities and made them resolved to reshape the rural party, to review its composition and to resort to more influxes of urban party workers. Beginning in 1928, a number of partial purges were instigated. During 1928, seven *oblast* and *guberniya* organisations were screened with the aim of ridding them of those who manifested insufficient vigour in the grain collections: as a result 2 130 (13 per cent) of party members involved were expelled.[57] Along with investigations of the Smolensk and Astrakhan party organisations, singled out '*pour encourager les autres*', these screenings prepared the way for the 1929–30 full purge in providing the authorities with the required examples of degeneration within party and state organs.

The displeasure with the rural party composition was expressed tellingly in a November 1928 C.C. plenum resolution.

> In the composition of the rural organisations, the specific weight of the proletarian elements still remains absolutely minute, and the number of kolkhoz members is negligible. In certain cases, they are found to include a considerable proportion of well-to-do peasants, and sometimes also elements which have drawn near to the kulaks, degenerated and become completely alien to the working class.[58]

The question of social differentiation within the rural party did not remain a matter of socio-economics; with the political conflict in the higher echelons of the party in 1928 and the related grain crisis, it soon became couched in political overtones. When the political leadership split over the rate of industrialisation and over the nature and durability of the 'extraordinary measures', a campaign was launched in the press against those labelled as 'Rights'. What interests us more here is how a tense atmosphere was generated in 1928–29 against those economically strong communists, who were usually categorised henceforth as Rights or conciliators, and what effect this might have had on the rural party membership's perceptions.

Gradually, commencing in 1928, the membership was made more aware that excessive prosperity, links with the class enemy and resistance to radical, socialist change would no longer be tolerated. An investigation of 535 communist households in Kremenchug *okrug* in the Ukraine revealed that 10 per cent of the communists were well-to-do and concluded that:

> These communists not only do not fulfil party decisions, not only do they not appear as examples for the broad peasant masses in the transformation of small, individual peasant holdings into large collectives, but become an hindrance on the path to collectivisation and represent a clear expression of the Right deviation.[59]

This was one of the early condemnations of rural party members as an 'expression of the Right deviation'. The circumlocution testifies to the as yet ill-defined nature of the deviation, but henceforth those rural communists who were wealthy, those not in *kolkhozy*, were faced with the opprobrium of being classified as Rights. The campaign against those in the party was linked with severe criticism of the non-party *kulaks* and connections of a social and political nature were drawn between the two elements. A perhaps unintentionally pathetic tale of how the authorities had fomented class division and created a rift between party members and class aliens, and of how they hoped to widen further such a rift is evident in the case of a communist named Zhukov who was held up to ridicule for having written the following poem to his girl-friend, the daughter of a former trader deprived of his electoral rights:

> I am a communist, you the daughter of one deprived of rights,
> What is the different between us? Tell me,
> Tell me oh beautiful, young girl,
> And in so doing you will show me the path to happiness.[60]

Perceptions may well have altered at all levels of the party: the leadership became dissatisfied with the rural party performance and once and for all in this decade the rural communist knew where he stood. The problem of social differentiation, which was recognised as such only in 1928, was to be resolved by propaganda and threats among the membership but more forcefully by party purges conducted in the same year and on a broader scale in 1929–30. Paradoxically the purge of rural ranks in 1929–30 was the launching pad from which enormous peasant recruitment would rise almost simultaneously. But in the 1920s there were very few manifestations of concentrated, long-term, well-planned preparations to build support among the rural party ranks for the new policies. There was much that was abitrary in the way the rural party's fortunes rose and fell:

> In sum, Soviet recruitment of rural party members before 1930 did not lead to impressive qualitative results, tended to emphasize the recruitment of categories other than peasants, and was divorced from the goal of collectivisation of agriculture.[61]

The urban influxes to which we have already referred as one measure in the party's programme for the countryside in 1928, affected the composition of the rural cell cadres, specifically the post of cell secretary. At the beginning of 1928, 20.8 per cent of rural cell secretaries were workers by social composition, but only 3.2 per cent were workers by occupation;[62] a year later the former had risen to 29 per cent.[63] This suggests that people with a non-rural background were introduced from outside to lead a significant number of cells. On arrival at their cells, the new secretaries would take up employment either in some form of rural administration or co-operative or work in the agricultural household of relatives who had remained on the land; this explains why the number of workers by occupation was quite low. They needed to take up some remunerative work because very few rural cell secretaries occupied their posts on a full-time, paid basis: in 1928 only 8.1 per cent of them were 'freed', full-time, paid party workers, whereas in industrial cells they represented 36.6 per cent.[64] This testifies to how the rural party lagged behind its urban counterpart. Some 65.1 per cent of rural cell secretaries were of peasant origin, but this declined to 41.1 per cent according to occupation, of whom only 25.8 per cent were engaged exclusively in agriculture in their own household or in a kolkhoz: in other words, 15.3 per cent of rural cell secretaries held their party post, worked their agricultural holding and dabbled in some other paid activity, most likely in rural administration or in some other economic organ. 45.8 per cent were categorised as 'others' by occupation, employed entirely in Soviets, co-operatives, schools, whilst in the urban cells a smaller proportion (27.2 per cent) belonged to this employee category.[65] The findings for the composition of cell bureaux were in all aspects very similar and also indicated how the rural cells were less advanced from the point of view of the regime's ideals than those cells in industry and the towns.

The rural party was intended to be supported by other groupings and organisations, but several of these suffered from the same failings as the party. The party census of 1927 recorded nearly 49 000 *komsomol* cells in the countryside with 1.1 million members, when the party's strength was considerably less at 17 456 full cells with 264 055 communists.[66] Even so, this did not make their combined forces remotely ubiquitious: of peasant households in 1927 only 0.7 per cent included a party member and 1.1 per cent a member of the *komsomol*.[67] When policies turned to more socialisation in 1928–29, the *komsomol* was riddled with the same shortcomings as the rural party with regard to social composition and political outlook, although the *komsomol* was not devoid of all value to the regime and in some cases acted as a focus through which the talents and vigour of the young could be chanelled. Of more doubtful value as a subsidiary support were the non-party activists. Prior to mass collectivisation and industialisation, the non-party activists were considered to be those who attended open party meetings, read party literature and supported publicly the party's slogans; later, activism became equated with shock work in production. Without a precise term of definition, grandiose claims have been made for the number of non-party peasant '*aktiv*'. S.F. Markov states that at the beginning of 1928 in the RSFSR alone there were two million, a figure which grew to over 4.5 million in mid-1930.[68] This does not mean that there were, in addition to the rural party and *komsomol*, almost five million genuine, committed supporters of radical social change in the countryside. If there had been, the collectivisation programme would not have been as problematic as it was.

The grain procurement crisis of 1928 proved to be a major experience for the rural party. Having bull-dozed demands through *skhod* meetings and having used extreme measures of threats and searches against peasants, middle ones as well as *kulaks*, relations between the rural party and the peasantry were transformed irrevocably from the state of peaceful co-existence that had reigned during NEP. The above mentioned purges of 1928 made the rural party a less tolerant institution, less tolerant of its own foibles and those of the peasantry generally, a process reinforced by the growing influx of urban party workers. After experience in the 1928 grain collections, the rural party was directed to use more administrative methods to compensate for its inability to coax the peasantry towards a more socialised way of living and producing. Sheboldaev, first party secretary of the lower Volga *kraikom*, who was well placed to know the truth of the matter, noted ironically at the sixteenth party conference in April 1929 that during the grain collection crisis the local rural party organisations 'from month to month "were growing into" [*vrastali*] extraordinary measures'.[69] But this need to resort to excesses stemmed from underlying weakness. E.H. Carr has identified the rural party's major failings prior to 1929, echoing the main themes of this chapter: 'Whether the party sought to control or to woo, its manpower and points of contact were hopelessly inadequate for the task'.[70] More prone to coercive methods, the rural communist party became more alienated from the peasantry. As collectivisation developed during 1928–30, the rural party was caught in no-man's land: on account of the way it had behaved during and after 1928, it had been sufficiently alienated from the peasants to be generally distrusted by them; but, because of its poor showing in measures of socialisation, that is its unwillingness or inability to switch abruptly and show commitment to the new general line that was taking shape in 1928–29, it was not sufficiently trusted by the central party authorities to be chosen to play the major role in collectivisation, for which outside agencies were often preferred. A case can be made for the view that the rural communist party remained in this ambivalent position until the end of the first Five Year Plan when the central authorities finally lost all faith in it.

The nature of the NEP was debated heatedly. Whether it was an advance on the road to socialism, as advocated by its proponents, or a retreat, as claimed by its detractors, it was not designed as a programme of rapid societal transformation, even less of rapid socialisation; it was gradualistic and not a useful preparation for mass collectivisation as undertaken with little forethought in 1929. Whereas Soviet historiography refuses, in the main, to accept that collectivisation as carried out in 1929 was a denial of NEP, we have argued that collectivisation was a quantitative and qualitative leap unforeseen in the 1920s.[71] The preparations and final decision to collectivise were crammed into a few short weeks towards the end of 1929. Policies designed to placate the peasantry in the 1920s were shattered by the collectivisation drive, which disjointed rural organisations, especially the rural communist party, to such an extent that it would take several years for them to adapt.

2 Collectivisation in the Years of the First Five Year Plan

This brief survey is presented with the aim of putting the party's organisation and activities in context. Several works are already available on the general features of collectivisation, in particular its early stages.[1]

Before the summer of 1929 the collective farm sector grew at a modest pace.[2] In the late summer and early autumn of 1929 more ambitious projects were underway: inter-*kolkhoz* conferences, the establishment of farms like *'Gigant'* with an area of 135 000 hectares and the creation of 'districts of comprehensive collectivisation'. Various interlocking campaigns were encouraged in the context of attacks in the press and at meetings on the danger of low tempos and on the members of the right-wing within the party. The number of households collectivised rose from one million households on 1 June 1929 (3.9 per cent of the total) to 1.9 million on 1 October 1929 (7.5 per cent).[3] Further increases were noted in October in the major grain regions. The central authorities had some grounds to believe that rapid collectivisation was feasible.

This thinking was reflected in the C.C. plenum meeting of 10–17 November 1929, one of the most momentous gatherings in the history of the Soviet communist party. The ground work for the meeting was laid by the publication of Stalin's 'Great Break-Through' speech on 7 November and several articles in *Pravda* attacking the party's right wing; these were intended to achieve iron unity at the plenum and to bring waverers into line. The plenum was important for discussing a dramatic foreshortening in the tempo of collectivisation. Subsequently, a resolution on the rates of collectivisation was ready on 5 January 1930 and published in *Pravda* on the following day. This was a most important document laying out the time limits for collectivisation in the various regions and was imbued with the spirit to push the movement along. The resolution noted that the area of collectivised land would exceed the Five Year Plan mark of 30 million hectares as early as the spring of 1930. It continued to state:

the collectivisation of such major grain areas as the Lower Volga, Mid-Volga and North Caucasus can in the main be completed in the

23

autumn of 1930 or in any case in the spring of 1931; the collectivisation of other grain areas can in the main be completed in the autumn of 1931 or in any case in the spring of 1932.[4]

It did not remark in any detail what was to happen in the grain deficit and national minority regions. This was rather characteristic of the vagueness of much of the legislation at the turn of the year.

Thus the decision came about to seek mass collectivisation. Sometime between the deliberations of the sixteenth party conference in April 1929 and the November C.C. plenum, Stalin and many of his associates came to regard the phasing out of individual agriculture and a policy of mass collectivisation as an intergral part of their overall programme. Many factors were behind the decision: some concrete, economic and political, others less tangible.[5]

Once the decisions on collectivisation and dekulakisation had been taken, the campaigns raged throughout the Soviet countryside during the months December 1929–March 1930: after this 12–16 week period, things would never be the same again. Multitudinous brigades and plenipotentiaries swept through the villages, comprising urban workers, urban party workers, party and Soviet workers from the *krai* and *raion* centres, to exhort, urge, persuade and threaten the peasants into the collective farms. The countryside was turned topsy-turvy by a host of meetings. An integral part of collectivisation was the expropriation of *kulak* property and the exile of many of them to remote regions. By the end of 1930, 300 000 households (one and a half million people) had been expropriated. Dekulakisation served at least three purposes: ideologically, it was an assault on the rural class enemy; politically, it instilled fear into all peasants and warned them of the grave consequences of resistance; economically, it provided the economic foundations for the burgeoning *kolkhozy*. As a result of these campaigns, the number of peasant households encompassed by the *kolkhozy* leapt dramatically from 1.9 million households (7.5 per cent of households in the USSR) on 1 October 1929 to 4.6 million (18.1 per cent) on 1 January 1930, 8.0 million (31.7 per cent) on 1 February 1930 and 14.5 million (57.2 per cent) on 1 March 1930.[6]

The collectivisation drive took off so quickly that legislation and detailed instructions were left in its wake, only following later.[7] A model statute on the organisation of the *artel* form of collective farm was only confirmed by the Central Executive Committee and the USSR *Sovnarkom* on 1 March 1930. This was a grievous delay, as it meant that peasants had been unsure of their future prospects when joining a *kolkhoz*. Clarification had been urgently needed since the *artel*, with its intermediary level of socialisation between the *toz* and the commune, entry into which represented a considerable leap into the unknown for the ordinary peasant, became the predominant type of collective farm in the winter of 1929–30: whereas 22.7 per cent of all collective farms in October 1929 were *artels*, by May 1930 the proportion was 76.9 per cent.[8] There was resultant confusion, disarray and deep concern that no instructions were issued on how to organise the *kolkhoz* labour force, how to remunerate *kolkhozniks* and to what degree livestock and small animals were to be socialised. The Soviet collectivisation system also failed to provide any compensation for socialised property; a prosperous middle peasant lost irrevocably up to half his income on joining the *kolkhoz*, after his contribution to the indivisible fund and the payment of an entry fee. The peasants responded to this uncertainty in one of the few ways at their disposal: they slaughtered their animals and stuffed their bellies before joining the *kolkhoz*. This had a very severe, long-term effect on Soviet agriculture.[9]

In the spring of 1930 a retreat in policy occurred due to several reasons: the intensifying slaughter of animals, the danger posed to the spring sowing by the helter-skelter campaign, combined with the manifestations of peasant unrest and cases of open rebellion. Stalin's 'Dizzy with Success' article caused the biggest stir.[10] Criticising local party authorities, he pleaded moderation and consolidation, themes reiterated in the C.C.'s resolution of 14 March 1930.[11] Once the voluntary principle was restored to collectivisation, huge numbers left the *kolkhozy*: on 1 March 1930, 14.59 million households (57.2 per cent) were in *kolkhozy*, a figure which declined to 7.13 million (28.0 per cent) on 1 May and 5.49 million (21.5 per cent) on 1 September.[12] In an attempt to stem the tide, a whole array of economic benefits were granted to the *kolkhozy* and their members in the spring of 1930; but, as can be seen from the foregoing figures, this legislation was not entirely successful.

The period April–November 1930 can be viewed as one of comparative calm on the agricultural front. The authorities recorded some gains and losses. Despite the outflow from the *kolkhozy*, the proportion of households within the collective sector did not sink below 20 per cent. The spring sowing was salvaged and, given the circumstances, was quite a success, especially for the *kolkhozy*. Later, the 1930 harvest and procurement campaigns provided the opportunity to complete the systematisation of the grain procurement machinery. Launching the campaign, organising and supervising it was the responsibility of the party secretaries. The technical apparatus for actually doing the job was provided by the agricultural co-operative organisation *Khlebotsentr* and its local branches, whence the grain was transferred to the state agency *Soyuzkhleb*. This framework replaced the numerous, central, republic and local organisations which had formerly competed with each other.[13] Even so, until October 1932 when co-operative influence was finally removed, a division of labour existed between co-operative and state agencies: namely, *Narkomzem* (The Peoples' Commissariat of Agriculture), the co-operative system of *Kolkhoztsentr* and the mixed system of *Traktorotsentr*. The local organs of *Narkomzem* – the *oblzu* and *raizo* – provided general technical supervision and policy guidance over *kolkhoz* production. The *kolkhoz* unions of *Kolkhoztsentr* at *oblast* and *raion* level focused on the organisation and direction of new *kolkhozy*. By the decree of the Central Executive Committee of 1 October 1932 *Kolkhoztsentr* and all secondary co-operative unions (the *kolkhozsoyuzy*) in the *kolkhoz* system were abolished. The *kolkhozy* were placed under the operational control of the *Narkomzem* and its local organs, the *raizos*, which were responsible for the distribution of plans and delivery quotas among the *raion*'s *kolkhozy*. *Traktorotsentr* was abolished and the MTS system totally integrated into the national *Narkomzem* bureaucracy.[14]

The rationalised system, blessed as it was by fine weather in the summer of 1930, resulted in an abundant harvest and a successful grain procurement campaign. Estimates on the size of the harvest vary between 71.5 and 83.5 million tons.[15] The grain procurements extracted from this harvest amounted to 22.139 million tons (26.5 per cent of the total crop), which represented a considerable improvement on the harvests of 1928 and 1929 when procurements were 10.7 million tons (14.7 per cent) and 16.8 million tons (22.4 per cent) respectively.[16] From this point of view, collectivisation could be judged a success.

Thus the scene was set and the winter months of 1930–31 served as a convenient moment to strike out once more on the collectivisation front. Modest monthly increases were reported in the last months of 1930, but it was the December C.C. plenum that sounded the clarion call. It set the target figures to be achieved during 1931 as 80 per cent of households in the first zones of major grain regions, not less than 50 per cent in the second zone of lesser grain areas and at 20–25 per cent in the grain deficit regions; in the USSR as a whole at least 50 per cent collectivisation of the total number of households was the objective.[17] The national goal was achieved with time to spare with a proportion of 54.2 per cent by August 1931. The collectivisation campaign of 1930–31, like that of the previous year, was accompanied by an intensified dekulakisation drive, but was dissimilar in other respects: not as much zeal was manifest in its conduct because officials at all levels had been chastened by the disciplinary measures taken against perpetrators of excesses the previous spring; it involved larger numbers of *kolkhozniks* acting as promoters of the collective farm system; and it was pervaded by an air of inevitability, which meant that the peasants were unable to delude themselves that collectivisation would go away. Towards the end of the first Five Year Plan (1 July 1932), the proportion of collectivised households reached 61.5 per cent.[18]

All in all in early 1931 there was some cause for self-satisfaction among the party leadership with regard to agricultural affairs generally. But the full ramifications of collectivisation and its concomitant procurement campaigns were yet to be faced. Nor did agriculture function in splendid isolation; it depended on vital inputs from an industrial sector that was encountering severe growth pains. After 1930 industry could no longer rely on taking up spare capacity; it was faced with a shortage of capacity and materials. The down-turn in industrial growth affected tractor and lorry production, which was unable to compensate entirely for livestock losses. The unrelenting drive to overcome the lag in industry entailed renewed pressure on agriculture to provide more in raw materials for the factories and in food for the expanding urban population, yet investment in agriculture was limited because state credits were restricted, materials directed from the countryside to major industrial projects and *kolkhoz* manpower urged to work on industrial sites. All this served to undermine the fragile foundations of the newly created socialised agricultural system. When this coincided with ill-considered procurement campaigns in 1931–32, it brought the Soviet regime close to collapse and resulted in the death by starvation of millions of peasants.

The beginning of the problem may well have been the good harvest of 1930. The state aimed at and succeeded in obtaining a large amount of procurements from this harvest, as a result of which its expectations for the future were raised, misguidedly as it turned out. The grain procurements from this harvest amounted to 22.139 million tons. Given the Soviet leadership's propensity to enthusiasm at this time, it is not surprising that the planned figures for the 1931 harvest were set at 24.161 million tons.[19] Despite the fact that in 1931 the Mid and Lower Volga, Western Siberia, Urals and Kazakhstan suffered a drought with a dry, hot summer followed by a wet autumn which hampered the harvesting, the grain procurement plans of *Narkomtorg* (The People's Commissariat of Trade) were maintained and the harvest assessed at 78 million tons, when in fact it turned out to be nine million tons less.[20] During the last months of 1931, the grain procurement plans were reduced for areas where the harvest had failed, but to compensate for this, plans were increased for the major grain regions of the Ukraine and North Caucasus: the ramifications of this action were to last for several years and have dire consequences for the peasant population and rural party of these areas.

The energetic grain procurement campaign of 1931, which was in embryo that of the following year, eventually procured 22.85 million tons, and although this was one-and-a-half million tons short of an optimistic plan, it represented 32.9 per cent of the gross harvest.[21] Intense pressure was brought to bear in the Ukraine; by January 1932, this republic's grain procurements from the 1931 harvest reached 6.98 million tons, when they had been 6.92 from the much more bountiful harvest of 1930.[22] In 1930 the Ukrainian *kolkhozy* had delivered to the state 36 per cent of their gross harvest, whereas in 1931 this leapt to 61.8 per cent, and the respective figures for *kolkhozy* in the North Caucasus were 44.6 and 63.4 per cent.[23] These figures are quite portentous if one bears in mind Moshe Lewin's assessment of the needs of the NEP peasantry: in rough figures they required 12 per cent of the gross harvest for seeds, 25–30 per cent for livestock, up to 30 per cent to feed themselves and approximately 6 per cent as reserves, giving a minimum total of 73 per cent.[24] Admittedly the *kolkhoz* peasantry of 1931–32 would have fewer needs for livestock, but it was impossible for them to bear such procurements of 1931 without severely damaging the production cycle, by eating into their seed for the coming sowing, and without reducing sharply the amounts they consumed.

Signs of discontent came in a well-publicised scandal in *sovkhozy*, located in the main in the Ukraine, at the same time as which Stalin and the party leadership launched a campaign against 'rotten liberalism'. Other manifestations of deeper difficulties came with reports of the progress of the spring sowing of 1932: as of 5 May, the Ukraine had fulfilled its spring sowing plan by 26.3 per cent and on 25 May had only attained 57.9 per cent of its plan, but even worse was the break-down for some of the Ukrainian *oblasts* with Vinnitsa at 48.6 per cent and Kiev at 36 per cent.[25] Eventually the Kiev *oblast* only accomplished 64.1 per cent of its plan and in the spring of 1932 the Ukraine as a whole fell three million hectares short of the 1931 sown area.[26] It may well have been such depressing figures as these which had some influence on the resolutions on the introduction of *kolkhoz* trade in May 1932. It was hoped no doubt that by allowing the peasantry to sell off their surplus on the open market, after they had met their procurement obligations in full, that this would provide a major incentive for production; but the 1931 grain procurement campaign had been such a wrench for the peasantry and, more significantly, cut into their seed reserves, so that in the Ukraine the peasant-*kolkhoznik* probably had little choice in increasing production and concentrated solely on survival. The state of the southern regions was one of demoralisation.

This reality was faced, to a limited extent, and the grain procurement plans for 1932 were reduced from their planned figures of December 1931, set at 29.48 million tons, to 20.5 million tons.[27] During the late summer and autumn of 1932 the full effects of the years before filtered through: by the end of July only 45 per cent of the planned monthly grain deliveries had been collected in the USSR, whilst in the Ukraine by 20 October only 38.5 per cent of the annual and 20.1 per cent of the monthly plan had been fulfilled.[28] On 1 September only 15 per cent of the national plan had been achieved, compared with 27.3 per cent at the same time in 1931.[29] On 5 July Rumyanstev, first secretary of the Western *obkom*, sent a top-secret letter to all *raikoms* on how to deal with 'cases where kolkhozy fall apart' and how to adopt severe action of economic pressure upon those who insisted on leaving *kolkhozy*.[30] This latter trend, caused in the main by peasants fleeing the countryside to work in the towns, was only curbed with the introduction of the passport system in November 1932, but by then another reason was to save the urban population from the sight of emigrating starving peasants.

Caught in a vicious circle of their own making, unwilling and unable now to admit the underlying causes of the failure, the central authorities, their concessions having proven, as so often in history, too little and too late, were obliged to turn the screw and insist on more repressive measures against the peasantry as a whole, in which the rural party was to figure prominently – as a victim: the central authorities must have felt that the carrot had failed and that now only the stick remained. The Central Executive Committee-*Sovnarkom* decree of 7 August 1932 signalled the beginning of brutal retribution for the theft of *kolkhoz* property, with sentences ranging from the death penalty by shooting to a lesser ten years' confinement with confiscation of property in mitigating circumstances.[31] Reports of the law being implemented soon figured in the press: one from Ul'yanovsk recounted how the leader of a gang, who had stolen grain from the field and beaten up a night-watchman, was sentenced to be shot.[32] This decree, like that of the *Sovnarkom* and C.C. dated 27 September 1932 on ways to increase the harvest yield, can be interpreted as attempts to salvage the best of a deteriorating situation by hoping to cut down losses on the one hand, and on the other by increasing the amount of produce from a reduced sown area. Neither was to be entirely successful.

The campaign did not abate as the year drew to a close. Yu.A.Moshkov reports euphemistically that in the autumn and winter of 1932, some *kolkhozy* in the Ukraine and North Caucasus 'left the organisational influence of the party and state'.[33] Savage reprisals were taken to destroy this opposition and to prevent it contaminating other areas further afield. *Kolkhozy* and *sovkhozy* which had completed their plans had further quotas dumped on them and all grain was removed, even that necessary for future seed and payment of work days. A well-tested means of action was to curtail all supplies, manufactured goods and credits to those *raions* and *kolkhozy* that failed to achieve their plans, which in conditions of critical shortages may well have condemned at least a proportion of these populated areas to starvation. This latter method was threatened by V. Shubrikov, one of the Mid-Volga *kraikom* secretaries, who warned that, although 75–80 per cent of *kolkhozy* had completed their plans, those of the remainder who sabotaged fulfilment would be subjected to 'severe measures', such as the closure of all cooperative, Soviet and state trade, the discontinuation of all credits and the full, immediate payments of all debts.[34] When one realises that severe measures were also adopted in White Russia, then the picture shows that there was a crisis of confidence in *kolkhozy* and the party through a whole swath of the western and southern regions of the Soviet Union. So critical was the situation that the army was employed in bringing order. It is probably not an exaggeration to affirm that this was a critical moment in the survival of the Soviet state. In spite of all this, manifest success was not forthcoming. The harvest at 69.8 million tons was worse than the previous bad year and the planned procurements of 20.5 million tons were not achieved for a second consecutive year with only 18.7 million tons being gathered, and once again the Ukraine did particularly poorly.[35]

A major theme of our argument has been that it was economic causes which led to the rupture of any remnant of *smychka* between state and peasantry. The root of the problem was not faulty organisation, even less was it the 'fault' of the party organisations that they were unable to fulfil the duties set them by the higher authorities. The tasks set the rural party and other rural non-party institutions were often in fact impossible to fulfil, and when vigorous efforts were made to do so as best as possible, a famine ensued. This argument, with specific reference to the rural party, is taken up in a later chapter.[36]

3 The Rural Communist Party 1929–32: Membership, Location and Occupation

This chapter examines the changes brought about in the membership of the rural communist party by the impact of collectivisation, and considers how far these changes were adequate to the new demands placed upon the party. T.H. Rigby has distinguished several processes at work in the transformation of the rural communist party membership: the purging of peasant communists resistant to collectivisation; the recruitment of non-party activists in the formative phase of the collective farms; and individual communists joining collectives.[1] This useful framework, with slight modifications will be employed here.

THE PARTY PURGE OF 1929–30

Few positive steps were taken to prepare the rural party membership for mass collectivisation. However, the authorities had not been completely dilatory or negligent in laying foundations for the now clearly enunciated objectives. Prior to 1929 the recruitment of *kolkhozniks* had been 'very, very weak',[2] but in that year 8000 were recruited.[3] This was at least a beginning. In addition during 1929 greater pressure was exerted on existing party members to join the collective farms. Concerning the poor peasant aspect of recruitment, the large majority of peasants joining the party ranks in the latter half of 1929 were poor peasants with 58.8 per cent of those accepted freed from taxation and 24.2 per cent paying only up to 10 rubles.[4] And yet it was the party purge, essentially a somewhat negative measure, which was the main preparatory stage in moulding the membership.

The small-scale purge of 1928 and the various screenings of party organisations in 1928–29 provided the basis for the plans for a general purge. There were already hints at the November 1928 C.C. plenum that the rural party would be in the forefront of any purge; a resolution demanded 'far firmer measures than those taken in recent years to purge party organisations, by expelling from them elements which used their membership . . . for aims of personal greed and ambition, elements of petty bourgeois degeneration who mingled with kulaks and so forth'.[5] One of the features of the purge, especially in the countryside, was its close attention to the socio-economic class of those before the purge commissions. Early in 1929, on behalf of the Central Control Commission (C.C.C.), E. Yaroslavsky, in a letter to all local control commissions, advised that the rural purge should focus on the economic standing of each party member.[6] But the purge was not conducted solely in terms of economic class. The party also frankly stated that its objective was to remove those who were lukewarm in their support for the policies of collectivisation and industrialisation. These two aims frequently coincided. The local party organisations seemed to understand clearly where they stood on this matter. Even before the purge was underway, the Vladimir *gubkom* estimated that 33 per cent or more of its rural communists deserved to be removed in the purge for inactivity in collectivisation and elections.[7]

In the spring of 1929 it was decided to conduct the purge of rural cells at a time which would least interfere with agricultural work, and its approximate dates were set at 10–15 May to 1 July 1929, between the spring sowing and the harvest. This proved to be far too optimistic and the purge dragged on in most areas until the end of the year. Preliminary figures on the purge of the rural party were published in the autumn of 1929, but much more comprehensive data were available in the summer of 1930. These showed that 21 582 cells with 282 586 members had been investigated and 47 753 (16.9 per cent) expelled.[8] Comparatively the purge fell most heavily on the rural party. The purge of the whole party resulted in 170 000 expulsions, about 11 per cent of the current membership, which after subsequent rehabilitations reduced these figures to 133 000 (8 per cent).[9] Only 8 per cent of the membership of industrial cells was removed and 10 per cent of non-production cells in administration and education, but the equivalent figure in rural cells was 16 per cent.[10]

No detailed national break-downs have been available of the reasons for expulsion, but the above disproportionately heavy purging of the rural ranks supports E.H. Carr's contention that: 'it is reasonable to assume that known sympathisers with the Right opposition, more numerous in the countryside than in the town and factory, were effectively eliminated'.[11] This probably included many who had joined the party in the years of 'High NEP'.[12] There are also some indicators of what social grouping bore the brunt of the purge in the rural party. It appears that well-to-do communists, who had more to lose financially from the socialisation of property and were therefore believed to be more likely to resist the process, were singled out. Preliminary results received by the autumn of 1929, based on information gathered from 1070 cells in 23 *okrugs*, showed that of those communists in the high tax bracket 100–150 rubles, 40.6 per cent were expelled, compared with 11.6 per cent among the poorest groups who were freed from taxation.[13] According to information culled from the Soviet archives by B.A. Abramov, 65.8 per cent of those purged in the first half of 1929 were excluded on the basis of their economic position and class.[14] Similarly a break-down by social-economic grouping of those purged by the spring of 1930 reveals that among those investigated 6.7 per cent of *batraks* and agricultural workers, 9.5 per cent of *kolkhozniks*, 14.2 per cent of employees and 19.8 per cent of individual peasants were expelled.[15] Thus the purge rid the party ranks of many of those who had prospered in the NEP years, those most likely to disapprove of the regime's new course.

The party purge was accompanied by purges in the government, trade unions and Soviets. The Western *oblispolkom* (*oblast* executive committee) report for 1929 showed that of 616 village Soviet chairmen in 26 *raions*, 304 (49.8 per cent) were removed in the course of the year, of whom 102 were brought to trial: of this 304, some 102 were removed for deviation from the class line, 11 for bribery, 113 for inactivity and 78 for other reasons.[16] Similar results were recorded in a sample of 26 Ukrainian *okrugs*.[17] Between a quarter and a half of those expelled in these areas were purged because of resistance to the party line or at least passive resistance through apathy and inertia, which were often the best or only means to 'resist' orders from above. As some regional figures reveal, the rural Soviets were sharply punished for their mediocre performance as collectivisation speeded up. In the Mid-Volga, between the 1928–29 elections and spring 1930, 82 per cent of village Soviet chairmen were dismissed, 18 per cent of deputies recalled and 15 per cent of Soviets dissolved completely.[18] In a few weeks during February and March 1930, 23.4 per cent of all village Soviets in the Don *okrug* of the North Caucasus were dissolved.[19]

The purge in the countryside served several purposes. It was a sharp warning to the reluctant and recalcitrant; it paralysed criticism and prevented the Right leaders gaining a hearing among the rank and file; it halted or at least retarded economic differentiation among rural communists; it cleared the decks for the future actions of collectivisation. Temporarily at least the party and rural administration were in disorder, but were no different in this from the rest of the countryside at the turn of the year 1929–30. Perhaps the regime's representatives would have been better able to adapt to collectivisation, if they had not been overhauled in the midst of great social transformation. This point supports the view that much of the regime's approach to mass collectivisation was poorly prepared and *ad hoc*.

RURAL PARTY RECRUITMENT AND MEMBERSHIP 1929–32

The Setting and Framework

Owing to conflicting objectives, overlapping priorities and negligence, a gradual build-up of the rural party quantitatively and qualitatively did not occur in 1928 and 1929, the years just prior to and at the beginning of the first Five Year Plan. The recruitment of peasants in these years was at best erratic.[20] Nor did membership and organisation in the rural party keep pace with other sectors. Between January 1928 and January 1930, the number of rural party members grew by 14.8 per cent, whilst the party as a whole increased its membership by 28.7 per cent. Simultaneously, the number of rural cells grew by 23.7 per cent, while the total number of party cells increased by 24.6 per cent.[21] The more rapid growth of rural cells compared with membership meant that during the two-year period the average number of communists in a rural cell declined from 13 to 12, whilst in the towns it rose from 52 to 54.[22] As a proportion of the whole party, the rural party declined from 22.4 per cent in 1928 to 20.2 per cent in 1929, staying at this level in 1930.

This unpropitious expansion in the rural party was a direct consequence of the aim of increasing the proportion of workers by occupation in the party to 50 per cent, a goal that was retained in 1929–30. The rural party itself came to include more urban workers recruited from enterprises situated in rural areas, urban workers imported from industrial centres and co-opted into the rural party and agricultural workers and *batraks*; according to the C.C. resolution of 7 January 1929, *batraks* were to comprise 40 per cent of all rural recruits during the subsequent two years.[23] In his speech '*Zadachi partiinoi raboty*' at the beginning of 1930, Kaganovich attempted to reconcile the overlapping if not contradictory aims of party recruitment. He stressed the continued priority of the needs of the urban party, but tried to draw a balance by not neglecting excessively the rural party:

We cannot demand in the countryside the same tempo of party growth and of cell organisations, as in the towns. Here we must display a necessary restraint, but this restraint must correspond to the specific demands of the pace of the socialist reconstruction of the countryside.[24]

It is within these somewhat ambivalent parameters that the party's recruitment policy of genuine rural peasant and *kolkhoznik* elements must be judged.

Party Membership 1930–32: Recruitment and Composition

It was in these years that rural party recruitment policies were adapted to the demands of mass collectivisation, and began to compensate for poor preparation in earlier years. 1930 was a crucial year, in which the number of *kolkhozy* expanded so prodigiously. The situation facing the rural party at the beginning of the year was not promising. Its 28 500 cells and candidate groups were to supervise 597 359 population centres, some 21 inhabited places for each cell; moreover, when collectivisation stabilised in June 1930, there were some 86 000 *kolkhozy* and 69 829 rural Soviets.[25] If the rural party was not to be submerged by collectivisation, it was essential to establish numerous cells in the collective farms and to recruit large numbers of *kolkhozniks* to man them. The party authorities appreciated this and laid out guidelines for party recruitment policies in the countryside in a resolution of 6 February 1930, which stated:

The widespread collectivisation and implementation of the policy of liquidating the kulak as a class, on the one hand, and the small size of rural party organisations on the other, require an expansion of the ranks of rural organisations with more agricultural and state farm workers, and a more determined drawing of the foremost kolkhozniks, especially poor ones, into the party. There is to be a vigorous recruitment of those who have shown initiative in the organisation and strengthening of kolkhozy, who have been active and resolute in the struggle with the kulak ... and who have been proven in active work for the implementation of current politico-economic campaigns and the fulfilment of kolkhoz obligations towards the Soviet state.[26]

These stipulations were to be repeated frequently throughout the year. The party's aim was to foment class division within rural society and ally itself with those who would support its strategy. Some of the foregoing criteria for recruiting people were probably complementary:

for example, it was more likely that poor *kolkhozniks* participated most actively 'in the struggle with the kulak', as it was they, as poor peasants and *kolkhozniks*, who had most to gain from the dekulakisation programme.[27] Within a few months a significant group of *kolkhozniks* distinguished themselves most obviously as being potential supporters of the regime, or at least acquiescent in its policies, by remaining in the collective farms during and after the huge spring outflow.

The resolution of 6 February fitted well with existing developments. In 1930 the clear discrimination in recruitment already practised in 1929 was continued: of 384 940 applications in the first quarter of 1930, 16.2 per cent of urban workers who applied were rejected, 8.4 per cent of *batraks*, 19.4 per cent of *kolkhozniks* and 55.4 per cent of individual peasants.[28] Proportionally few *batraks* were rejected, but in absolute numbers their recruitment was less important to the party than urban workers and *kolkhozniks*. A remarkable development in 1930 clearly shown in these figures is that the *kolkhozniks* were being treated almost as equals with the urban proletariat. This was a major impact of collectivisation on rural party recruitment and reflected a major change in the political centre's attitude to the countryside. The available figures on recruitment are presented in Table 3.1.

Quantitatively considerable success is evident from the data in Table 3.1, which indicates how the rural party acquired greater comparative prominence: on 1 January 1930 the rural element in the entire party was 20.2 per cent, but this rose to 23.4 per cent one year later.[29] In the first quarter of 1930 rural recruits, excluding employees who would have been few in number, represented 20.5 per cent of all recruits to the party, but rose significantly to 33.8 per cent for the year 1930 and 37.2 per cent for 1931. The bulk of this rural recruitment was taken up by *kolkhozniks*, who were regarded as the best potential allies of the regime's policies: the rate of *kolkhoznik* recruitment more than doubled during 1930 and was maintained at a higher level throughout 1931 and into 1932. In this the rural party maintained its class line: of *kolkhozniks* recruited in the second quarter of 1932, it was claimed that 60.7 per cent were former poor peasants.[30] The recruitment of individual peasants was meagre during these years, but it is perhaps surprising that as many as 20 000 in 1930 and nearly 11 000 in 1931 were allowed to join the party. Many such communists were located in regions where collectivisation was intended to be slow, for example the Tadzhikistan and Karakalpak regions. Such individual peasants probably pledged to join a *kolkhoz* at the first opportunity; in areas where convenient *kolkhozy* did not exist, the *raikoms* and cells no doubt adopted a lenient approach in the hope

Table 3.1   Rural party recruitment (by occupation), 1929–32

Year (or part thereof)	Agricultural workers and batraks	Individual peasants	kolkhozniks
(percentages refer to the proportion of all recruits to the whole party)			
1929	—	—	8000[a]
first quarter 1930	19 119 (8.6%)[b]	4128 (1.8%)[b]	22 554 (10.1%)[b]
second quarter 1930	—	← peasants = 20% →	
fourth quarter 1930	—	—	53 000[d]
1930	56 539 (8.2%)[b]	20 667 (3.1%)[b]	150 814 (22.5%)[b]
first quarter 1931[e]	15 694	4617 (1.8%)	70 942 (28.7%)
second quarter 1931[e]	15 774 (7.1%)	2605 (1.2%)	75 719 (34.0%)
third quarter 1931[e]	14 990 (6.6%)	1913 (0.9%)	73 099 (32.2%)
fourth quarter 1931[e]	18 220 (6.1%)	1756 (0.6%)	75 752 (25.2%)
1931[e]	64 678 (6.5%)	10 890 (0.7%)	295 502 (29.6%)
first quarter 1932[f]	—	1484 (0.7%)	60 273 (25.8%)
second quarter 1932	—	—	⎫
third quarter 1932	—	—	⎬ 155 225[g]
fourth quarter 1932	—	—	⎭
1932	—	—	215 498[h]

Sources: (a) T.P. Bernstein, 'Leadership and Mobilisation in the Collectivisation of Agriculture in China and Russia: A Comparison', unpublished Ph.D. thesis, Columbia University 1970, p. 249; (b) *Partiinoe stroitel'stvo*, No. 17, September 1931, p. 40; (c) *Partiinoe stroitel'stvo*, No. 17, September 1930, p. 30; (d) *Partiinoe stroitel'stvo*, No. 13, July 1931, p. 5; (e) *Partiinoe stroitel'stvo*, No. 7–8, April 1932, p. 54; (f) *Partiinoe stroitel'stvo*, No. 15, August 1932, p. 52; (g) *Istoriya KPSS*, vol. 4, book 2, p. 89, based on archive sources states that 614 000 *kolkhozniks* were recruited to the party between July 1930 and the end of 1932. We presume that approximately 50 000 were recruited in the third quarter of 1930 and thus are able to arrive at this derivation of 155 225; (h) total arrived at by adding together figures for the four quarters of 1932.

that these individual-peasant communists would act as agitators for the formation of *kolkhozy*.

Our information on *kolkhoznik* recruitment in 1932 is not precise and we are unable to differentiate between the final three-quarters of the year. Recruitment to the rural party did not halt in the first half of the year; in fact the rural party increased its size quite considerably from 700 000 in January to 832 580 on 1 July.[31] Unfortunately one cannot state that recruitment in this six-month period was 132 000 because there is no exact correlation between a net increase and recruitment in party statistics.[32] T.H. Rigby, writing of the whole party, takes the down-turn in recruitment in 1932 for granted: 'In the course of 1932 the recruitment rate was progressively reduced, and enrollments for the year totalled less than half the figures for 1931'.[33] This certainly applied to the rural party, whose large organisations in the North Caucasus and Ukraine were undergoing a severe purge in the last months of 1932.[34] A cessation of all recruitment was announced on 11 December 1932, and one can imagine that party officials were made aware to some degree of what was in the offing and had reduced their recruitment rates in the weeks preceding the announcement. Accordingly one can surmise that recruitment in the last quarter of 1932 was minimal. Even so, the recruitment of *kolkhozniks* in 1932 did not follow exactly Rigby's pattern and remained at over two-thirds of its 1931 level. But taking into account the above reasoning, and the fact that 60 000 were recruited in the first quarter, it seems likely that a majority of the new members joined in the first half of the year. The effects of recruitment on the rural party size and composition are reflected in Table 3.2.

When comparing the total membership of the rural party at the beginning of each year and the recruitment conducted in the intervening years, major discrepancies are revealed. For example, between January 1930 and January 1931, the rural party grew from 339 201 to 516 897, and yet, judging from Table 3.1, in this year there was a minimum recruitment of 228 020, and thus we are left with a shortfall of 50 324 for 1930; similarly there was one of 187 967 for the period 1 January 1931– 1 January 1932.[35] These gaps are due to the fact that party members were expelled or left the party continually in numbers sufficient to account for these apparent disparities.[36]

The mass recruitment of collective farmers had a profound impact on rural party composition and the *kolkhoznik* became the major figure in the rural party. Another major element in the expansion was the agricultural workers and *batraks*, which from the end of 1929 composed between 15–20 per cent of the rural party membership. Between December 1927 and June 1930 this rural 'worker' contingent increased in absolute terms from 29 800 to 82 500, and as a proportion of the rural party grew from approximately 10 to 22 per cent.[37] In addition to this, in the first four months of 1930, 18 000 of the so-called '25 000-ers' were transferred from urban party organisations to rural ones.[38] Between 1 January and 1 April 1930 the rural party grew in size from 339 201 to 377 714, a net increase of 38 513, which included the intake of 25 000-ers mentioned above, who therefore represented 47 per cent of rural party growth in this crucial period.[39] If one includes these urban worker influxes in the rural party's 'worker' element for the summer 1930, then it rises as a proportion to 26.4 per cent.[40]

The accelerated recruitment greatly expanded the rural party ranks, which had only grown by 60 000 in the three years 1926–28 and had a membership of just over a third of a million when the first mass collectivisation drive was underway in January 1930. Two and a half years later the rural party was transformed; with a minimum membership of 832 000 in mid-1932, had recruitment trends continued, it would have reached the million mark in 1933 and been on the verge of becoming a mass organisation, instead of an isolated élite.

So far we have concerned ourselves primarily with quantitative indicators, but it is necessary to ask what underlying effects this massive recruitment had on the rural party membership's quality. The C.C. resolution *'O roste partii za 1930 god'* (On party growth in 1930) concluded that the results of 1930 were satisfactory and 'correspond with the tempo of socialist construction and the tasks of the party at this given stage', as Kaganovich would have wished.[41] However, scepticism about this optimistic appraisal is in order. Certainly in 1930 and the two following years the party devoted great efforts to the recruitment of huge numbers of *kolkhozniks* and agricultural workers. But there existed severe 'objective' difficulties which could not be quickly surmounted. As was argued earlier, the peasantry and the rural party were neglected in the 1920s.

It is quite difficult to evaluate the quality of rural communists and one is obliged to use the terms of reference employed in party literature without knowing how rigorous they were. But patchy information on the qualifications and abilities of rural recruits reveals few features of excellence. Of all new recruits to the rural party in the third quarter of 1931, only about 25 per cent had gone through some course of political training, only 12.9 per cent had been members of the *komsomol*. Among *kolkhoznik* recruits in the same period (73 099), only 20 per cent were awarded the vague, at times spurious, title of activist.[42] Of all *kolkhozniks* recruited in 1931, 28.9 per cent had passed through political schools and circles, and some five per cent were illiterate.[43] Illiteracy was to remain a problem in the more backward areas for some years. In the first and second quarters of 1932, among *kolkhoznik* recruits some improvement on the previous year was discernible: over 34 per cent had attended political schools; this was quite an achievement when in the first quarter of 1932 only 34.7 per cent of urban worker recruits had undergone similar training.[44] The scattered evidence seems to indicate that the majority of new recruits had not made any strong effort prior to joining the party to ally themselves with the forces of socialism, although

Table 3.2 Rural party size and composition (by occupation), 1928–32

Date	1 Agricultural workers and batraks	2 Individual peasants	3 kolkhozniks	4 residual[a]	Rural party size[b]
1 July 1928[c]	24 119 (7.6%)	145 148 (45.7%)	16 915 (5.3%)	131 421 (41.4%)	317 603
1 October 1929[c]	46 892 (13.4%)	134 178 (38.3%)	61 148 (17.5%)	107 782 (30.8%)	c.350 000
1 January 1930[c]	64 669 (19.1%)	78 474 (23.1%)	85 335 (25.2%)	110 552 (32.6%)	339 000
1 January 1931[c]	77 330 (15.1%)	44 256 (8.6%)	291 498 (56.4%)	103 813 (20.1%)	516 897
1 April 1931[c]	86 601 (15.5%)	33 605 (6.0%)	354 283[i] (63.3%)	85 511 (15.3%)	c.560 000
1 January 1932	113 145[d] (16.2%)	14 480[d] (2.1%)	426 059[e] / 517 356[d][ii]	146 316 (20.9%) / 55 019 (7.8%)	700 000
1 July 1932	c.125 000[g] (15.0%)	12 468[f] (1.5%)	557 964[f] (67.0%)	137 148 (16.5%)	832 000

Sources: (a) this column is obtained by subtracting columns one, two and three from column five. The calculated residual coincides on the whole with Soviet sources, see S.P. Trapeznikov, *Istoricheskii opyt KPSS v osushchestvlenii leninskogo kooperativnogo plana,* p. 222 and *Partiinoe stroitel'stvo,* No. 9, May 1930, p. 21; (b) for rural party membership figures and sources, see Appendix 1; (c) *Partiinoe stroitel'stvo,* No. 17, September 1931, p. 39; (d) *Partiinoe stroitel'-stvo,* No. 9, May 1932, p. 51; (e) *Partiinoe stroitel'stvo,* No. 11–12, June 1932, p. 47; (f) my derivations from *Partiinoe stroitel'stvo,* No. 21, November 1932, p. 48; (g) this is an estimate based on the facts that there were at this time few genuine agricultural workers and *batraks* left in the countryside to be recruited, and during the first Five Year Plan their proportion remained stable between 13–19 per cent.

Notes: (i) The figure for *kolkhozniks* in the party on 1 April 1931 surpasses by some 50 000 the starting figure of *kolkhozniks* in the party on 1 January 1930 *plus* those recruited in the interim: this was made up by *batrak* party members and individual peasant party members joining the collective farms and being classified as *kolkhozniks.* A process which balanced this to an extent, which we are not able to quantify, is that of *kolkhozniks* leaving the rural party organisations for industry or education, being expelled from the party or leaving it 'mechanically' by not paying party dues and so forth.

(ii) This figure of 517 356 *kolkhozniks* by occupation is flatly contradicted in *Partiinoe stroitel'stvo,* No. 11–12, June 1932, p. 47, which gives the figure of 426 059. They are made slightly more compatible by the fact that the higher figure refers to *kolkhozniks* by occupation in all party organisations, whereas the June 1932 source refers only to rural cells: of course the number of *kolkhozniks* by occupation not in rural cells would not be great, except for some scattered single communists, and so the discrepancy remains large. Which of the two figures is to be preferred? The source of which gives 517 356 *kolkhozniks* leads to a total of 644 981 *kolkhozniks,* individual peasants and *batraks* and others, with a total rural party membership of 700 000: this means the residual for employees is a mere 56 000 or 8 per cent of the rural membership. This percentage is ridiculously low and casts severe doubts on the usefulness of the figure 517 356 in our specific analysis of the rural party.

in many rural areas opportunities to do this may not have presented themselves very frequently.

The calibre of rural communists was not helped by the inability of the rural party, to an even greater extent than the rest of the party, to devise a technical-administrative system, capable of assimilating and processing efficiently the many hundreds of thousands of new candidates to the party. The deepening problem is manifest in the following data: whereas in January 1930 some 29.2 per cent of all party members were candidates, the figure in the rural party was 43.3 per cent; in January 1931 the respective figures were 38.9 and 54.4 per cent and by January 1932 these figures had risen to 43.3 and 60.2 per cent.[45] In certain areas, such as the Western *oblast* with many rural communists scattered in numerous small *kolkhozy*, the percentage of candidates reached 70–80 per cent.[46] Of the 43.4 per cent of all party members who were candidates in January 1932, 42 per cent were overdue for transfer to full membership. Among agricultural workers who were party candidates the figure was 61.5 per cent, and 250 of these had been candidates for as long as five years and more, instead of the usual probationary period of one year. Among *kolkhoznik* candidates 30 per cent were overdue for transfer.[47] Candidates lingered in this status for two major reasons. Firstly, the local party committee or cell did not think the candidate merited promotion to full membership, either because of a lack of educational and political knowledge or of enthusiasm and effort. Secondly, the filing system of the rural party was non-existent or chaotic; the promotion of candidates was often bogged down in a morass of red-tape and confusion.

As we argue elsewhere,[48] with the economic failures of 1932–33, the blame was laid unfairly on the rural party and a decision taken to purge its ranks extensively. The economic difficulties were not the fault of the rural party and it was beyond its scope and means to remedy them. But this is not to deny that the quality of rural party membership was exceptionally poor. The rapid mass recruitment of poorly trained, poorly educated peasants did not compensate for the inadequate preparation of the 1920s; the belated response was undermined and flawed by its internal contradictions.

THE LOCATION OF RURAL COMMUNISTS

Collectivisation transformed the countryside and changed the lives of those who lived in it; rural communists were no exception. For much of the 1920s most of the rural party was locked into its peasant environment. A minority of rural communists, however, were in the forefront of the collectivisation movement even before the collectivisation drive of 1929, as is depicted in Table 3.3.

The Process and the Debate

Material from several sources indicates that the communists who joined the *kolkhozy* before the end of 1928, that is before great pressure was brought to bear on party members, were motivated by a sincere belief in

Table 3.3   The level of collectivisation of peasant-communists and all peasant households, 1928–30

Date	Percentage of peasant–communist households collectivised	Percentage of all peasant households collectivised[d]
January 1928	6.0[a]	1.0
July 1928	13–14[b]	1.7 June
October 1929	37.0[a]	7.5
January 1930	52.0[a]	18.1
April 1930	75.3[c]	38.6

Sources: (a) V.P. Danilov, *'K kharakteristike obshchestvenno-politicheskoi obstanovki v sovetskoi derevne nakanune kollektivizatsii'* in *Istoricheskie zapiski*, No. 79, 1966, p. 15; (b) *Izvestiya TsK VKP (b)*, No. 1 (260), 16 January 1929, p. 5; (c) S.P. Trapeznikov, *Istoricheskii opyt KPSS v osushchestvlenii leninskogo kooperativnogo plana*, p. 225; (d) R.W. Davies, *The Industrialisation of Soviet Russia, vol. 1. The Socialist Offensive. The Collectivisation of Soviet Agriculture, 1929–1930*, Table 17, pp. 442–3.

the desirability and need for collective agriculture. They were therefore often willing to embrace it in its most extreme form, the commune: a sample survey in Siberia, the Volga and North Caucasus regions in 1928 gave the party layer in communes as 18 per cent, *artels* 4.9 per cent and *tozy* 6.1 per cent.[49] But there is little doubt that there was considerable initial resistance to collectivisation on principle among party members. Moreover, in 1925–28 collective farming was still very much a matter of trial and error. During a discussion which took place at the end of the 1920s in the Novosibirsk *okrug* on whether to set up an *artel*, a party member named Moskvin stood up and warned of how the situation had been in the middle of the decade:

> If you want to be left without your pants, go ahead and get together. I tried last year and joined a machine association; but it collapsed and I was left without my cows. So I advise you not to do this.[50]

But opposition among party members was often based on a frank preference for individual farming. I. Gladkov wrote from Barnaul *okrug* that: 'We have . . . party members who openly declare "we have milk, a horse and a cow – go and collectivise those who have nothing" '.[51] On the basis of the rural party conferences held in 1929, a party journal concluded that 'the majority of rural communists are not entering and do not wish to enter the kolkhozy'.[52]

Particular pressure to join the *kolkhozy* was exerted on the well-to-do elements within the rural party and in effect the rural party underwent dekulakisation before the peasant masses. Party members, unlike the ordinary peaasants, were, at least in 1928–29, given the option of joining the *kolkhozy* or leaving the party.[53] Some did in fact leave the party. The campaign for drawing all peasant communists into the *kolkhozy* took off in the party press in January 1929 with the publication of a discussion article by M. Vareikis, not to be confused with I. Vareikis, the first party secretary of the Central Black Earth *obkom*.[54] It is probably not coincidental that this press campaign occurred so soon after the intimations of a forthcoming purge at the November 1928 C.C. plenum. Vareikis was in favour of giving the benefit of the doubt to party members who were not well-to-do in a number of mitigating circumstances (such as long distances from *kolkhozy* and the potential break-up of a communist household on joining): they were not to be forced to join *kolkhozy*.[55] This discussion article provoked a sharp reaction from many commentators, who argued that Vareikis had adopted far too lenient an approach in allowing for mitigating circumstances which were so prevalent that they would have led to only a dedicated minority of the rural party joining the *kolkhozy*. The debate on the circumstances in which peasant-communists should or should not join the *kolkhozy* was a genuine one, just as the question of entry of the non-party kulak provoked a real exchange of views.

The campaign to recruit communists to the collective farms had substantial results. From October 1928 to October 1929 the proportion of communists who had joined the *kolkhozy* rose from 6.3 per cent to 37.3 per cent, while by the latter date only 5 per cent of peasants had joined.[56] The national campaign was accompanied by a range of measures at local level. On 22 August 1928 the plenum of the Moldavian *obkom* noted 'the low percentage of rural communists in kolkhozy' and proposed 'to party cells within the next six months to overcome this situation'. In January 1929 the same plenum hardened its attitude by obliging communists to join *kolkhozy* and to establish them where they did not already exist; this latter proviso prevented party members from using the excuse that there were too few *kolkhozy* to join in their particular area.[57] A similar decision was taken by the Lower Volga *kraikom* on 14 February 1929, and in early 1929 the Mid-Volga *kraikom* insisted that 80 per cent of its rural communists were to be in 'production co-operation' by the end of the spring sowing: the language and style of action were to be repeated exactly one year later.[58]

Party members sometimes reacted in ways which were later found on a mass scale among the non-party peasants. One party member stated: 'If they send me by force, I will go [into the *kolkhoz*], but first I will squander my holding in booze'.[59]

The Reasons

Our evidence so far confirms the judgement of M. Lewin relating to party members of *kolkhozy* in 1929:

> During the previous years nothing had been done to prepare the Party cadres for the important tasks that lay ahead of them, and all of a sudden they were being called upon to act as pioneers in a revolution which they did not understand and which was not of their choosing.[60]

But there were a number of reasons to explain why party members did in fact join *kolkhozy*.[61] One factor was certainly that some peasant party members were poor: for example, in 1927 some 20 per cent of rural party members in the RSFSR and Ukraine were without working animals or machinery. These peasants may well have been persuaded of the advantages of collective agriculture.[62] Secondly, some party cadres who belonged to the middle-level party committees of the *ukom* were recruited to the party in the heady days of the Civil War, and may well have held radical views on the collectivisation of agriculture. But the third and major factor in promoting party members into the collective farms consisted of the threat of the party purge. In many ways Vareikis and his fellow thinkers were arguing against the trend of the times. Strong psychological pressure was brought to bear on party members. It was proposed that in the forthcoming party purge rural communists should be asked 'and what did you do for the collectivisation of agriculture?'[63] One of the hard-liners of Biisk *okrug* advocated the dissolution (*rospusk*) of party cells that did not demonstrate initiative in the collectivisation process.[64] Early in 1929 E. Yaroslavsky in a letter on behalf of the Central Control Commission advised that the rural purge should concentrate on the economic position of each party member, including whether he was in a *kolkhoz*.[65] In instructions on the purge published in *Pravda* in May 1929, with reference to peasant members, extra attention was to be focused on the economic strength of the household to which they belonged, and to whether they were involved in any party duties in the co-operatives and especially in the *kolkhozy*.[66] The screw was tightening.

The proportion of rural communists reported to have been expelled for refusing to join a *kolkhoz* varied during the year. In preliminary figures published in the autumn of 1929, seven per cent of those expelled were purged for not joining a *kolkhoz*, a figure which declined to 4.7 per cent in the more comprehensive data available in the summer of 1930.[67] This proportion decreased further when Yaroslavsky, at the sixteenth party congress of June 1930, quoted the figure of 3.6 per cent of rural party members expelled for refusal to join a *kolkhoz* and for hiding grain surpluses, whereas in the above preliminary figures for September 1929 these joint figures equalled 10.2 per cent.[68] These in fact are not particularly high levels of expulsion but since in All-Union surveys usually only one ground for expulsion was cited, instances of party members refusing to join the *kolkhozy* are probably hidden behind the headings for expulsion such as 'distortion of the party line'. The figures also imply that rural communists were less persecuted in the later stages of the purge in 1930 by which time many had entered the collective farms and could no longer be accused of this particular misdemeanour. One should not be too surprised that the number and proportion of those expelled for refusing to join a *kolkhoz* are not significantly higher. The *threat* of the purge was successful in persuading party members of the advisability of joining *kolkhozy*: '*pour encourager les autres*' was definitely one of the main justifications of the rural purge. Judging by the increased proportion of party members who had joined the *kolkhozy* by the end of 1929, it appears evident that most rural communists had been made aware of the direction of the 'general line' concerning the collective farms, and were prepared, reluctantly in some cases, to follow it.

Regional data presented in Table 3.4 clearly reveal the consolidation of the communist party in the collective farms, and show both that the party was the vanguard, and that during the exodus of the spring of 1930 it also acted as a rearguard.

Table 3.4 shows that the involvement of rural party members was widespread and strong, not only in the major grain regions, but also in such areas as White Russia and the *oblasts* of Moscow and Leningrad where, with a lower level of collectivisation, there would have been fewer incentives to join.[69] Important figures are those for the months of April and July 1930, which testify that the peasant-communists remained in the *kolkhozy* at this time, while peasants generally left the *kolkhozy* in huge numbers. There was some outflow of party members from the *kolkhozy* in the period April – July 1930 but this was very small in the major grain regions and moderate in such consumer areas as Moscow and Kirgiziya.

Whilst a proportion of the figures for peasant-communists was artificially inflated and inflated in 'paper *kolkhozy*', as were all figures

Table 3.4   The percentage of peasant-communist households in collective farms compared with all peasant households (in brackets) in 1930

Region	1 January 1930	1 April 1930	1 July 1930
Lower Volga	83.2% (58–70%)	97.0% (54.0%)	96.3% (36.1%)
Mid Volga	65.8% (41.7%)	92.7% (43.8%)	90.6% (27.0%)
North Caucasus	71.4% (48.1%)	88.8% (67.0%)	90.0% (50.2%)
Ukraine	62.1% (15.9%)	85.8% (46.5%)	—
Siberia	55.4% (5–19%)	75.8% (43.0%)	—
Urals	72.8% (38.9%)	92.9% (57.8%)	—
White Russia	62.7%	90.5%	—
Moscow	46.4% (14.3%)	76.5% (12.5%)	67.0% (7.3%)
Leningrad	40.3%	71.0%	—
Kirgiziya	15.2%	38.5%	—

Sources: The percentages referring to all peasant households are from R.W. Davies, *The Industrialisation of Soviet Russia, vol. 1. The Socialist Offensive. The Collectivisation of Soviet Agriculture, 1929–1930*, Table 17, pp. 442–3; those for communists in January 1930 are from V. Vlasov, in *Partiinoe stroitel'stvo*, No. 9, May 1930, pp. 19–29; percentages for communists in April 1930 are from *Partiinoe stroitel'stvo*, No. 11–12, June 1930, p. 18; those for communists in July 1930 are from ibid., No. 18, September 1930, p. 16.

for *kolkhozy* during the first months of 1930, the rural communists were personally firmer in their commitment to collective agriculture than the ordinary peasant-*kolkhoznik*. However, their 'faith' in the *kolkhozy* may have been somewhat superficial and should not be overemphasised. The rural communist would have been more wary of 'deserting' the *kolkhozy* than the ordinary peasant and more aware of the consequences for himself of such an action, bearing in mind past warnings made during the purge. The rural communist was at times more faithful on principle to collective agriculture, but at the time of the exodus also much more conscious of the possibility of a future zig-zag in policy in favour of the *kolkhoz* system, which did indeed occur with the renewed drive of the autumn-winter 1930 and the first months of 1931. Perhaps the communists came to realise before the peasants generally that there would be no turning back the clock. The fact that the rural communists were first in and last out of the *kolkhozy*, if they left at all, can in part be attributed to the increased discipline within the rural party as a consequence of the recent purge. The threat of discipline in the rural party and the party as a whole was to be a major theme of the next decade, although it would not always be as successful in achieving the required aims as it had been in encouraging the rural communist to join the *kolkhoz*. For several years to come rural party members would put up recalcitrant resistance to orders from above. Then they were to be purged with a vengeance.

THE OCCUPATION OF RURAL COMMUNISTS

The question of the occupations of peasant rural communists is approached in three ways. Firstly, we consider the information available on the proportion of rural communists working directly in agricultural production; secondly, we examine the party layer in a number of posts; and thirdly, these two preceding threads are brought together when we present material on the numbers and proportion of rural communists in specific work areas.

In the mid-1920s only 45.3 per cent of rural communists worked exclusively on their holdings and 12.6 per cent shared their time between their holdings and paid administrative work; presumably this left some 40 per cent working completely in non-agricultural activities.[70] By January 1928 the proportion of employees had risen to 44.5 per cent. The percentage then dropped sharply to 29.9 per cent by January 1930.[71] The party journal *Partiinoe stroitel'stvo* claimed that the proportion of 'administrative-economic employees' in the rural party declined to 20.4 per cent (103 542) on 1 January 1931 and 19.6 per cent (135 182) on 1 January 1932.[72] T.H. Rigby is most sceptical about this and states that:

> Although in 1932 only one fifth of kolkhoz communists were 'officially' registered as 'managerial and nonmanual workers', a careful study showed that the actual proportion was in most cases 70 to 80 per cent.[73]

There were numerous reports that rural communists avoided production work. One *komsomol* cell secretary refused quite bluntly to move into production work and several others declared that: 'it is not dignified for a communist or *komsomol* member to walk behind a plough'.[74]

We endorse Rigby's view that only a minority of rural communists worked directly in production, but it is difficult to furnish detailed documentation. Soviet sources vary and are frequently contradictory. Nationally the proportion of rural communists working directly in production officially fluctuated between 49.4 per cent in 1930, 58.2 per cent in 1931 and between 30–35 per cent and 76.3 per cent in 1932 alone.[75] Regionally the picture was even more confused with the proportion in production in 1932 amounting to 5–10 per cent in the North Caucasus, 35.7 per cent in the Lower Volga and 60 per cent in the Central Black Earth and Mid-Volga.[76] These wild discrepancies may be explained in large part by the mobilisation of rural communists for temporary field work during the spring and summer peak agricultural months. For example, in the Petrovsky *kolkhoz* in the Novobug *raion*, Ukraine, at the time of the spring sowing of 1930, 45–50 per cent of party members were busy in production work of various sorts, but once this campaign had finished, this cell reverted to normal practice as did 'many others', and usually only 25–30 per cent were engaged in production work.[77]

Evidently there was a problem. The C.C. made its most important statement on the issue in a resolution dated 15 May 1932, which instructed local party organisations to prohibit 'inappropriate transfers' of party members, *komsomols* and non-party people from production into non-production work.[78] The objective set was for 70 per cent of rural communists to work directly in agricultural production,[79] but, despite some instances where this was achieved, it is essential to note that this call was so frequent, so persistent and so repetitive that it is unlikely to have ever been successfully fulfilled before the war.[80]

The problem existed because, having achieved a large influx of communists into the *kolkhozy* in 1929–30, a conflict of interests arose between the desire to maintain the proletarian ideal that communists would work in production, and the urgent need to promote them into administrative posts. Local rural communists themselves sought out administrative positions and this wish was supported by the party's need to supervise and control the nascent socialised economy. Thanks to directed training programmes, promotion and recruitment, the party layer among *kolkhoz* chairmen in the North Caucasus was a very large 88.6 per cent in 1931 and 72.4 per cent in the Lower Volga in the same year.[81] The *kolkhoz* chairmen in these samples were predominantly of peasant origin (over 80 per cent), the proportion of workers, 10–15 per cent, being explained by urban influxes.[82] Some of the peasants who joined the party in the early stages of collectivisation evidently experienced significant social mobility: this was one of the rewards available for those who supported the regime.[83]

As recruitment accelerated, the rural party disposed of more manpower resources to deploy in large numbers throughout the *kolkhoz* administrative hierarchy. Table 3.5 shows to what extent the party permeated the administration posts in the *kolkhozy*.

Table 3.5   The percentage of *kolkhoz* administration members with party or *komsomol* membership in the Soviet Union and North Caucasus, 1929–31

Region	1929 party	komsomol	1930 party	komsomol	1931 party	komsomol
USSR	14.0%	4.6%	22.2%	5.6%	31.6%	9.2%
North Caucasus	12.6%	4.0%	30.9%	3.1%	44.1%	6.5%

Source: E.I. Lar'kina, *Podgotovka kolkhoznykh kadrov v period massovoi kollektivizatsii*, p. 98.

This party layer among such a large grouping as *kolkhoz* administration members was significant. Table 3.5 suggests quite strongly that the rural party obtained greater administrative control of *kolkhozy* in key grain areas like the North Caucasus, where it also disposed of comparatively large rural party organisations. The absolute numbers involved in the above developments must have been large. With 57 000 *kolkhozy* in 1929, 86 000 in 1930 and 211 000 in 1931, and assuming three or four members in each *kolkhoz* administration, the percentages in Table 3.5 mean that in the USSR as a whole in these years respectively there were 28 000, 66 200 and 233 000 rural communists in the *kolkhoz* administrations, although not necessarily working as such full-time: approximately this represented 8 per cent of the entire rural party membership in 1929, 20 per cent in 1930 and 45 per cent in 1931. Such a trend was maintained throughout the first Five Year Plan and beyond. In October 1933 over the whole country, only 34.2 per cent of the *kolkhoz* party membership were ordinary *kolkhozniks*, 15.7 per cent brigade leaders and 11.1 per cent were *kolkhoz* chairmen.[84] Presumably many others (40–50 per cent) were heads of production branches, as they had been in 1932.[85] One can safely conclude that for most of the first Five Year Plan and afterwards, a significant majority of rural communists held important posts of responsibility, authority, supervision and control at various levels in the production hierarchy on either a full-time or part-time basis; only a minority resembled their non-party colleagues in the *kolkhozy*, and laboured full-time in the fields.

Thus during 1929–32 rural party membership had been transformed to keep in line with developments in the collectivised countryside. The party had grown in size and changed its composition to seek close links with the collective farms and other economic units such as *sovkhozy* and the machine tractor stations (MTS).

The two following chapters examine respectively the organisations in which these party members were present and the operations and policies carried out by them.

4 The District Party Committee (*raikom*): Organisation, Structure and Personnel 1929–32

As it became more enmeshed in the control and supervision of the rural socialised economy, the rural party increased its level of organisational sophistication and introduced organisational changes to meet social, political and economic circumstances. This chapter discusses how the party at district (*raion*) level reacted organisationally to the new demands made upon it during the first Five Year Plan.

A most prominent debate on organisation in the period 1925–50 revolved around the issue whether to organise on the basis of functions such as personnel, propaganda, culture and inner-party work and so forth, whereby functional departments supervised their relevant subject in all subordinate party organisations, or to adopt a system which followed production branch lines, wherein the party department supervised all functions within a particular branch of the economy such as transport, heavy industry or agriculture. During the 1920s a functional system of organisation was taken for granted; in the years of the New Economic Policy, when the national economy was comparatively less developed, anything else would have been inappropriate. This functional system remained much in vogue until 1934, when it was argued that such a structure was poorly adapted to enforce unified party control over the various branches of the economy and government. In 1939 a further reorganisation was put into effect, which involved almost a complete return to the functional scheme that had prevailed prior to 1934. This was partly because the purges of the mid-1930s had engendered a crisis of personnel. Under the 1934 system responsibility for the selection of cadres had been divided among numerous competing industrial-branch departments, and the return to functionalism met a temporary need. As early as 1939 and in the post-war period, there was a partial and then full return to the production principles of the 1934 structure, and these arrangements (with some modifications and expansion) have been retained until present.[1]

In the rural party's substructure everything was less rigid and clear-cut. Much organisational reform was misunderstood and poorly explained, and demarcation of authority between party units was left ambiguous. Most important in the rural party, there were fewer means of verifying that orders were obeyed as they were communicated downwards through the party hierarchy.

THE EVOLUTION OF THE *RAION*

During the 1920s the *raion* and the *raikom* gained in stature until in 1930 they emerged as the central link at the middle-lower levels of the administrative hierarchy, acting as an intermediary between the central authorities at *krai* and *oblast* level on the one hand and the village and the *kolkhoz* on the other.

Outlines of a new administrative system to replace the existing *volosts*, *uezds* and *guberniyas* were accepted by the Central Executive Committee in March 1921. By the beginning of 1924 change was underway, but

Figure 4.1   The party administrative hierarchy during the first Five Year Plan

Pre-1929	Summer 1929	Autumn 1930	Spring 1931
republic	republic	republic	republic
guberniya	krai or oblast	krai or oblast	krai or oblast
uezd	okrug		
		raion	raion
	raion		
volost			
rural cells	rural cells (10)	rural cells (10–20)	rural cells (20–35)

Note: Figures in brackets refer to approximate number of party cells in an average *raion*, not taking into account regional variation.

change was gradual. Until the 1930s the old and the new units existed simultaneously in different parts of the country. The party hierarchy during the first Five Year Plan is presented in Figure 4.1.

Some statistics as presented in Table 4.1 will give an idea of the size of these administrative units and the populations they contained.

The rationalisation and enlargement of the administrative units throughout the 1920s was an economic and social–political process: a means of reducing the number of units and thereby simplifying the administrative machine and one which, it was hoped, would require less manpower and fewer finances. Unfortunately for the peasant, the gradual disappearance of the *volost* detached him further from the centre of local administration and from the party, requiring him to travel further to the new *raion* centres. Until 1929 the *raikom*'s status was equivalent to that of the *volkom*. The years 1928–30 saw the steady progress of the role of the *raion* and the party centre, the *raikom*. Confirmation of the *raion*'s growing importance was made at the

Table 4.1 Size and population of some administrative units before and after 1929

Administrative unit	Old system (prior to 1929)	
	Number of rural Soviets	Number of inhabitants
one *guberniya*	1200 village Soviets[a]	1 380 000 inhabitants[b]
one *uezd*[c]	136 village Soviets	210 367 inhabitants
one *volost*[c]	14 village Soviets	22 040 inhabitants
	New system (1929)	
one *oblast*	1600 village Soviets[a]	3 500 000 inhabitants[a]
one *okrug*[c]	299 village Soviets	583 988 inhabitants[d]
one *raion*[c]	22 village Soviets	44 814 inhabitants[d]

Sources: (a) My estimates based on *Administrativno-territorial'noe delenie soyuza SSR i spisok naselennikh punktov* (M. 1929), pp. 12–21. These are only average figures which cannot take into account considerable regional variations; (b) E.H. Carr, *Socialism in One Country*, vol. 2, p. 296. This refers to the average population of a *guberniya* in the RSFSR in 1924; (c) *Administrativno-territorial'noe delenie soyuza SSR i spisok naselennikh punktov* (M. 1929), eighth edition, pp. 20–1; (d) These represent average populations in the RSFSR, but covered variations depending on population densities, of from 1 013 340 in an *okrug* and 62 622 for a *raion* in the Central Black Earth *oblast* to 230 799 and 26 759 respectively in the Far Eastern *krai*, *Administrativno-territorial'noe delenie soyuza SSSR*, pp. 12 and 21.

sixteenth party congress in the summer 1930, but no alteration made in the party statutes at what would have been a convenient juncture to do so.[2] It was left to the C.C. resolution of 6 August 1930 to determine more fully the *raikom*'s authority: the *raikom* and *gorkom* (town committee) could now confirm new worker or peasant recruits, and the required length of party membership for a *raikom* secretary was extended from three to five years.[3] And yet it should not be thought that the party apparatus within the *raikom* prior to 1930 was particularly large. With the number of communists within the boundaries of a *raion* varying between less than 100 and as many as 300, the *raikom* staff available to supervise them could be as sparse as a single secretary and perhaps one or two assistants.[4]

THE ABOLITION OF THE *OKRUG*

The abolition of the *okrugs* as an administrative unit and the transfer of their staffs to the *raions* is treated here as an example of how administrative and organisational reform was carried out at the local levels and of how party cadres resisted the central authorities' commands for party mobilisation with obdurate recalcitrance.

Several excuses, some valid, some less so, were advanced for the abolition of the *okrugs*. Claims were made that party organisations subordinate to the *okruzhkom*, such as the *raikoms* and large party cells, were expanding rapidly, taking on more responsibility: it seems that these bodies were pushing upwards in the party hierarchy leaving the *okrugs* nowhere to go.[5] The *okruzhkoms* were criticised for their inattention to the *raikoms*. The party at okrug level was also condemned as a useless intermediary, which merely delayed the passage of directives to lower units for a week or as long as a month. An appealing justification for phasing out the *okrugs* and replacing them with *raions* was that this would reduce party and administrative costs.[6] However, raionisation did not entail large reductions in the party's wage bill, as the *okrug* workers were to retain their salaries on moving to the *raions*, and as the *raion* party organisation acquired more responsibilities, so the *raion* party staff would be remunerated accordingly.

A C.C. resolution adopted on 15 July 1930 abolished the *okrugs*. It instructed that all *okrug* enterprises and budgets be taken over by the *raions*, together with their administrative authority. The C.C. directed the *krai* and *oblast* apparatus to adopt a stance of 'face to *raion*'.[7] The party authorities wanted the *raikoms*, who were to have greater control over the cells and countryside as a whole, to be in more or less direct contact with the *obkoms* and *kraikoms*, which were only one step away from the Organisational–Instruction Department of the C.C. (*Orginst*); thus ultimately, the *obkoms* and C.C. were to benefit. With their new increased duties and responsibilities, the *raikoms* were to leave minor matters to the rural Soviets and *raion* executive committees, which received their own budgets and were in charge of social, cultural institutions within their territory.

Any fruitful development of the *raikom* was hampered because of a shortage of cadres. At the sixteenth party congress in June 1930, just prior to the resolution, J.V. Stalin posed a question and, as was his style, answered it:

> Are the raion party organisations provided adequately with the necessary workers in order to bear all this varied work? There can be no doubt that they are provided most inadequately with workers.[8]

Therefore, the most important section of the 15 July 1930 resolution stipulated that, in order to buttress the *raions*, 90 per cent of *okrug* staff be transferred there. Not only *okrug* party workers were involved but all other workers in *okrug* institutions. The planned abolition of the *okrugs* envisaged the release of 100 000 *okrug* workers (party and non-party) to the *raions*, with the final result being that 10–12 experienced party workers would be transferred to each *raion*.[9] However, a warning of lurking dangers was already available. The *raion* party organisations were supposed to have been well supplied with party workers from the *guberniya* and *uezd* levels, that is higher party authorities, and yet in 1929, 82 per cent of *raion* party workers in the Central Black Earth *oblast* were drawn from the former *volosts* or villages, whilst only 18 per cent had experienced *guberniya* or *uezd* work.[10]

Many of the *okrug* staff did transfer to the *raions*. *Pravda* reassured them that this did not imply a 'punishment' or a 'demotion'.[11] But many must have felt resentment at what they regarded as a demotion in leaving the *okrug* centres for what they saw as the backwoods of the *raions* with their poor facilities. Once there, the *okrug* workers tended to be nominated to the best posts, no doubt to the chagrin of those *raion* workers already present. Even so, the *okrug* workers, party and non-party people alike, resisted the move to the *raions* and the authorities were obliged to resort to all the psychological, propagandistic and administrative techniques at their disposal.

The staff in Kozlovskii *okrug* even pre-empted the resolution by disbanding themselves and drifting away to the *oblast* centres.[12] Within a fortnight other reports were coming in that as soon as the resolution was published, some *okrug* workers were obtaining transfers to the *oblast* centres.[13] A *Pravda* editorial on the day following the resolution's publication was quick to warn the *kraikoms* and *obkoms* from poaching more than their allotted share of *okrug* staff.[14] To escape orders they disliked, the *okrug* personnel employed an amazing variety of subterfuge and trickery: excuses given by party members, remarkably similar to those used the year before in refusing to join the *kolkhozy*, referred to family problems, illness and the need to study.[15] In Central Asia the okrug party secretaries departed on their summer vacations never to be seen again, in neither their *okrug* nor the new *raions*.[16] In the Vladimir *okrug*, to cover up the deficit of *okrug* workers arriving in the *raions*, the *okruzhkom* ordered a merry-go-round of transfers back and forth between *raions* to make it appear that new people were frequently turning up; in the North Caucasus efforts to circumvent the transfer were 'epidemic'.[17] Nor was there any proper verification that those people transferred ever actually reached their destination, and there were many cases of those who 'mixed up their addresses' (*oshibilis adresom*) and 'didn't arrive' (*ne doekhali*).[18] Others were less subtle and simply stone-walled in their refusal to be transferred. There was the case of the *okrug* worker in Ostrogozhskii, named Vold'man, who sent a succinct telegram to the *raion* to which he had been assigned, which read simply: 'Don't bother waiting for me. Yours, Vold'man.'[19] Nor was it only the *okrug* workers who were undisciplined. Despite the remonstrations of the central authorities, the North Caucasus *kraikom* creamed off 17 per cent of *okrug* party workers and kept a further 7 per cent as a mere reserve without any specific duties.[20]

To combat this recalcitrance and outright disobedience, the C.C. responded with two resolutions of 6 and 11 August 1930 reaffirming the necessity of transferring 90 per cent of the *okrug* staffs to the *raions*. The *Pravda* edition of 29 August carried headlines across half the page promoting the transfer, as well as complaining that this was not being achieved and warned that those who refused would be expelled from the party.[21] Reports of expulsions were published to encourage stragglers: in Pyatigorsk two *okrug* party workers were expelled and four more by the Remontinskii *raion* control commission.[22] Similarly, a party cell secretary was expelled for going to Moscow instead of a rural *raion*; other communists refusing to go to the *raions* were labelled deserters.[23] The expulsions, judging from available sources, seem not to have been massive in number, but were certainly an important part of the package of measures adopted by the central authorities in their administrative battle with the *okrug* staff. It testifies to the vigour of the conflict that the *obkoms* and C.C. saw fit to use this final sanction and is characteristic of the interrelationships between the various levels within the party hierarchy. When the centre could not coax, cajole or command its subordinates into submission, it expelled them, but there is little doubt that many of the *okrug* party personnel escaped such reprisals and arrived successfully where they wanted. Expulsions from the party over administrative squabbles did not necessarily signify a victory for the party authorities, more often this phenomenon was a pointer to their defeat: this inability to control the lower levels without administrative sanctions is an important theme in our study.

Before evaluating how successfully the 15 July resolution was carried out, it is worth noting a curious feature of how the party committees chose to implement it. The resolution specified that its instructions were to be completed by 1 October 1930. Seemingly without rhyme or reason, the *obkoms* and *kraikoms* were soon intoxicated by the desire to overfulfil the 90 per cent figure and to finish the reorganisation before the target date. This approach was not necessary, nor does it seem called for by the C.C., and could only contribute to impair the resolution's proper fulfilment.[24] Administrative reforms of this type did not require alacrity, but care, attention and patience. In the Central Black Earth, where 173 *raions* were to replace 12 *okrugs*, the *obkom* decided to complete the change by 1 September and to send 95 per cent of *okrug* staff to the *raions*.[25] Quickly following this decision, M. Khataevich, first secretary of the Mid-Volga *kraikom*, announced that in this *krai* the reform and transfer would be finished during August.[26] Despite sensible warnings that a too rapid phasing-out of the *okrugs* would mean that they could not assist the *raions* during the transition phase, the regions continued their helter-skelter race. The completion dates set by the *kraikoms* and *obkoms* themselves were: Lower Volga – 1 August, a mere two weeks after the publication of the resolution, so presumably this *krai*, like others, had made prior arrangements; the Central Black Earth *obkom* brought forward once again its date to 10 August, coinciding with that of the Western *oblast*; the Urals *obkom* and North Caucasus *kraikom* aimed for 15 August and the Ukraine for 1 September, with only the Siberian and Northern *kraikoms* retaining the original date of 1 October.[27] One would presume that such haste in a complex reorganisation of the rural administration could only be pernicious, so why did the party organisations seek to accelerate the process? Firstly, and typically, they may have done so in an attempt to outbid each other, to display their zeal and efficiency, although this does seem foolhardy, especially after the censure incurred for chasing wild percentages during the collectivisation drive only a few months earlier. Secondly, and more vague, it may have been due to an element in the communist party psyche to overcome obstacles with as much bravado and fanfare as possible. Thirdly, and more practically, it may have been caused by the need to free party forces from administrative technicalities at the end of the harvest and during the vital grain procurement campaign.[28]

Was the reorganisation and its transfer of 90 per cent of the okrug staffs involving 100 000 party and non-party people a success? Partial and complete results of the transfer tend to suggest that it was not entirely successful. One source claims that by the beginning of 1931 some 85 000 officials had been transferred from 203 *okrugs* to *raions*, a figure which is repeated in a recent Soviet history of the party.[29] But there is much material which contradicts this finding. Regional data point to only partial success; by October/November 1930 in the Central Black Earth *oblast* 71 per cent of okrug workers had been transferred, 64 per cent in the Urals *oblast* and only 54 per cent in the Mid-Volga *krai*.[30] By the summer of 1931 the proportion for the Central Black Earth had only risen to 75 per cent, whilst that for the Ukraine was still well below target at 56 per cent.[31] A *Pravda* editorial of 16 October 1930, by which time even in the C.C.'s estimation the transfer ought to have been complete, admitted that on average 40–50 per cent of the *okrug* staff were in the *raions*. The Soviet historian S.F. Markov, in a more recent article, puts the figure at only 'over 50 000'.[32] In short, many difficulties were encountered in this transfer and it seems most improbable that 80–90 per cent of the supposed 100 000 *okrug* personnel actually reached the *raions* and stayed in them. The haste, the recalcitrance of state workers and party members and the inherent difficulty and complexity of the administrative reform explain why at best it was only a partial success.

The consequence was that the party at *raikom* level, and non-party organisations, were not reinforced with experienced personnel in the years 1931–32 to the degree that had been intended by the party authorities. Information relating solely to *raikom* party personnel is rare but one source does give precise figures. It is stated that in the rural *raikoms* prior to the okrugs' abolition there were 6295 responsible workers (*raikom* secretaries, *raikom* department heads and their assistants) and 2000 technical workers (clerks, accountants and the like), whereas after these were 11 067 and 2831 respectively.[33] Thus the increase in the number of *raikom* personnel was in fact less than 6000. During 1930 the number of rural *raikoms* was reduced from 3012 to 2466, as they were consolidated and enlarged in some cases.[34] With some

14 000 *raikom* personnel, the average number of full-time party workers in each *raikom* was six. The rural *raikom* staffs were further enlarged in immediate subsequent years, which suggests that this initial transfer was not entirely adequate to growing demands.[35]

This miniature case study is an excellent example of how the party authorities could not impose their will. Despite the threat of purge, this was a failed mobilisation, unlike the drive for rural communists to join *kolkhozy* in 1929–30, which had employed similar administrative tactics, encountered similar recalcitrance and yet on the whole proved generally more successful. The differing results can be explained by a couple of reasons. The entry of communists into *kolkhozy* was a top-priority campaign, an essential prerequisite of collectivisation, and greater propaganda and pressure were probably employed in the process. There is also the difference that in the mobilisation to join *kolkhozy* the communists were most often ordinary, rank and file members, whereas the *okrug* staffs were composed of qualified, experienced party cadres in a variety of institutions. The *okrug* party workers disobeyed orders and, on occasion, did so with open assuredness, even arrogance. They were not cowed, nor did they fear the retribution of their superiors. They were sure of losing themselves in the party's bureaucratic network. They were confident of their ability to play the system and win the game.

THE *RAIKOM* STRUCTURE AND ORGANISATION

The *raikom* organisational structure which prevailed from 1930 until the beginning of 1934 is discussed here. It was within this organisational framework that the *raikom* conducted its operations in the Soviet countryside and co-ordinated with its cells, a process discussed in a subsequent chapter.

In 1930, with the abolition of the *okrugs*, it was realised by those responsible for party organisation that links in the chain of command between the *obkoms* and *raikoms* would need to be quickly overhauled and in most cases created from scratch. During the initial stages of the relationship with the *raions* in 1930–31, the *obkoms*' work methods with regard to the *raikoms* were orthodox, not to say unimaginative: often they resorted to 'paper leadership' (*bumazhnoe rukovodstvo*), sending letters and telegrams, usually with a threatening content without differentiating between different *raions*. Often the *raions* were simply ignored: some *raions* in the Ukraine did not see a living soul from the *oblast* centre for three to four months.[36] Throughout the summer of 1930 notice was given of the intention to ameliorate the *obkoms*' contacts with their numerous, new subordinate *raikoms*: one priority was to ensure telephonic or telegraphic contact between the units. In the years 1930–33 the party became more enmeshed in economic questions as a result of which the *obkom* organisation-instruction departments (*orginst*) found themselves with a greatly increased workload of supervising the party-economic affairs of a larger number of smaller units in the shape of the *raikoms* compared with the former *okrugs*. To cope with this, an expansion in the number of *obkom* staff and non-staff (part-time, unpaid) instructors was envisaged.[37] Still, towards the end of 1930 the *obkoms* were in dire need of some reorganisation to supersede the loose arrangements that had been allowed to persist.

A scheme was formulated whereby party, Soviet and trade union organisations at the *oblast* level instituted measures to allocate their *raions* into a particular sector according to their predominant branch of economy, and selected leading workers in the *oblast* to supervise a particular sector. This was taken up on a nationwide scale when the 'Introduction to the Orgburo Plan' (*Vvedenie k planu Orgburo*) of March 1931 launched the production-territorial sectors in every *obkom*. These sectors were subordinated to a sub-department (*otdel*) newly created within the existing organisation-instruction department (*orginst*) of all *obkoms*, *kraikoms* and national republic committees. The number of *raions* belonging to each sector was allowed to vary between 10 and 25. The *raions* in each sector were to be of the same type of economy, defined as heavy or light industry, livestock, grain, flax and so on. The reorganisation at *krai/oblast* level was accompanied by one in the C.C. apparatus in order to adjust its work to the existence of the new sectors. The rationale of this organisational reform is plain to see. The C.C. apparatus formalised its relations and control over the *oblasts*, making C.C. instructors responsible for what went on in 'their' *oblasts*. Lower down in the hierarchy, the procedure was repeated in the *obkoms*, although the sectors were not without their teething problems.[38] The introduction of the production-territorial sectors in the *obkom orginst* was also a major step towards a transition to party organisation on a production basis. Indeed, by the end of 1931 the Moscow *obkom*, always a forerunner in organisational innovation, retained only three functional sectors for party organisation (*stroitel'stvo*), party cadres and statistics, together with 10 production-territorial sectors, of which two, transport and war industries, were wholly production orientated.[39]

To return now to our consideration of the *raikom*'s structure, a first major point is that it was much more stable than its personnel. Regardless of the party's 'face to production' during the first Five Year Plan, the party apparatus above cell level continued to be organised on a functional basis until 1934. The *raikoms* based themselves on this functional principle but for reasons of finances and manpower, as well as their smaller range of duties, they were not an exact replica of the apparatus at the C.C. and *obkoms*. Figure 4.2 depicts this *raikom* structure.

The most important department in the *raikom* was that of organisa-

Figure 4.2   The *raikom* structure, 1930–41

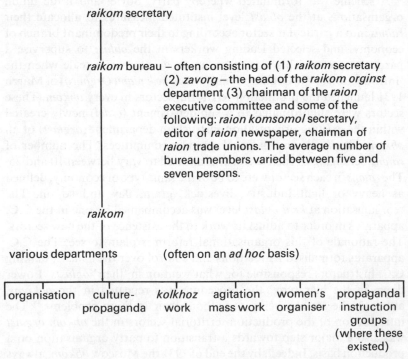

raikom secretary

raikom bureau – often consisting of (1) *raikom* secretary (2) *zavorg* – the head of the *raikom orginst* department (3) chairman of the *raion* executive committee and some of the following: *raion komsomol* secretary, editor of *raion* newspaper, chairman of *raion* trade unions. The average number of bureau members varied between five and seven persons.

raikom

various departments   (often on an *ad hoc* basis)

| organisation | culture-propaganda | *kolkhoz* work | agitation mass work | women's organiser | propaganda instruction groups (where these existed) |

Note: At the seventeenth party congress in 1934 the various *raikom* departments were replaced by a system of instructors who were in charge of a specific number of cells, but by about 1936 some departments (especially for cadres) were being reintroduced, again often on an *ad hoc* basis, see Chapter 11. *Source:* This diagram is adapted from M. Fainsod, *Smolensk Under Soviet Rule*, p. 113.

tion, headed by the *zavorg*, which dealt with all internal party matters concerning party members and cells. Other *raikom* departments included those for culture-propaganda and agitation-mass campaigns, whose titles indicate how the rural *raikom* was expected to concentrate its interest on mobilising its members and especially the non-party peasantry. Instead of a department dealing with women's issues, the *raikoms* made do with an organiser. Other departments were also established on an *ad hoc* basis depending on the regional, social-economic conditions. The functional system of party organisation percolated through the hierarchy to encompass the cells: indeed, during 1930, there occurred an excessive proliferation of various complex functional sections and departments of dubious quality, which soon faded away for want of support.

The most significant attempt to modify the organisational structure of the *raikom* prior to 1934 was the introduction of instruction-propaganda groups. Their introduction had been proposed in the far-ranging programme of the *Orgburo* Plan of the spring 1931, whereby each *raikom* was to establish an instruction-propaganda group comprising two or three full-time party workers to supervise the work of the rural cells.[40] Where these instruction-propaganda groups did exist, they were not expected to idle their time in the relative comfort of the *raion* centre, but to work in their allotted cells for 'at least twenty five days a month'.[41] This was the theory, but the rural party, and in this case the *raikoms*, lacked sufficient numbers of qualified party members to put it into practice, and instruction work at the *raikom* and *obkom* levels was notoriously neglected in any case.[42] One can conclude that the difficulty in setting up these groups was a long-standing one in that they were absent in many *raions* in 1932 and 1933.[43] But the defects in the establishment and functioning of the groups show how the rural party's organisation was not smooth running and how, once again as with the mobilisation of *okrug* staff, central party directives were simply not implemented at the grass-roots, often, but not always, because of objective impediments.

Although the structural framework of the *raikom* was quite stable in the period of 1929–33, occasionally the economic-production demands of the socialised economy made upon the *raikoms* were such that a self-reorganisation was undertaken without the permission, or any resultant censure it seems, from the central party authorities. For example, in 1932 the Buzuluk *raikom*, in the Mid-Volga, a key *raion* in the early days of collectivisation, reshaped its organisational department by creating three new sectors for party work based on production: one for party work in *kolkhozy* and MTS, one for *sovkhozy* and another for enterprises and transport.[44] On its own initiative the party at grass-roots dispensed in some cases with functionalism and preferred to adopt a variant on the production principle more suited to its working environment, in which production was the focus. This puts the 1934 reorganisation in better perspective: not totally an instigator of change, in part a response to it.

Comparatively little organisational innovation was introduced in the latter half of 1931 and throughout 1932. The authorities were seeing how the system brought in during 1929–31 would operate. When they did not like what they saw, the rural party was greatly reduced in size and necessary organisational changes were made during the years of the second Five Year Plan: to the cells in mid-1933 and to the *raikoms* early in 1934.

RAIKOM PERSONNEL

Before examining the *raikom* personnel, a few words are in order on their working environment, which will illustrate further the multifarious problems faced by the rural party workers at the lower levels.

We have already noted that some of the *okrug* staff were reluctant to reside in the *raions*, one of the principal reasons for this being the poor living conditions prevalent in the rural *raions*. Many *raions* were not furnished with basic amenities to cater for newly arrived people, who sometimes went without accommodation and food supplies.[45] Complaints were voiced on their behalf, but it seems that many *raion* cadres were obliged to accustom themselves to poor or non-existent housing and canteen facilities, and even to sleeping on table tops.[46] These grim conditions resulted from the backward nature of Russian rural life and from the fact that the central authorities had many other priorities to consider. The standard of living in the towns in this period was far from luxurious, but the rural regions were comparatively more primitive: of 1 177 rural *raion* centres in the RSFSR in 1932, only 343 had electricity and a mere 60, those usually adjacent to factories, had running water; even in the Moscow *oblast* only seven out of its rural *raion* centres had running water, 23 were electrified and 35 supplied with communal baths.[47] Nearly all villages, *kolkhozy* and *raion* centres spent their long winters illuminated by kerosene and candle, or stood in darkness. The *raion* centres and their *raikoms* were plagued by the absence of telephone and telegraph links with their immediate superiors: many *raikoms* relied for their contacts with their superiors and subordinates in the cells on party couriers, who carried the mail long distances on horse-back taking days or weeks over round trips. Remote *raikoms* could be isolated from the outside world for long periods of time in bad weather. Nor did this state of affairs automatically improve with time. In 1934, when the *raikoms* were reorganised and *raikom* instructors introduced, each to supervise a group of party cells, most were not supplied with vehicles or horses, but had to make do with a bicycle, if they were fortunate; the not so lucky ones were obliged to tramp many miles on foot to and fro between the cells, which must have greatly reduced the frequency of their visits and their general efficiency.

Thus conditions were so bad as to deter many party workers from remaining in the rural *raions* and lowered the morale of those who did stay. In addition, the primitive communications system retarded the development of an efficient political-economic network. The revenge of backwardness was such that not only agriculture lacked tractors and machinery, but even the party did not dispose of the wherewithal to perform its job properly.

Who were the people who lived and worked in these conditions? We are able to make reasonably reliable *approximations* on the total size of the *raikom* apparatus in 1931–32. The leading personnel were the *raikom* secretary, a number of department heads varying from three to five, who each had one or two assistants, as well as one to five technical staff. Thus the full-time apparatus of a small *raikom* would number in the region of 10–15 and that of a larger one between 20 and 25. This was an appreciable growth on the average number of six in 1930. The *raikoms*, as their scope of work expanded, resorted to using 'non-staff' workers, who were employed on a part-time basis and not remunerated for their services. Often these non-staff instructors were party activists living and working in the *raion* centres, who could spare up to a dozen or more hours a week on the *raikom's* paper work. The employment of non-staff instructors, compared with full-time staff, was usually on an approximate ratio of two to one, which means that the total numer of full-time and non-staff apparatus workers varied between 20 and 55. This latter figure may seem quite substantial, but whatever the number, they were invariably burdened with a lot of work. Our estimates are supported by reference to some specific examples: in the Western *oblast*, where *raions* were comparatively small in size, the full-time *raikom* apparatus staff rarely exceeded 15–20; in the Moscow *oblast* prior to 1934, when a reduction in *raikom* apparatus size took place, there were 11–17 full time staff in the *raikoms* and *gorkoms*.[48] The *raikom* staff size had expanded considerably over the years: prior to mass collectivisation in 1928–29 the recommended size varied between a single secretary and half a dozen workers, and even after the abolition of the *okrugs* towards the end of 1930, the average *raikom* apparatus numbered no more than six people. The number of party apparatus workers in the countryside in 1933 had increased by 61 per cent compared with that of 1930, and it was claimed that this growth took place particularly in the lower apparatus, which included the *raikom* personnel.[49]

The number of rank and file party members supervised by the *raikom* staff within the boundaries of a *raikom*'s jurisdiction varied considerably. For example, in the Rzhevsk *raion*, Western *oblast*, a non-grain region with small *kolkhozy*, there were 411 communists in mid-1932 (a time of peak membership in the rural party generally), whereas in the Buzuluk *raion* in the Mid-Volga at the beginning of 1932, there were already 3 682 communists.[50] The party membership in these *raions* is large, particularly in the latter of the two, when one considers that with 700 000 rural party members and approximately 2 500 *raions* at the beginning of 1932, the average *raion* party membership was 280. However, such an average figure for *raion* party membership cannot be very meaningful without including endless regional-economic variations, which is not possible with available sources.

The principal post within the *raikom* was that of *raikom* secretary, whose unenviable job it was to act as intermediary between *obkoms* and cells, passing down admonishments and threats to the party rank and file. In 1928, of 1 596 *raikom* secretaries, a high proportion were workers by social origin (51.9 per cent), with 28 per cent from a peasant background and 20 per cent employees and others. Their length of party membership was remarkably long: 76.8 per cent could date their presence in the party to before 1921, 14.5 per cent between 1921–23, and 11.7 per cent from 1924 and after. [51] At a time when *raikom* secretaries required constitutionally to be of one year's membership, this was a valuable feature of their experience. It would seem that already the post of *raikom* secretary was regarded as somewhat exceptional. The *raikom* secretaries' length of party membership (*stazh*) must have differentiated them quite markedly from their other 'younger', subordinate committee members, many of whom belonged to the mid-NEP generation of party recruits, and buttressed their prestige and authority. Information on the background of 2 457 *raikom* secretaries in June 1931, presented in Table 4.2, allows us to discover what changes had taken place since 1928.

Table 4.2 Composition of *raikom* secretaries, June 1931

| | Social position | | | |
	Workers	Peasants	Employees	Not known
number	1 364	519	540	34
%	55.6	21.2	21.9	1.3

| | Length of party membership | | | |
	Before 1921	1921–28	Since 1928	Not known
number	1 524	860	48	25
%	62	35	2	1

| | Branch of former work | | | | |
	Party	komsomol	Studies	Soviet and others	Not known
number	1 516	15	102	233	104
%	67.1	0.7	4.5	23.1	4.6

| | Level of former work | | | | | |
	Republic and krai	okrug	raion	Lower	From study	Not known
number	134	857	842	168	113	343
%	5.4	34.9	34.3	6.8	4.6	14.0

Source: Partiinoe stroitel'stvo, No. 11, June 1931, p.12.

This information is most revealing in conjunction with our earlier material. It shows that the influx of *okrug* workers, a considerable proportion of over one third of the sample, only brought about moderate improvements in the secretary group in terms of social composition and length of party membership. The worker contingent rose from 51.9 per cent to 55.6 per cent, which would have included such urban influxes as the 25 000-ers and is therefore not wholly attributable to the *okrug* intake. There was a noticeable drop in those with party membership before 1921, from 76.8 per cent to 62 per cent, but this was to be expected with the intervening years as more recent recruits rose in the party hierarchy. This comparison suggests that the influx of *okrug* party workers was not designed primarily to improve the composition of *raikom* secretaries, but rather to strengthen numerically the *raikom* as a whole and qualitatively such posts as *raikom zavorg* and other department heads.

The figures in Table 4.2 also reveal that a reasonable proportion of party workers could be considered as adding to the post of *raikom* secretary: that is 34.9 per cent former *okrug* workers, 5.4 per cent from the republic and *krai* level and 4.6 per cent from study, giving a total of 44.9 per cent, although there were noticeable regional variations. Quite a surprisingly large number underwent rapid promotion from positions below *raion* level directly into the *raikom* secretary post (6.8 per cent), and undoubtedly, a larger proportion followed a more conventional route into the lower ranks of the *raion* apparatus before progressing to the post of secretary. The figures also show that *raion* party workers could maintain a realistic hope of becoming *raikom* secretaries (34.3 per cent), although this does not imply that a *raion* worker would become secretary of 'his' *raion*, that is the *raion* in which he had worked prior to his promotion, because frequently the *raikom* secretaries were 'imported' and 'exported' between *raions* in order to prevent 'familiness' and systems of mutual guarantees.[52]

According to another quality indicator, though, the standard was not so good. The level of political education among a sample of 1 358 *raikom* secretaries in 1931 was not very high: 24.6 per cent had completed *komvuzy*, 23.8 per cent 'special schools', 23.7 per cent Marxist-Leninist circles and 23.4 per cent had no political training. When one realises that much educational work at the circle level was most rudimentary, the poor standard is more striking. However, this information does indicate an improvement in comparison with that for all *raikom* secretaries, not just a sample, pre-June 1930, that is before the abolition of the *okrugs*, which showed that 47.1 per cent were without systematic training.[53] Despite efforts in the interim, by 1933 the *raion* personnel's educational level was little improved compared with that of 1931: among a representative sample of 30 000 leading *raion* workers, most of whom, but not all, were party members, only 10.2 per cent had special, higher or middle education and only 17.2 per cent had passed through special short courses.[54]

Inadequate political training and education was one of several reasons for a peculiar characteristic of rural party personnel matters, and within the party as a whole: the rate of turnover. The problem of turnover was a chronic one. In 1931 the numbers of party members moving from one party organisation to another in the party as a whole, not just the rural party, was approximately 125 000 every three months, and in the first quarter of 1932, this rose to 138 000.[55] This was at a time when in 1931 the party membership numbered 2 212 225. Moreover, the above figures only include officially recorded movements and future checks of party records revealed that many thousands had transferred themselves without the knowledge of their party committees. The following information on the Ukraine is typical. In the period of approximately one and a half years from the abolition of the *okrugs* to mid-1932 there had been 288 changes of *raikom* secretaries (80 per cent).[56] The position had become so grave in the Ukraine by 1931 that the Ukrainian C.C. declared that *raion* party workers could not be removed without its consent.[57] In Central Asia and Kazakhstan it was usual for the *raikom* secretaries to change three to five times within a year.[58] The turnover rate among *zavorgi* was generally higher than that for *raikom* secretaries: in the Lower Volga in 1931 the figures were 89 per cent for *zavorgi* and 71 per cent for *raikom* secretaries; during a one-year period in the Central Black Earth *oblast* the figures were 52 per cent and 35 per cent respectively, and among heads of culture-propaganda departments 65 per cent, agitation-mass campaigns department heads 57 per cent and women's organisers 60 per cent.[59] In a survey of turnover in 20 leading *raion* posts, party and non-party, conducted in 1932–33, the rate of turnover amongst *raikom* secretaries was near to the average.[60] The turnover rate among the instructor apparatus at *obkom* level was even higher: for example, in the Urals and Nizhegorod *kraikoms* their annual rate of turnover was 150 per cent, 250 per cent in the Lower Volga *kraikom* and 174 per cent in the North Caucasus *kraikom*.[61] Thus in comparison with other posts the turnover rate among *raikom* secretaries was not particularly high, and this remained the case until 1935 when, with abolition of the political departments, the *raikom* secretaries acquired more prestige, and perhaps greater stability.

The above represents a major element in M. Lewin's 'quicksand society'. He saw part of the problem as:

> All echelons of local administration . . . and in the party apparatus itself, its obkomy and raikomy . . . adopted the habit of leaving in good time before they were fired or penalised, transferred, muted, degraded, purged . . . (recalled, summoned) or arrested.[62]

These high turnover rates played havoc with the rural party's generally weak organisation, preventing the emergence of necessary reserves to replace those *raion* workers who were incompetent. The turnover rate became so prodigious that it was proposed in the party organisational journal that each *raion* be permitted a nucleus of leading party workers to be left in their posts for four–five years continuously.[63] The Central

Black Earth *obkom* resolved along the same lines to retain party and Soviet workers at their posts for a three-year period: the various purges during 1933–38, in addition to normal transfers, were to wreck these quite sensible ideas.[64]

The party authorities stated that the causes for high turnover lay in the following: inadequate study of cadres prior to their promotion, especially at *raion* level and below; insufficient practical assistance given to the cadres from above; lack of attention to the education, training and raising of the cadres' ideological–political awareness; and cadres were not deployed in posts which brought out the best of their capabilities.[65] Kaganovich argued similarly when he stated:

> We do not have a properly established system for studying our workers and their business – like qualities for when we select and deploy them. We often suffer, not from the fact that we lack people, but from the fact that we do not know them.[66]

Although making a valid point, Kaganovich overstates the case. More often than not, the real problem facing the rural party was a shortage in pure numbers of party members to meet numerous tasks in the economic units of *kolkhoz, sovkhoz* and MTS. Other factors also contributed to high turnover. The *obkom* party leadership conspired to increase it by disbanding groups of *raikom* staffs to extirpate 'familiness'. Party members were also transferred at their own request when they became bored and dissatisfied. Of course, a major cause was that many were removed on account of their poor performance, which could include incompetence and/or corruption or else lack of vigour in conducting campaigns which had severe consequences for the peasantry.[67]

Transferring incompetent *raion* staff from one posting to another was not a solution, but merely perpetuated the problem, resulting in a merry-go-round of ephemeral party staffs unable to come to grips with their tasks in every new setting. The authorities would only have got to the root of the problem by resorting to more severe disciplinary action in the form of dismissals, demotions and expulsions from the party. Yet the reasons why they did not do this are not far to seek. The number of trained, experienced party workers who could fill middle and leading level posts in the *raions* was limited. The failure of the authorities to adopt more stringent measures may also suggest that for a time they appreciated that local difficulties were more deep-rooted and not always, nor entirely, due to poor personnel, nor even less to sabotage. If they did believe this, and it is highly conjectural, they kept it to themselves. Publicly the authorities insisted that any shortcoming could be overcome by the proper selection of conscientious, capable party workers. This was no more than an illusion for public consumption among the party rank and file. High turnover was a symptom of the personnel's low calibre and a further impediment to the accomplishment of duties for those capable, industrious workers who did exist.

Throughout the first Five Year Plan one objective had been to strengthen the middle level (*raikom* secretaries and cell secretaries) in the rural communist party. Some success had been achieved, but it was by no means complete. The *raikom* had become the most important party-administrative link in the Soviet countryside, and as a consequence expanded in size and personnel. The foregoing discussion has pointed to some of the difficulties involved in achieving this. It will be interesting now to compare our findings on the *raikoms* with the those for the rural party cells: they are on the whole similar.

5 The Rural Communist Party Cell 1929–32

As the rural socialised economy expanded and the number of production-economic units multiplied during the first Five Year Plan, particularly in 1929–31, the communist party organisation turned 'face to production' and it was the party cells which were most involved in and affected by this innovation. This chapter considers how the rural party cells reacted organisationally to their new working environment and concentrates on a number of principal features: the massive increase in cell numbers in the attempt to keep pace with the rapidly expanding collective farm sector; the increased complexity and sophistication in the structure of cells, as they endeavoured to adapt to new conditions; and the problems encountered in the above processes.

THE RURAL PARTY CELL ADJUSTS TO MASS COLLECTIVISATION 1929–32

The build-up of the rural party cell network had not been promising prior to mass collectivisation. Rural cells were deployed primarily on a non-production basis and concerned themselves little with individual agriculture, and even less with the collective farms. The number of *kolkhoz* cells did expand to accompany the flow of communists into the *kolkhoz* in 1929, but there were still only 1 514 *kolkhoz* cells in mid-1929, when *kolkhozy* already numbered over 50 000. The number of *kolkhozy* rose from 54 899 on 1 June 1929 to 67 446 on 1 October 1929, to 106 000 of 10 March 1930 and dropped to 84 050 in May 1930. In the same approximate period the total of all rural cells and candidate groups increased by a mere 2 000 from 27 039 in mid-1929 to 28 500 at the beginning of 1930, and to 29 204 in April 1930.[1] On this latter date there was still only one rural party unit for every three rural Soviets.[2] Kaganovich, the Politburo 'specialist' on party organisation, admitted at a C.C. conference on 13 January 1930 that: 'If we formulate it sharply and strongly, in essence we have to create a party organisation in the countryside'.[3] Having just embarked upon a hectic campaign of mass collectivisation, this was a most remarkable statement and highlighted the rural party's grievous position. Many future problems in organisation can be explained by inexperience and haste.

The objective in 1930 was to create a rural party cell network that would facilitate and ensure the supervision of the newly socialised sector comprising *kolkhozy*, *sovkhozy* and MTS. Both in industry and agriculture the clarion call in party organisation was 'face to production'.[4] The fundamental reason for party reorganisation was to bring the party closer to production activities, and thereby to achieve control of collectivisation and industrialisation. But how was the rural party to achieve this in practice? What form did these new agricultural-production cells take?

The only organisational life-line available to the rural party was to resort to the tried and tested structural model of the urban party cells located in the factories, which seemed especially appropriate to an urban minded party functioning in rural Soviet Russia.[5] From the point of view of organisation (and at times production), the *kolkhozy* and *sovkhozy* were transformed in the minds of the policy makers into agricultural factories. Such an organisational framework was introduced not without some reservations. The adoption of factory type systems did permit the cutting of corners in implanting rural party cells in the economic units. However, because the rural cells were being organised in a socio economic environment which was predominantly alien (so recently petty-bourgeois in the minds of party theoreticians) and because the rural party membership was recognised to be quantitatively and qualitatively weaker than its urban counterpart, it was generally appreciated that this transposition should not be carried out artificially or uncritically. A vivid image of the danger of imbalance was conjured up by one party commentator when he warned that unthinking imitation of factory organisations and work methods 'would be like putting adult's clothing on a child'.[6]

The rural party cells did not, however, become standardised and the variation of types during the first Five Year Plan was one of their most striking features. They were so different in form and structure for a number of reasons. Firstly, they differed so as to be able to accommodate party members in the best possible way in order to overcome the problem of scarcity of rural communists in many areas. Secondly, they had to adapt to many different local socio-economic conditions. Thirdly, and specific to the transition period of 1929–30, on many occasions the centre lagged behind developments in the regions and allowed organisational affairs to take their own course. The political centre did not provide the *raikoms* and cells with definite guidelines of how they were to adapt to the new circumstances: the party press more often than not reported faits accomplis in organisation. The *kolkhoz* movement of the winter 1929–30 was so swift that in order to fill the political-organisational vacuum the cells were forced to reorganise 'as they went along' (*na khodu*).[7] When reviewing the initial stages of collectivisation at the sixteenth party congress in the summer 1930, Kaganovich, speaking of cell organisation, noted how the localities had been given a relatively free hand: '. . . the C.C. has not regulated this party practice, so as not to impede the initiative of the localities – we are now studying this experience'.[8] A less complacent interpretation of the events might be that the centre neglected the localities. If things turned out well, the centre could award itself the praise; if not, the blame could be distributed among the party at regional level to be communicated downwards.

It has been possible to distinguish almost ten types and sub-types of rural party cells operating in the early years of collectivisation. The four most straightforward forms were: 1) the *kolkhoz* cell which operated in a single *kolkhoz* and was widespread throughout the country; 2) the *sovkhoz* cell and 3) the MTS cell, where party forces were generally at their strongest; and 4) the territorial cell, located in villages, co-operatives or more often in the Soviets, which sought to supervise the relevant institution as well as the local population. Other more complex structures were variations on these themes.

As the *kolkhozy* were created, where there were enough party members, and this was more easily achieved in large *kolkhozy* which were formed out of several villages or even whole Soviets, *kolkhoz* cells were set up. *Kolkhoz* cells were created by a combination of establishing them from scratch in the newly formed *kolkhozy* composed of new party recruits, or simply by transposing territorial-based cells from the villages and Soviets.[9] When party members were drafted into the new *kolkhoz* cells from territorial ones, if three communists remained in the territorial cell, they still constituted a rural cell. In this way the rural party could increase the absolute number of all types of cells, raise the proportion of *kolkhoz* cells and retain as well a core of territorial cells, which were still necessary in the years when large numbers of peasants remained uncollectivised.

In an effort to encompass as many production activities as possible, the party cells in larger *kolkhozy* sub-divided into constituent cells often between four and ten in number, established like 'shop' (*tsekhovaya*) cells in factories: thus was formed what was variously termed the party collective or general *kolkhoz* cell (not to be confused with the inter-*kolkhoz* cell which encompassed several party cells at *different kolk-*

hozy).[10] This type of cell was particularly suitable for the large *kolkhoz* party organisations (and was also employed in *sovkhozy* and MTS) located in the grain regions, and in fact developed from experience gained in the North Caucasus, Lower and Mid-Volga, whereas in the non-grain areas simple *kolkhoz* cells predominated or the inter-*kolkhoz* cell joined up scattered party members in numerous small *kolkhozy*. The party collectives were to be composed of at least 15 communists and contain a minimum of two shop cells, some candidate groups and a network of party organisers in the economic-production sectors, variously called *sektor*, *chast'* or *uchastok*. Examples of the party collective, very large ones, were to be found in the Khoper *okrug*, Lower Volga, a leading *okrug* of mass collectivisation where the rural party had to adapt more quickly and radically than elsewhere. In this *okrug* three *kolkhozy* alone – *Znamya Kommunizma, Krasnyi Putilovets* and *Bolshevik* – extended over 120 000 hectares with a population of 19 000, including 200 party members and candidates in nine party cells. With each collective farm having four or five economic branches, these party cells were rationalised into three party collectives, one for each *kolkhoz*, consisting of three shop cells each.[11]

Out of the chaos of early 1930 was also born the inter-*kolkhoz* cell, an extension of the party collective, which went beyond the confines of a single *kolkhoz* and joined together, supposedly in one corporate party organisation, several small party cells and single communists from various collective farms under the leadership of a larger, central *kolkhoz* cell; these inter-*kolkhoz* cells, the central one and its constituent ones, could themselves be broken down further into shop cells. Inter-*kolkhoz* cells were adaptable and developed in most regions, but predominantly in those areas with small *kolkhozy* and scattered communists such as White Russia, the Western, Leningrad and Moscow *oblasts*. Many arguments would follow on how far the inter-*kolkhoz* cells could extend themselves.[12] This was the beginning of something very significant in party cell organisation in which lay the seeds of future innovations such as the support points and political departments.[13]

Party collectives at a single *kolkhoz* and inter-*kolkhoz* cells were introduced to give the lower party links greater cohesion and to overcome the cells' isolation and consequential communication difficulties. It seems that the localities created spontaneously an intermediary link between the *raikom* and cells to make everyone's administrative life more bearable. The sub-cells were provided with closer supervision within a party collective than if they remained on a one to one basis *vis-à-vis* the *raikoms* or *okruzkoms*, who could pay them comparatively little time and attention. It was even adumbrated that at some future date the *raikoms* could dispense with single cells and operate through five to seven party collectives and inter-*kolkhoz* cells.[14] Such a scheme was not really feasible, especially in areas such as White Russia and the Western *oblast* where the *kolkhoz* party organisations were small and numerous and individual peasants were to continue to exist for several more years: it would have required too many collectives to supervise so many units. Nor was it likely that the inter-*kolkhoz* system would take over entirely because, as their internal structure became more complicated, they encountered their own organisational problems. Some were uniting constituent cells over a distance of 30–40 *versts* with the resultant perennial difficulty in holding party meetings and providing a regular lead from the party collective centre, based usually in the largest constituent *kolkhoz*.[15] The party organisation model very much in the ascendant at this moment was one where the *raikom* supervised all types of cells and no challenge to its authority was to be tolerated, but, as we will see in a discussion of the support points, the regime's outlook, or that of some of its spokesmen, was ambivalent.

The other two types of production-orientated party cells were those in *sovkhozy* and MTS. These were very similar in structure to the *kolkhoz* cells. They could either be simple cells, or, and this was more frequent in *sovkhozy* and MTS where the party was strongest, they formed complex party collective structures, centred solely on the single *sovkhoz* or MTS, and on occasion those in the MTS incorporated surrounding *kolkhozy*.

The simple territorial cell responded to the problem of the scarcity of rural communists. One should not doubt that the danger of rural communists being swamped in the countryside and even in the *kolkhozy* was a real one: although communists in *kolkhozy* increased from 81 957 on 1 June 1929 to 313 200 in May 1930, during the same period their number per 100 *kolkhoznik* households declined from 8.3 to 5.3.[16] Their isolation outside the collective farms was even more accentuated. To combat this and to provide scattered communists with some sort of focal point and sense of solidarity with their fellow party members, rather than leave them isolated in ones and twos and small cells, larger 'group cells' (*kustovaya yacheika*) were formed on a territorial principle uniting any and all who lived and worked in the villages, institutions, schools and *kolkhozy* of a given vicinity. This type of cell therefore went against the current trend by not making a clear distinction between *kolkhoz* (production) cells and other (territorial) ones. In the climate of 'face to production' it could hardly be regarded as a satisfactory development, but indicates how local party organisations tried to stick together at a time of great flux and confusion. This sort of cell seems to have been common in the Western *oblast*, where *kolkhozy* were small and numerous, the non-collectivised sector still significant and the rural party comparatively small in size. During the transitional period in the early months of 1930 some territorial cells in areas with less than 50 per cent collectivisation (calculated approximately), although officially designated as territorial cells, monitored new *kolkhozy* not possessing their own party organisation. Conversely, *kolkhoz* cells supervised the non-collectivised peasantry, when time was available. In other words, while collectivisation ebbed and flowed, the demarcation between production and territorial cells was vague, and once the *kolkhoz* cells became consolidated in later months and years, they were instructed to turn somewhat more attention to the individual peasants. Cells were not standardised in early 1930 nor even in later months, and unusual anomalies in cell organisation existed. Obviously cell secretaries were making the best of things in the light of their limited or non-existent experience. Until later in the year, providing the cells did not infringe excessively the principle of face to production in the areas of mass collectivisation, it was very much a case of '*on s'engage et puis on voit*'.

At last in the autumn of 1930 the authorities took stock of what had happened in the rural party cell organisation and provided some clarification with a guideline (*polozhenie*) on *kolkhoz* party cells dated 26 August 1930, which was confirmed in a C.C. resolution of 11 February 1931.[17] Remarkably, whilst dotting the organisational 'i's, *the polozhenie*, in force in effect from September, endorsed almost everything that had arisen within the rural party cell system in the hectic winter days of 1929–30. In other words the C.C. was fully satisfied with a cell system which had sprung up with little forethought and planning in a matter of weeks. Theoretically the cell general meeting elected a bureau every six months with a maximum of seven full members and two candidates; party cells of less than seven members confined themselves to electing a secretary possessing at least one year's party membership, who was only rarely a full-time, paid party worker and yet whose job it was to write bureau agenda, lead daily work and co-ordinate with the *raikom*. *Raikom* decisions were obligatory for the cells: the subservient position of the cells was confirmed.[18] The cells' responsibility for recruiting party members and transferring candidate members to full status was reaffirmed as were such duties as ensuring fulfilment of party tasks by members, presence in production, attendance at party meetings, payment of dues and dissemination of relevant party decisions among the non-party peasantry. The C.C. decision also indicated the role of the party groups, which were encouraged more in 1931 and especially in 1932, to which we will refer later.

Another feature of the rural party cells was the proliferation of functional sectors within the party collectives. It was more a reflex, artificial copy of reorganisation that was taking place at the *oblast* and *raion* level. One recommendation for the number of functional departments within party collectives was three to five, with a maximum of six to seven, to include some of the following: party study, agitation, work with poor peasants, work among individual peasants, party recruitment, leading of production campaigns and socialist competition in *kolkhozy*, and work among women; the choice of departments was often dependent on local circumstances.[19] This appears to have become, with local modifications and resultant intricate organisational squabbles, quite common. It was probably advantageous to the party collectives that, as they were responsible for political and economic affairs over a large area and among a large population, they should endeavour to allocate responsibility amongst themselves and to establish requisite organisational sectors based on functions, a system so much in vogue at the time. But this variety of heterogeneous production sectors with their production 'shop' cells and grandiosely titled functional departments superimposed on ever smaller units were more and more unable to find the necessary manpower with time and energy to make them properly operative.

It is reasonable to conclude that the cell reorganisation, which was a major element in the rural party face to production drive of 1929–32, was accompanied by a considerable amount of confusion and controversy concerning the principle and details of organisational transformation. Much of this sprang from the *ad hoc*, haphazard way in which changes was introduced, and is only one example, but a very important one, of how the rural party was unprepared for what faced it and of how it had to act spontaneously and hurriedly in new circumstances. Put briefly, the rural party at cell level could have been better organised than it was, if the central party authorities had had a clearer vision of their objectives for the rural party. Nevertheless, despite the confusion and waste of time and energy, major change did occur.

The Support Points

An examination of the support points serves as another case study in our analysis of the rural communist party organisation and mobilisations. The support points are interesting in themselves for at least four reasons:

firstly, their introduction in the party organisation provided heated discussion on the role of an intermediary link between *raikom* and cells; secondly, centred as they were at MTS, *sovkhozy* and large *kolkhozy*, they represent an early indicator of how greater thought was paid to the MTS and *sovkhozy* as potential control centres of rural economic and political life; thirdly, and related to the previous point, they were forerunners in embryo form of the important political departments which superseded them in 1933–34; finally, and most important in a strict organisational sense and most relevant to one of our major themes, they highlight how organisational innovation was introduced to the rural party at grass-roots level without sufficient detailed instructions and clarification of how units were actually to be set up and behave.

In March 1931 support points were introduced at MTS, *sovkhozy* and large *kolkhozy*. They represented a developed, strengthened version of the inter-*kolkhoz* cell. Greater cohesion was sought at the rural cell level, which would also aid the *raikoms'* co-ordination and communication with these lower units. It was the intended role of the support points to act as an assistant intermediary link. But the idea of a lower intermediary link was not welcome in all quarters.

In the debate on the suitability of the inter-*kolkhoz* cells and support points both sides sought to assist the *raikoms*, but could not agree where their real interests lay. They were unable to agree whether a lower intermediary link between *raikom* and cells would be an aid or a nuisance to the *raikoms*. Those who disapproved of the proliferation and expansion in authority of party links beneath the *raikoms* may well have thought that, having dispensed with the *volkoms* (party committees at the *volost* level) and having sought to assert the position of the *raikoms*, it was inadvisable to promote so soon the growth of lower level units beyond the basic cell stage. Others, and they seem to have constituted the influential majority in the policy-making groups for party organisation in the Secretariat and C.C., came quite quickly to the realisation that, with the expansion of the socialised economy and the increased demands upon all party units, combined with the massive growth in party membership in 1930 with no let-up in sight, and the augmentation in cell numbers and *kolkhoz* cells especially, the *raikoms* alone were no longer capable of providing a continuous lead to so many small, economic-party units, and that it was imperative to introduce some form of intermediary that could ease the *raikoms'* work load and reduce the number of party units with which the *raikom* had direct dealings. It is also worthwhile to note that the support points, unlike the later political departments, were created before major stresses and strains were detected in rural economic affairs towards the end of 1931 and more so in 1932. They were more than a mere reflex response to economic and political difficulties.

The support points originated in a package of far-ranging measures incorporated in the 'Introduction to the Orgburo Plan' (*Vvedenie k planu Orgburo*) of spring 1931, which sanctioned the reorganisation of cells at MTS, *sovkhozy* and large *kolkhozy* by the 'unification' (*ob"edinenie*) of a number of small cells into a full party committee (*partkom*). These were to function under *raikom* control, which also retained responsibility even for the constituent cells within the support points.[20] Certainly the initial aim was to set the independence of the support points within strict limits. A C.C. conference held sometime in March–May 1931 discussed the support points and clarified some issues concerning their structure and composition. Support points could be established in base cells that contained at least 15 communists (full members and candidates), and where the whole support point united at least 50 communists (including those from the base cell) from among the surrounding, constituent cells: they were intended to be quite large party units. They did not bring party coverage to *kolkhozy* or other bodies that did not already possess some party representation. They could give general assistance to villages and Soviets without party organisations, but their priority was to party cells.[21]

From their inception in the spring they proliferated appreciably in several areas by the end of the year. In the North Caucasus their number grew from 12 in May 1931 to 79 two months later.[22] By September 1931 they had become quite widespread in the Central Black Earth *oblast*: here 214 were set up in 66 *raions* composed of 1 003 cells, including 6 244 members and 8 319 candidates. This was quite an achievement, as an approximate estimate of all rural cells in this *oblast* would not exceed 2 000; thus the support points here supervised approximately half the rural cells and presumably a large majority of *kolkhoz* cells.[23] In Uzbekistan at the beginning of 1932, there was a total of 63 support points in this national republic,[24] which is a significant number, as one would expect the agricultural production centres of MTS, *sovkhozy* and large *kolkhozy* to be comparatively less well developed here; on the other hand the weaker rural party cells required more co-ordination and mutual assistance. Judging from this limited evidence, it appears that the support points became a significant feature in the rural party network in 1931–32.

However, within a few months of their introduction problems surfaced. These problems arose so swiftly that one wonders whether all the implications of the support points had been thought out thoroughly enough in advance. A general heresy in party organisation was detected by critics of the support points: they threatened to organise their own miniature fiefdoms and tended to usurp, or the *raikoms* to relinquish, immediate authority over the cells.[25] To combat this, the support points were given plain warning not to exceed their authority, although the extent of their authority was unclear because of the initial imprecise C.C. instructions: this was not the first time, nor certainly the last, when the failure to give a clear, detailed lead in a complex organisational reform caused confusion. In any case, it is likely that once a party body was created and allocated responsibility, it sought to obtain as much authority as possible over its subordinates within its own territory. Also the *raikoms* were unable, or unwilling, to control the support points: the *raikoms* may have condoned this expansionism beneath them as a means to lessen their own workload and to simplify communication by using the party committees (support points) as their intermediaries and disseminators of instructions. Neither were the central party authorities keen to revamp or go to the extreme of replacing the support point system so soon after its inception. This would have caused great confusion and upheaval and the authorities themselves would have lost face: it must have seemed a better policy to give the support points further opportunity to overcome their teething problems. On 5 December 1931 the C.C. published two brief resolutions reasserting the role of the support points, the implication being that criticism to date had now served its constructive purposes.[26] The support points continued their existence through 1932, attracting much less attention as the year progressed and the rural economic situation deteriorated. The support point party committees were not cited as organisational culprits in the 1932 débâcle, unlike the *raikoms*, and the support point principle was retained and refined in the conception of the political departments, introduced at the beginning of 1933 to overcome serious economic and political troubles.[27] The party committees faded from the scene at the beginning of 1933 for two major reasons: firstly, they were supplanted in most cases at the MTS and *sovkhozy* by the political departments, although the latter were not introduced into large *kolkhozy*; secondly, with the drastic reduction in rural party numbers that resulted from the 1933 purge and those that followed, numerous heavily manned party committees were not feasible.

The support points show how the attempt by the central party authorities to introduce organisational reform was hampered once again. The shortcomings of the support points were most often to do with their structure, their size and deployment, and less to do with any recalcitrance on the part of their personnel, as had been the case with the abolition of the *okrugs*. It shows that, because of a lack of awareness of potential difficulties by those who issued the insufficiently detailed orders, instructions were not fully understood by those who had to carry them out at the local levels, and therefore frequently misinterpreted. Much of the policy on rural party organisation seems to have been haphazard and even contradictory: the support points, their predecessors the inter-*kolkhoz* cells, and their descendants the political departments, all posed a potential or real threat to the authority of the *raikoms* and brought much jurisdictional wrangling in their wake, which reached a crescendo in the arguments and rivalry between the *raikoms* and political departments. Although this was not a major cause of economic difficulties, these defects in organisational matters did not help the rural cadres in their implementation of policy.

Little altered in the type and quality of cell organisation after the spring of 1931 until the major reorganisation of June 1933. This interim period saw less change and innovation because the rural party was endeavouring to make a success of the structure established in the previous years.

RURAL CELL NUMBERS AND THEIR DEPLOYMENT

The most radical transformation concerning cell numbers and their deployment was the increase of rural cells situated at production sites, especially the *kolkhozy*, and the decline in numbers of cells located territorially at villages and Soviets. During the period of greatest upheaval in the countryside between 1 July 1929 and 1 April 1930, the number of *kolkhoz* cells increased by almost 8 000, whilst territiorial cells diminished by 6 000; between 1 July 1929 and 1 July 1932, the respective figures were a rise of 42 500 and a decline of 15 000. Full information is contained in Table 5.1.

So many cells were created at *kolkhozy* to satisfy the theory of 'face to production' and, more practically, to accommodate the hundreds of thousands of *kolkhozniks* recruited to the party in these years. Judging from Table 5.1, it is possible to distinguish periods of accelerated expansion in the growth of *kolkhoz* cells, followed by relative calm, although a significant net increase in the number of all rural cells did not take place until the first half of 1931.[28] The initial take-off in *kolkhoz* cell numbers occurred in the winter months of 1930. The *kolkhoz* cells

Table 5.1 Numbers of rural party cells and candidate groups* and their deployment, 1929–32

Date	Total number of cells and candidate groups	sovkhoz no.	%	M.T.S. no.	%	kolkhoz no.	%	Territorial no.	%
1 July 1929	27039	1270	4.7	—	—	1514	5.6	24254	89.7
1 April 1930	29204	1635	5.6	58	0.2	9250	31.7	18252	62.5
1 October 1930	31874	2199	6.9	223	0.7	13132	41.2	16319	51.2
1 January 1931	33325	2466	7.4	229	0.9	14964	44.9	15596	46.8
1 July 1931	42113	3916	9.3	1137	2.7	25562	60.7	11497	27.3
1 January 1932	45165	5194	11.5	1897	4.2	29984	66.4	8084	17.9
1 July 1932	63135	7075	12.2	2645	4.2	44045	69.8	8740	13.8

Sources: (1) July 1929 – January 1932, Partiinoe stroitel'stvo, No. 11–12, June 1932, p. 46. All gross figures are my derivations; (2) 1 July 1932, Partiinoe stroitel'stvo, No. 21, November 1932, p. 46. Here the percentages are my derivations.
* As a proportion of all party units during the first Five Year Plan period, candidate groups remained fairly constant at about 20–30 per cent.

expanded considerably in absolute terms and as a proportion of all cells in the first half of 1931, again in the wake of the accelerated tempo of collectivisation, and the rate of increase subsided in the latter half of the year. The huge expansion in numbers of kolkhoz cells in the first half of 1932 is less directly related to trends within collectivisation than to the need to incorporate even greater numbers of collective farmers recruited in 1931 and early 1932. The numbers of territorial cells did not decline in the first half of 1932 and it may be assumed that a figure of 8–9000 was regarded as a basic minimum for cells located in the Soviets, villages and co-operatives, if the party was to maintain a presence in the non-collectivised sectors of the Soviet countryside, admittedly a meagre one. The proportion of cells that were production- or territorially-based matched reasonably closely the proportions of rural communists deployed in them, as is shown in Table 5.2.

Nationally the size of the average rural party cell grew during the first Five Year Plan from 13 in 1929 to almost 16 at the beginning of 1931 and 1932.[29] These national averages concealed variations in cell types according to regions as information indicates in Table 5.3.

In 1931 in the North Caucasus the average kolkhoz cell was already very large, containing 28–30 communists, whilst at the same time in the

Table 5.2 The numbers and proportions of rural communists located in different types of cells, 1930–32

Date	Rural party membership	Territorial cells	Production cells	Of which kolkhoz cells
June 1930[a]	404 600	263 000 (65.1%)[b]	141 000 (34.9%)[b]	115 000 (28.4%)[b]
January 1931[c]	513 588	226 816 (44.2%)[d]	286 772 (55.8%)[d]	234 000 (45.6%)[d]
January 1932[c]	700 951	111 385 (15.9%)[d]	589 000 (84.1%)[d]	461 000 (65.8%)[d]

Sources: (a) Kaganovich in *XVII s"ezd Vsesoyuznoi Kommunisticheskoi Partii (b)*: *stenograficheskii otchet* (1934), p. 557; (b) my derivations from ibid.; (c) *Partiinoe stroitel'stvo*, No. 11–12, June 1932, p. 47; (d) my derivations from ibid.

Mid-Volga and White Russion Republic the sizes were 14.5 and 10, and 16.3 and 11 respectively in 1932.[30]

Several conclusions can be drawn. Production-based cells, as well as becoming a larger proportion of all rural cells, encompassed a commensurate number of all rural communists. In particular *kolkhoz* and MTS cells expanded their average membership, whilst territorial cells shrank in size. The territorial cell was reduced in size most especially in an important grain region like the Ukraine, whereas the *kolkhoz* cells were strongest in these areas, most noticeably the North Caucasus. Proportionally as well the *kolkhoz* cells tended to be more important in the grain regions. For example, in the Ukraine, *kolkhoz* cells took a greater share among all rural cells than on the national scale: on 1 April 1930 and 1 October 1930 *kolkhoz* cells in the Ukraine represented 39.2 per cent and

Table 5.3 Average cell sizes in the Ukraine in 1930

	1 April 1930	1 October 1930
kolkhoz cell	11.6	16.2
MTS cell	13.4	16.5
sovkhoz cell	11.1	14.1
territorial cell	14.3	8.5
all cells	12.9	15.4

Source: My derivations from *Partiinoe stroitel'stvo*, No. 3–4, February 1931, p. 18.

67.1 per cent of the total, whereas in national terms the percentages were 31.7 and 41.2 respectively.[31]

These were the numbers and sizes of rural party cells. An important question is to what extent they provided party coverage over geographical areas and economic units. The problem of coverage, a perpetual one, was quickly encountered in the collectivised countryside at the beginning of 1930 when there were only 23 400 full party cells to supervise 70 000 rural Soviets and an almost equal number of collective farms. [32] Rural party cell coverage was best in the MTS and *sovkhozy* where during the first Five Year Plan it became almost complete. The total number of MTS and *sovkhoz* units rose little over 10 000 during the 1930s; by July 1932 there were 7700 *sovkhoz* cells and 2645 in the MTS.[33] In mid-1932 there were only 217 (10 per cent) out of 2100 MTS which did not possess a party cell, although the party layer among the work force in MTS and *sovkhozy* remained very low at 2–4 per cent.[34] The party's cell coverage of these units was impressive because of the relatively small numbers of units involved; the party was less fortunate in seeking to encompass the more numerous collective farms.

The ideal cell coverage of collective farms would have been to have one rural cell in every *kolkhoz*. On a national scale this was not a feasible target in the foreseeable future, and in fact was only attained in 1962.[35] Nevertheless, it remained an objective which the party could always strive to approach. During the first Five Year Plan some noteworthy improvement was recorded in the cell coverage of *kolkhozy*. Whereas in mid-1929 there were 44 *kolkhozy* for every party cell and candidate group, this number was reduced to four or five by mid-1932. Table 5.4 presents the picture nationally and with reference to a number of important regions.

At the beginning of the first Five Year Plan only 2 per cent of *kolkhozy* contained a party unit; towards the end of the plan period (June 1932) a fifth of all *kolkhozy* possessed such a party presence. The grain regions recorded the best results because here the *kolkhozy* were generally larger in size and fewer in number, and also because the party consciously concentrated its forces on these, the more important *kolkhozy* from the point of view of grain procurements. Judging from Table 5.1, it seems that at the end of the first Five Year Plan it was still only feasible to aim for complete coverage in a few selected areas, the most important grain regions, and even here actual results fell short of the objective. Moreover, where there was a party presence, the impact of a single communist or even a small party cell of three to eight communists in a huge *kolkhoz* with a population of hundreds or thousands was

Table 5.4   *Kolkhozy* and the proportion of them with a party cell or candidate group: nationally and regionally, 1929–33

Region	1929	1930	1931	1932	1933
USSR	67 446 (2.3%)	85 950 (12.5%)	211 000 (12.5%)	211 000 (Jan. 16.6%) (June 20.2%)	—
Ukraine	14 306 (0.1%)	20 745 (Apr. 17.0%) (Oct. 10.7%)	35 000 —	25 300 (20.5%)	24 100 (summer 27.3%)
North Caucasus *krai*	6452 (1.6%)	3715 (14.2%)	5700 —	5000 (60.0%)	5000
Lower Volga *krai*	3230	1448 (93.6%)	3300 (61.1%)	3350 —	3300 —
Mid Volga *krai*	2812 —	3544 —	6000 (23.0%)	5200 (51.9%)	6300
Central Black Earth *oblast*	3301 (1.9%)	5004 (16.2%)	16 700 (8.5%)	15 300 (13.4%)	15 800 —
Western Siberia	— —	— —	12 000 —	10 700 (26.4%)	11 400 —
White Russia	1027 (4.0%)	3023 (5.3%)	7400 (3.9%)	9600 (6.5%)	9400 (6.5%)
Western *oblast*	1011 —	2666 —	15 000 —	16 800 (6.0%)	17 900 (July 4.4%) (Sept. 5.5)

Sources: (a) for *kolkhoz* figures, see *Sotsialisticheskoe stroitel'stvo*, (1934), p. 160; (b) for *kolkhoz* cell numbers, see Appendix 3; (c) percentages are derived from the above sources and it should be noted that they are only approximate, since the two sets of data do not always coincide exactly in their chronology.

sometimes negligible. Despite the large scale recruitment and the breaking down in size of party units in 1933, the rural party did not approach its goal of a cell or candidate group, nor even a single communist in each *kolkhoz*. In the non grain-consuming regions, the rural party's hold and presence was most precarious even in 1932 at the time of its greatest size. In the Moscow *oblast* 85 per cent of *kolkhozy* and 50 per cent of rural Soviets did not contain independent party organisations.[36] At the beginning of 1932 in Georgia, there were 3550 *kolkhozy* and 285 *kolkhoz* cells (8 per cent of *kolkhozy* covered); in the Western *oblast* during the summer and autumn 1932, the number of *kolkhoz* cells and candidate groups rose from 782 to 987, but this was a meagre figure in comparison with the *oblast*'s 17 000 collective farms (6 per cent coverage).[37] With regard to the northern, western and central consuming regions, it was confessed that 'it must be borne in mind that the great number of rural Soviets and especially kolkhozy are completely without either a cell or a candidate group, and many of them do not even have in their composition a single party member or candidate'.[38]

This quantitative information on the disposition of the rural party's organisation and manpower resources indicates that the rural party was forever short of the necessary numbers to provide an ubiquitous or pervasive presence in the countryside. This could only have a detrimental effect on the quality of its work and undermine basic policy objectives.

DEVELOPMENTS AT THE SUB-CELL LEVEL

The turn to 'face to production' in organisation during the first Five Year Plan saw the rural communist party extend over a broad geographical expanse centring itself at production points: this can be seen as a horizontal process. In 1931, and more so in 1932, the rural party had the manpower resources, or thought it did, to sub-divide its units further and to permeate all economic units internal to the *kolkhoz*, MTS and sovkhoz: this process can be seen in vertical terms.

Such a process could be promoted by making better use of party groups and party organisers in the production sections and especially in the field brigades. Party groups and party organisers were accepted as proper means of organisation in the autumn 1930 *polozhenie*. Party groups consisted of full members and candidates working in production sections or brigades, who could number in practice between two and ten and were in some cases indistinguishable from cells, except that they did not have a full secretary but were headed by a party group organiser, and the group as a whole was part of the full cell and subordinate to it. A party organiser was a single party member who represented the party at the lowest production levels where there were insufficient communists to form groups, which was often the case. Their extensive use was encouraged gradually throughout 1931; in the autumn of that year, for example, the Berezovskii *raikom* was chastised in the party's organisational journal for its 'simple fear of breaking up the party cells into smaller units' (*prostaya boyazn' razukrupneniya yacheek*).[39]

This breaking down the size of party units (*razukrupenie*) was the organisational theory to make the rural party network more pervasive. The proliferation of party groups and party organisers in the *kolkhoz* brigades and *sovkhoz* production departments was given major impetus by two complementary C.C. resolutions in the first half of 1932. The first, dated 4 February, urged the 'organisational-economic strengthening of *kolkhozy*' and focused attention on the brigade.[40] The second C.C. resolution, dated 15 May, called for the direct involvement in production activities of as many as 70 per cent of rural communists.[41] Some party organisations, for example, the Lower Volga *kraikom*, interpreted these resolutions as expressing an underlying aim of achieving a party presence in all *kolkhozy*, and even in all brigades.[42] By May 1932 in the Lower Volga there were 1200 party groups and 2867 party organisers for the 7000 *kolkhoz* brigades.[43] The party groups were intended to promote quick completion of sowing, to ensure that the *kolkhozniks* remained in the brigades for at least one year, to hold daily 10–15 minute meetings of the party groups to discuss individually communists' work, whilst not interfering in the one-man management of the brigade leader; on completion of sowing, the *raikoms* were to organise party groups in meetings to review the sowing campaign and prepare for the coming harvest.[44] The groups and organisers were seen as a means to assist the crucial 1932 sowing and to bolster flagging work discipline.

The results achieved by the groups and organisers were variable. In the Mikhailov *raion*, Far Eastern *krai*, with a total of 36 cells, 47 party groups and 76 organisers were employed, but it was admitted that their work was patchy and depended on the zeal of the cell secretaries organising them. In the Millerovskii *raion*, North Caucasus, a party group of the Degtevskii cell, containing nine communists (quite large), carried out mass-party work and was exemplary in the thick of production, but it was noted that such groups were rare.[45] *Raikoms*, support points and ordinary cells were urged to train and assist the groups and organisers, making a further demand on their time and energies. Success was relative; and towards the end of 1932, when events overshadowed them as with the support points, the initial spurt of enthusiasm for groups and organisers may have dissipated. It also turned out that some of their success was artificial, with communists being merely attached to brigades on a haphazard, temporary basis, visiting the brigades only two or three times a month. These 'attached' people (*partprikreplennyi*) were granted the title of party organisers, when ideally they were intended to have been mobilised from among the *kolkhoznik* party members already working in the brigades or from communists working formerly in an administrative capacity, transferred permanently to production work in the brigades.[46]

The further the rural party tried to encompass the socialised, agricultural network, the more probable it became that the average calibre of party members would decline. One must remember what the party was seeking to achieve in its more exuberant moments. We have seen how the attempt for a party presence in every *kolkhoz* failed: to extend this objective to the *kolkhoz* brigades was unrealistic. In mid-1932 for example, at the height of the ambitious attempt, there were 211 000 *kolkhozy* each with 5–15 production brigades, depending on *kolkhoz* size, totalling between one and three million economic-production units, in addition to key units such as *sovkhozy* and MTS. Because of such limiting factors as these, in a major grain region like the Mid-Volga at the end of the first Five Year Plan only 24.2 per cent of brigade leaders were communists.[47]

A clear manifestation of how the rural party was over-extending itself is the quality of the personnel to which it resorted in order to ensure a presence in even a small proportion of brigades. It was broadly recognised that party organisers were 'young party people [recent recruits] poorly grounded politically'.[48] Several shortcomings needed to be rectified: those organisers who were candidate members were to be replaced or promoted to full membership, as candidates were regarded as wholly inadequate and inexperienced to give the required lead in production and organisation to the non-party peasantry; those who could not devote sufficient time to their duties as party organisers were to be replaced.[49] Although efforts were made to improve their calibre by providing more training courses and by ensuring close supervision, there is little evidence to suggest any major qualitative improvement in the party organisers' composition or achievements in 1931–33. Thus the two principal problems encountered in the turn to production brigades, as in many other aspects of rural party organisation, concerned quantity and quality.

There are several impressions which are most striking with regard to the rural party cells in the period 1929 to mid-1933. Firstly, and obviously, one is struck by the increase in their numbers from 27 039 in July 1929 to 63 135 three years later in mid-1932. This expansion in cell numbers was a corollary of the recruitment drive conducted during collectivisation, and necessary to accommodate new recruits. Secondly, there is the emphasis on the key production centres and the attempt to establish party units, large and small, in these places. The *kolkhoz* occupied the predominant position as the key to ensuring party control over the socialised peasantry. Particular attention was also paid to the party organisations in the *sovkhozy* and MTS with the innovation of the support points. The MTS acquired more political and economic importance as it became a control centre for supplementary extractions of agricultural produce from the *kolkhozy*. Thirdly, the variety in the structure and deployment of party units is apparent, and was a consequence of the efforts of the local party organisations to mould the party network to multifarious economic and population criteria.

However, all was not well with the reorganisation of the lower levels of the rural communist party in the years of the first Five Year Plan. As the changes occurred, a number of set-backs were suffered and defects uncovered. With raionisation the operation had been partially flawed by the inability to mobilise and transfer smoothly all the cadres intended – this transfer was noticeable as a failed mobilisation of personnel; the instruction-propaganda groups, which could have ensured more cohesive internal party relations between *raikoms* and cells – a very crucial point this – failed on the whole to materialise; where *raikom* staff were competent, this was no guarantee that they would not be frequently transferred to and fro; finally, again a question of internal party affairs, the central party authorities were not acquainted sufficiently with their subordinates, who were too numerous and too distant geographically. Similarly the cells had their share of problems. The most serious was the inability to extend the cell network over the majority of *kolkhozy*: without a party presence, there could be little party control or influence. The support points revealed how complex reforms in organisation were not properly explained to the local cadres in adequate detail, who then misinterpreted how, where and when to construct new models. This only epitomised the problem. There were different approaches to the rural cell framework and to intermediary cell levels on the part of those who framed organisational policy for the rural party. The authorities seem to have been unsure over the question of the orthodoxy of the inter-*kolkhoz* cell, which had created mutual support for many scattered small cells and their members and had simplified the relationship between the *raikom* and cell.

However, organisation was not the most important element in the rural party make-up; this concerned its performance. Organisation was a means to an end. Developments in the rural party structure at *raikom* and cell level were often a reflection or a response to deeper seated socio-economic phenomena present in the Soviet countryside. The organisation and deployment of party units certainly played a part in the shaping of the rural party's role and activities in the 1930s in addition to responding to them. The rural party organisation that had existed in the 1920s was wholly unsuitable to meet the demands imposed on the party during collectivisation, and for that simple reason it was reorganised. We have seen how this was carried out at the problematic grass roots, where it took more than loud orders to change reality. Nor was organisation the only factor which influenced the rural party's conduct. It was affected, negatively, by the small size of the rural party compared with the rural population; by its personnel of raw, inexperienced recruits or imported cadres who knew little about rural life; by the technological and administrative backwardness inherited from the past; and by the rupture and disjuncture caused initially by collectivisation and dekulakisation in 1929–31, which was accentuated by the misguided procurement campaigns of 1931–32. The party in action is the subject of the following chapter.

6 The Rural Communist Party and Collectivisation 1929–32

This chapter examines chronologically the role played by the rural communist party during the first Five Year Plan: its daily and seasonal chores, its part in the collectivisation process generally and in a number of extraordinary mobilisations of rural society. As we examine the rural party role, we also assess the working relationships internal to the party between *raikoms* and cells, and those between party units and other organisations and individuals. We conclude with a detailed discussion of the rural party in 1931–32, with special regard to the grain procurement campaigns of these years.

THE RURAL COMMUNIST PARTY: MID 1929–MID 1930

In 1929 the rural party was poorly prepared in terms of size, quality and organisational structure to sustain the stresses incumbent in the socialisation of peasant households and the control of agricultural production. The low level of preparedness in rural party composition and organisation combined to hinder its operational capabilities.

Before continuing further it is important to understand how this general weakness affected the relative weight that different party units could pull: in particular *raikoms* and cells. The communication of instructions passed down from the policy-making bodies in Moscow to the regional centres, who themselves had some limited autonomy in making policy and more in adapting it to local circumstances; it would be ridiculous to imagine that Moscow could control the minutiae of local life in the regions. The *krai/oblast* authorities, whether state or party, in turn communicated policies and precise orders (in theory, the orders were supposed to be detailed; in practice, this was often not the case) to their subordinates at the *okrug* (until mid-1930) and *raion*. With regard to the rural communist party, and many other institutions, it was the *okrug/okruzhkom* and *raion/raikom* that played the most important roles in co-ordinating and controlling the various program-

92

mes and campaigns conducted in the countryside during 1929–32; the party cells for most of the time played a subordinate and subsidiary role. The reasons explaining this difference in importance are not far to seek. The major distinguishing feature between the *raikoms* and rural cells, and one that had considerable impact upon their roles, was that *raikoms* were present nationwide at all the *raion* administrative centres into which the Soviet Union was divided. They were thus more all-embracing than the cells, which were deployed unevenly across the country. In addition, of course, the *raikoms* were senior in authority and contained more experienced party cadres. In those villages and *kolkhozy* that did not have a party organisation nor even a single communist, and these were the large majority, the party depended first and foremost on its representative, the *raikom*, and secondly on the use of plenipotentiaries who could be shipped to and fro to monitor events in a number of settlements; communists from the cells were also used for such peripatetic assignments: because they belonged to a particular cell based at a certain village or Soviet or production centre does not mean that they were obliged to be confined to a single location. Communists from the *raikoms* and cells were mobilised for various missions which involved travelling some distance in such campaigns as collectivisation and dekulakisation. They would be mobilised by their respective superiors to go where the action was, whilst, if for example they were cell secretaries, retaining responsibility for events in their own bailiwick.

The party forces in industry and agriculture were expected to act as initiators, promoters, co-ordinators, assistants and monitors, but, although during the first Five Year Plan they were encouraged to get as close to production as possible, they were never officially sanctioned to interfere with the principle of one-man management; in this the party's role has changed little over the years to the present day.[1] Most actual administration was in the hands of the Soviets and other state and economic organisations. 1929 was the transitional year when the change in style and content of the rural party's work set in. As well as mobilising rural communists to join the collective farms, the rural party developed techniques acquired in the 1928 grain crisis which were adaptable to new conditions; its more direct involvement in economic campaigns began in earnest. A C.C. resolution dated 29 July 1929 specified the details of the rural party's participation in the minutiae of rural economic life: with the aim of 'avoiding mistakes' in the accounting (*podschet*) of planned quotas, 'the party organisations must take direct participation in defining the method of composing and checking grain-forage balances'.[2] From the very beginning of the campaign, 'the intensified attention of the Soviet organs and the party' was to be directed to the full and prompt fulfilment of deliveries of all surpluses by the *sovkhozy, kolkhozy* and peasant households entering contract agreements. The local rural party involvement in the 1928 grain deliveries had been on an emergency, *ad hoc* basis, undertaken in what were thought to be wholly exceptional circumstances. Now the rural party's participation and responsibilities were extended and the party's contribution regularised: this was a significant break with the past. With each year the rural party was to become more and more embroiled in the annual grain collection campaign. In addition to the party and Soviets, the 29 July 1929 C.C. resolution mentioned the role of the trade unions and *komsomol*. The collections were meant to be co-ordinated affairs; the rural party rarely acted in isolation.

The steps towards laying plans for rural party operations had been taken towards the end of 1929. In the period December 1929–March 1930, the party's duties were dominated by the collectivisation and dekulakisation drives. The collectivisation process accelerated in the latter months of 1929. The party at *krai* and *oblast* level was instructed to push ahead at full speed; this urgency they communicated to their subordinates at *raikoms* and cells. With the C.C. resolution of 5 January 1930 the regions were given their overall targets. The standard Soviet planning procedure of control figures and quotas for grain collections and collectivisation then came into force. Actually to mobilise the peasant households into entering the collective farms was the responsibility of a variety of worker brigades, rural Soviet workers, plenipotentiaries from the *okrug* and *raion* party, and the rural party cell members, especially the cell secretary. As in the case of the grain collections, a modified version of the Urals-Siberian method was used. On arrival at a particular village, the state and party representatives would seek to hold a number of separate meetings of specific groups and strata of the local population. Once sectional meetings were over, having organised a caucus of support, the state-party representatives convened a general meeting of the village – not to be confused with the commune's *skhod* which in theory had been limited to heads of households – from which *kulaks* were barred.[3] The general meetings could drag on for hours with officials urging, coaxing, promising and threatening the peasants to get them to join existing *kolkhozy* or to set up entirely new ones. When a majority of those present had signed up, the decision was binding on the whole village or commune, with those rejecting the transition being allotted the worst lands on the edges of the *kolkhoz*. This was the model, but owing to the shortage of time permitted in accustoming the peasants to this fundamental change in their life style, and the uncertainty of the whole venture, many peasants refused point-blank. Rural communists, having had little experience of mobilising the peasants in the 1920s, when persuasion failed, resorted to coercion.[4]

The other related campaign which occupied the rural party's attention and that of the rural population at the beginning of 1930 was dekulakisation. In the collectivisation process the rural party rarely acted in isolation; this applied more so to dekulakisation. Local authorities were provided with their quotas. To obtain these figures, *troikas* were established at the *raion* and *okrug* levels, consisting of the first secretary of the party committee, the chairman of the Soviet executive committee and the head of the OGPU.[5] These worked through the *raikoms* and village Soviets to hold meetings of poor peasants and *batraks* in order to gain popular support for the arrest, expropriation and exile of the wealthier inhabitants. But in the eyes of the central authorities many Soviets and some rural party organisations were seen to be unreliable in this most arduous duty. This was not the first nor the last time that the rural party proved a disappointment for Moscow. This was why in many instances the major driving force behind dekulakisation was non-rural in composition. The local commissions or brigades that went about the actual arrest and expropriation in the villages comprised poor peasant–middle peasant activists often under the chairmanship of a worker 25 000-er.[6] In those areas where it existed and was not considered up to the task, the rural party was reinforced or replaced by urban outsiders.

The Role of Outsiders[7]

Whereas before 1929–30 'guardianship societies' had sought to develop general cultural, political and occasionally economic links between urban and rural life, urban workers were now in the countryside to assist the creation and stabilisation of the expanding socialised rural economy in the shape of *kolkhozy, sovkhozy* and MTS.

The most renowned example of urban workers transferring to the countryside was the 25 000-ers. It was the C.C. plenum decision of 17 November 1929 that recommended the recruitment of 'not less than 25 000 workers with adequate organisational-political experience' to supplement the promotion of *kolkhoz* cadres in rural areas.[8] About 80 per cent were sent to the major grain producing regions and national republics. It is noteworthy that 4000 were sent to the Trans-Caucasus (excluding Azerbaidjan), Central Asia, Kazakhstan and the Lower

Volga, and that less than one third of these were locally recruited urban workers, whilst 66 per cent were selected from the major industrial centres.[9] This highlights how the authorities preferred the reliability of outsiders in an extreme sense, that is not only urban workers but proletarians originating from distant towns who could have no possible ties with the local population, a tactic similarly employed with the political department staff in later years. On their arrival, 71 per cent of the 25 000-ers were allocated posts in leading *kolkhoz* work.[10]

Between 1928 and June 1930, 250 000 outsiders (workers and communists) were mobilised for temporary and permanent work, mostly the former, in the countryside. In the period June 1930 to June 1931, 200 000 urban workers alone was the corresponding figure, and it seems probable that this figure erred on the side of underestimation.[11] The trend in the use of outsiders was definitely upwards with 300 000 workers and 40–70 000 communists mobilised in the single year of 1933. These were considerable mobilisations of manpower and in the earlier years almost matched the size of the entire rural party (339 201 in January 1930).[12] The outsiders possessed a major advantage over their rural counterparts in how they used their numbers. They were not obliged nor intended to maintain a diffuse, national network; they could and did converge on the key agricultural regions; for example, 30 000 urban workers were employed in the 1931 spring sowing campaign in the North Caucasus and 109 000 during the first half of 1931 in the Central Black Earth. They could not encompass the vast countryside in its entirety, but they could saturate parts of it and exert a marked effect on certain districts. By the summer of 1930, 18.8 per cent of *kolkhozy* in the Soviet Union had 25 000-ers working in them and in a major grain region like the North Caucasus this rose to 40.3 per cent.[13] By concentrating their forces, the outsiders aimed for maximum impact.

The working relationship between urban outsiders and the local authorities was fraught with opportunities for misunderstanding and disagreement. Questions of authority and subordination were rarely solved and remained ambiguous. The urban outsiders mobilised were frequently experienced, long-serving proletarians and/or party members, although this by no means entailed that they were more experienced in or more suitable for work in rural conditions. But they were in any case usually vested with more authority than the local rural party representatives. In practice generally, urban outsiders and other plenipotentiaries, in their quest for success in trouble-shooting, paid little regard to the rural party cells and their communists; they would give them terse orders or by-pass them completely. Despite, and even judging by, the repetitive instructions to plenipotentiaries not to abuse or ignore the local rural party cell, little heed seems to have been paid.[14] This by-passing of the rural cells by outsiders adds weight to our view that at local levels it was more the *okrug* and *raion* and their respective party committees who could command respect, although they too could be browbeaten when the plenipotentiary was of sufficient authority. The relationship was not entirely one-sided and was tempered by a number of factors. When an urban worker was not a party member, the local rural communists were able to pull party rank. The local authorities had one further advantage in that very frequently the outsiders depended on them for basic living amenities. Whether they were well received not only affected this working relationship but coloured the outsiders' perception of their mission.

The role played by all types of outsiders must not be underestimated. They represented an essential supplement, large in numbers, to the local rural cadres and were used in most aspects of collectivisation and dekulakisation. Owing to their numbers and qualities, such as experience in production or party work, the outsiders acted as a significant support to the rural communist party and rural administration generally, who without their assistance were unlikely to have been able to cope and to overcome their own lack of preparation.

The chief preoccupations of the rural party were collectivisation, dekulakisation, involvement in economic processes and maintaining working relations with non-party bodies and urban outsiders. With the spring sowing and the concurrent outflow from the collective farms as a consequence of the restoration of the voluntary principle, the rural party had to reorientate itself. It is particularly interesting to see how local party cadres responded to Stalin's 'Dizzy with Success' article of 2 March 1930 which initiated the outflow. In his article Stalin condemned local officials for not taking into account local conditions and the voluntary principle behind collectivisation, and sought in this way to explain errors and excesses, whilst exempting himself and the C.C. from any blame, in a crude distortion of the facts. Some, and perhaps many, *raikoms* and cells disagreed with a policy change which invalidated so much of their recent efforts, or were more aware then the centre of how extensive the resultant retreat would be. Some lower level party workers were astonished, disappointed and disgusted with the duplicity of their superiors at the obkoms, in the C.C. and in the Politburo.[15] Even when taking the blame upon themselves, local committees could do so in the most grudging and ironical manner: the Ostrogozhskii *okruzhkom* confessed its errors but some *raion* party workers likened themselves to 'small people' in the role of musicians who carry out the producer's wishes like 'following a conductor's baton'; others were less subtle, 'Why come looking for faults in us when we are not guilty?'.[16]

When the *okruzhkoms, raikoms* and cells refused to admit the error of their ways during collectivisation, punishments followed swiftly in many places. The Lyubarskii *raikom* bureau was dissolved for gross deviation from the party line: the *raikom* secretary, the *raion* executive committee (RIK) chairman, the head of the land department were all removed from their posts and the *okruzhkom* plenipotentiary for this *raion* was recalled. All these were to face party disciplinary action and the procuracy was to investigate whether a case was to be answered in court.[17] In the Astrakhan *okrug* 198 people were brought to book, three whole *raikoms* dissolved and five *raikom* secretaries, 31 cell secretaries and 19 Soviet chairmen removed from their posts.[18] For one *okrug* this was quite a turnover of personnel for disciplinary reasons. Similar high figures were recorded in Stalingrad *okrug* where 66 people were brought before the courts; another 59 were arraigned in the Pugachev *okrug* and three *raikoms* dissolved.[19] Regular party elections were due in the spring and these were used as a further opportunity to demand more self-criticism on this issue.

It is not easy to evaluate the extent of this mini-revolt among middle and lower level party workers. There is no doubting the depth of feeling over the issue. Judging from our examples, several hundreds or one or two thousand were involved. This in itself is not an insignificant number of recorded cases, but may represent only the tip of the discontent. Seeing their colleagues demoted and brought to trial, some may have had second thoughts about refusing to recant and behave. Nor ultimately, and this is most important, could they hope to change radically any policy by their efforts alone. What was now demanded of the rural party membership in the *raikoms* and cells in 1930 and later years was to follow the middle course of the party's general line, neither deviating to the (Trotskyite) left nor to the (Bukharinite) right. This affair is also important in highlighting once again the theme of recalcitrance as displayed by local rural party members towards the central authorities' instructions, which we have already seen exhibited in the campaign to join collective farms and in the transfer of personnel from the *okrugs* to the *raions*: nor was this to be the final occasion on which the rural party membership failed to satisfy the centre.

What assessments were made at the time, and can we make, of the rural party performance in the initial stages of mass collectivisation? In 1930 the party began in earnest to reinforce its rural ranks and establish close links with the socialised economy by recruiting large numbers of collective farmers and accommodating them in an expanding network of rural party cells. In the chaotic circumstances, this consolidation and expansion was an achievement. On the other hand, given the rural party's ramshackle starting point, it was not difficult to find fault. One speaker at a January 1930 C.C. conference noted, with regard to the initial phase of collectivisation, that the rural party cells were so weak that the campaign had by-passed them, relegating them to the same position as the rural Soviets.[20] A few months later at the sixteenth party congress, Kaganovich, reviewing the preceding period came to some fairly scathing conclusions about the rural party cells' role and condition:

The tentacles [*shchupal'tsa*] [of cells in the countryside] were very weak quantitatively and very weak qualitatively . . . The cell as a productive, leading organising force in the present day still plays a minuscule role . . . the cell, as an independent organism . . . as we have in industry, in the [factory] shop, in Soviet institutions, functioned and functions badly in the countryside.[21]

As so often in the rural party's history in this era, these harsh remarks were true enough, but there was no discussion of fundamental questions regarding the timing of collectivisation and the level of the party's preparedness to cope with socialist transformation, or of the implications which stemmed from these questions, and as so often the culprits in poor organisational planning, most notably Kaganovich who was responsible for party organisational affairs, escaped criticism.

THE RURAL COMMUNIST PARTY: MID 1930–MID 1931

Beginning in 1930 the rural party settled down to function on a regular basis in the countryside in the fields of party and economic work. Attention is focused here on the major change in party activity: its turn to production, involvement on a day-to-day basis in the details of the rural economy. This includes a study of how the party operated during the agricultural procurements of 1930, the behaviour of and working relations between *raikoms* and cells, and the part played by the party in the major collectivisation drive of early 1931. Much of the material discussed here pertains to the party's routine operations, those which occurred on a weekly, monthly or seasonal basis, and is applicable to almost any period of the first Five Year Plan, while some aspects remain relevant for 1933 and beyond, although in the second Five Year Plan the rural party role changed dramatically.

Party Activities 1930–31

With regard to party work, the *raikoms* and cells developed the system employed in the 1920s. Apart from rearrangements necessary with the abolition of the *okrugs* and the rise of the support point cells, few changes occurred in the rural party's internal operations. The *raikoms* received their orders from their superiors and communicated them to the cells often in circular letters and memos. Before and after contact with cells, the *raikoms* held numerous, often interminable plenum meetings to discuss ways and means of implementing policies. Various other meetings were convened, often of a particular group of party workers, such as rural Soviet chairmen, cell secretaries, *raikom zavorgi*, communist *kolkhoz* chairmen and so forth. Communists were summoned to such meetings by terse notes sent to the cells informing them of the date and time of the meeting at which, they were frequently reminded, attendance was compulsory.[22] Frequent party meetings, discussions with many sectors of rural society, at least its élite elements, visits to cells and reports were standard fare in the rural party's regulation of mass-party and internal party activities.

The party's ever present duties included party recruitment, party education, political propaganda, maintenance of cultural facilities, liaison with non-party bodies with the aim of improving and expediting agricultural production and delivery. However, a major impediment to the proper communication, comprehension and implementation of plans was that rural party cadres and workers were continually pressed for time and overburdened with chores. Some rural party cells were left leaderless as the secretary and his deputy went out and about seeing to their duties.[23] Pressed for time and harassed for quick, manifest results, the local rural party workers were agreed on their major priority, one invariably of a strict, economic character. One cell secretary expressed it thus: 'For poor party work they won't "beat" [*pob'yut*] you, but for non-fulfilment in a campaign they will certainly thrash [*vzgrevut*] you'.[24] In other *raions* and cells communists were reported as saying, 'One thing only gets in the way of another, we'll finish the grain procurements first, then bother ourselves with the kolkhozy'.[25] This last example not only draws the distinction between economic and party work, but also differentiates between less and more important economic campaigns. In brief, as far as these party workers were concerned, the major priority was agricultural deliveries according to the state's plan. It was necessary to distinguish between priorities even within the economic sector because the local rural party workers had so many economic commitments. When compared with the 1920s the greatest transformation in the rural communist party was its 'turn to production' at the beginning of the first Five Year Plan. This change in operational activity made life more demanding and complex. One high-ranking party official, speaking in mid-1931, recognised this: 'it was one thing to guide [*rukovodit'*] the countryside three to four years ago and another thing to guide now the collectivised countryside.'[26] The importance of production and the party's role in it had been made clear in 1929: 'Party organisations as a whole and each communist individually must stand in the vanguard of fulfilling basic production tasks'.[27] In the countryside this entailed direct involvement in the *kolkhozy*. The major impact of collectivisation upon the party was to transform the deployment of rural cells and their work content. As many questions such as the role of the *mir* and the distinction between poor and middle peasants were swept away by the advent of the *kolkhozy*, often the rural cells and *raikoms* had little time for anything but *kolkhozy* and related matters like procurements.

In 1930 when, like many other institutions including the rural party, the *kolkhozy* and the *kolkhoz* unions were acclimatising to the new conditions, it was intended that the rural party would be closely involved in the economic-production activities of the *kolkhozy*, *sovkhozy* and MTS. This may have been due partly to the shortage in numbers and unknown reliability of *kolkhoz* chairmen and administrators, but quickly the party involvement in detailed economic questions acquired a momentum of its own. Theoretically, party organisations were not to impinge on the one-man management of *kolkhoz* chairmen or *sovkhoz* and MTS directors, but to guide and influence *kolkhoz* decisions by means of party fractions within the *kolkhoz* administrations. In the early days of collectivisation though, party fractions in *kolkhozy* were few and far between and, with the *raikoms* and cells held responsible for economic success and failure, there was an irresistible temptation to go beyond mere supervision and guidance. *Kolkhoz* and *sovkhoz* cells busied themselves with the planning of grain procurements, seed sorting, creating seed funds and with the technical and production aspects of economic campaigns.[28] Early in 1930 one rural cell secretary in the Kuban was praised for his work in actually formulating production-

financial plans, plans for crop rotation, land usage and work alloca-
tion.[29] Production-based cells orientated themselves towards the minutiae of the socialised production system: to struggle for work discipline
and against absenteeism, to devise methods to increase yields and ways
to reduce costs, to encourage shock work and socialist competition, and
to participate in production activities themselves. Their role was not
confined to work plan formulation but involved implementation as well.
These were the types of economic details handled at the lower levels; it
was the *raikoms* which had to co-ordinate economic objectives, to ensure
that each sector of their *raion* was on course for plan fulfilment. The
raikoms had to keep in sight the ends (plan fulfilment) and means (their
power to order subordinates): 'It is necessary for the raikoms to turn
their face to the economy and wherewithal [*tekhnika*] of their raions'.
The aim was for the *raikom* 'to become the boss [*khozyain*] of its raion'.[30]
One agricultural campaign blended into another: the harvest followed
by the threshing, the autumn sowing, autumn ploughing, long-term
preparations for the spring sowing and the spring sowing itself; these
were all directed towards one goal: agricultural procurements to the
state – the barometer of success.

The Grain Collections of 1930–31

Since the question of agricultural procurements was such a central one,
and relates to the following discussion on 1931–32, attention will be
paid here to the 1930 campaign. The campaign's format was modelled
on the experience gathered from the previous two years. Contracts were
drawn up between the state on the one hand and the *kolkhozy* and
individual farmers on the other. However, the contracts were little more
than a 'legal fiction';[31] in reality, the *raions* were allocated their quota,
which was sub-divided amongst the *kolkhozy*, middle and poor peasant
households under contract, and *kulaks*. The quotas were no longer
designed to extract a norm on a per hectare basis, the goal was to take
away all agricultural surpluses at fixed prices. Although the
procurements from the 1930 harvest would eventually prove satisfactory
to the authorities, the fact that there were too few industrial consumer
goods supplied to the countryside to act as an incentive to the peasants,
and not even enough currency in circulation to pay the peasants the
meagre fixed prices (one fifth the open market rate), engendered
complications for rural cadres at local levels, who were obliged to
overcome peasant reluctance to deliver.

The Monastyrshchi *raikom*, Western *oblast*, presents a vivid picture of how one *raikom* co-ordinated with its cells during the 1930 procurement campaign, how it communicated with them, the subjects it treated, and the tone and attitude it adopted towards its subordinates. The *raikom* contacted its cells on a variety of issues: the propagandising of measures taken by the regime such as the advantages to *kolkhozniks* in April 1930, and of Stalin's speeches; the collection of information on party members for various surveys; even the annual mobilisation of recruits to the Red Army involved the active participation of party cells, but no business took on quite the same character as agricultural procurements.[32] On 8 September 1930 the *raikom* via the cells made an urgent appeal to all communists and *komsomols* engaged in agriculture to deliver their grain surpluses within seven days.[33] As ever, the communists were expected to set an exemplary pace for the non-party peasants. On 1 November 1930 the *raikom* in a circular to all cell secretaries noted that grain procurements were progressing far too slowly, especially from *kulaks* and rich peasants, and 'categorically demands that measures be taken' to increase the tempo of the collections. The response to this circular must have been perfunctory, as a fortnight later (14 November) the complaint was reiterated: on this occasion the phrase 'the raikom categorically demands' had been omitted in the typed version of the circular, but later, on being vetted by the *raikom* secretary Korolev, this phrase was inserted in his own handwriting, and was obviously regarded as an important threatening part of the circular.[34] In mid-November the *raikom* categorically demanded once again an augmentation, this time in the flax procurement rate. This was followed a few days later by a further circular to the cells, surprisingly milder in tone, which merely suggested an improved tempo.[35] Perhaps the *raikom* did not want to exhaust its supply of 'categorical demands' and thought that a more guileful approach might be more rewarding. Sometime in August, the *obkom* itself had sent a communication to all cells pointing out that potato procurements had reached only 24 per cent of their plan and vegetables 10 per cent. The Monastyrshchi *raikom* took up this theme on 14 December to report to the cells that potato procurements were still only 39.8 per cent of target, once again it urged them to concentrate their energies on the *kulaks* and demanded that these contributions should be on their way in the next 24 hours.[36] On 17 August 1930 the *raikom* directed its cells to accelerate work on contracts from the winter sowing and a similar message was dispatched early in December concerning milk contracts.[37]

A most revealing instance of the *raikom*'s tensions and resulting tone is conveyed in two circulars concerning broader subjects of tax collections and loan repayments, although these were an integral part of the procurement campaign, forcing the peasants to sell to the state for want of cash to repay their debts and taxes. The first circular, dated 8 September 1930, ordered communists and *komsomols* to work on these topics, with cell secretaries sending in their progress reports every ten days. This provoked little resulting action. By 14 December, the *raikom* was reduced to the frenzied impotence of demanding 'for the last time' tax collections and prompt repayment of loans.[38]

The documents pertaining to the Monastyrshchi *raikom* in the autumn and winter of 1930 reveal several characteristic features of rural party operations. Firstly, the scope of topics treated by the *raikom* in its dealings with its own party cells is striking, nor does our list include other various subjects that were handled in conjunction with non-party institutions, who were berated in 1930–32 for not doing their fair share of work and for being too willing to shift the burden and responsibility on to the party. Secondly, and partly consequential to our first point, the *raikom* seems to have been perpetually harassed and pressed for time, and conveyed this haste and urgency to its cells. It is probable that the time schedules of the *raikom*, set by the *obkom*, were marginally less rigorous than the *raikom* was willing to acknowledge to its own cells: in this way it reduced the length of time available to the cells so as to ensure itself a breathing-space and a chance to recoup losses in the event of non-commission by the cells first time around. A certain underlying fear of failure and its consequences is discernible in the frenetic manner in which the *raikom* conducted its affairs: although transfer was more frequent than demotion and expulsion, *raikom* staff still tried assiduously to avoid any censure or blot on their service record for fear of being made an unfortunate example. Thirdly, the style and content of the materials are noteworthy. Most often the instructions were phrased in vague and general terms of 'measures to be taken' with only rare comment on how actually to go about the business concretely. This was a general feature of *raion* authorities, not confined to the Western *oblast*. The chairman of the Buddeiskii *kolkhoz*, in the Aleksandrov rural Soviet, Moldavia, complained to his *raion* authorities that 'You all tell me to do this, that and the other. But no one ever tells me how to do it'.[39] This fact underlines one of our foregoing points that many people were unable to provide pertinent, detailed information since so few administrators in the early 1930s had any long-term experience of collectivisation and procurements. The papers dispatched to the cells also show the relationship between the party links at the grass roots. The subservient position of the cells is obvious, but the *raikom* appreciated that its own success depended on the effectiveness and co-operation of the lower units, and was, therefore, compelled to employ a medley of supplications, promises, requests, recommendations, instructions, orders, demands, threats and abuse. As will be seen again, intricate human relationships, based on the need for apparent success, pervaded the rural party.

This is how one *raion* behaved in the comparatively smooth procurement campaign of 1930. However, this campaign was not entirely trouble free and in fact one or two features can be identified which point to the shape of things to come. Firstly, *ad hoc* bodies appeared to reinforce the procurement machinery: in the Central Black Earth these were entitled 'commissions of assistance to grain procurements'.[40] Secondly, severe measures were called for against those who were thought to be resisting the collections. The 'sowing and grain collection *troika*' of *Kolkhoztsentr* (a forerunner of the 1932 *troikas*) resolved that:

> leaders of kolkhozy who delay and disrupt the collections must be put on trial immediately, and kolkhozy retaining their grain must be deprived of their loans, and the supply of agricultural machinery to them must cease.[41]

Thirdly, and most relevant, were the first reported appearances after mass collectivisation of significant party resistance to the grain procurements. This was something more serious than usual run-on-the-mill misdemeanours. A variety of offences was cited against a background of '*kulak*' terror and arson, designed no doubt to convey a more charged atmosphere. In some *raions* of the Central Black Earth – Shchuchenskii, Kozlovskii, Karachanskii – there was reported inadequate pressure against *kulaks*. Slightly more grave were cases of individual communists or even whole cells not carrying out the grain procurements properly, as in Gryazinskii, Bolshepolyanskii, Gremyachenskii *raions* and others. The most serious incidents occurred in the V. Lapatinskii, Staro-Yup'evskii, Mikhailskii, Muchapskii *raions* and others where communists refused directly to carry out procurements, refused to accept plans, requested to have them lowered and 'deserted' from duty.[42] Local rural communists were refusing openly to obey orders when not exorbitant procurements were being extracted from a comparatively bountiful harvest.

The Second Collectivisation Drive 1931

There was little movement in the level of collectivisation on a national scale in the summer, autumn and winter 1930. There were two major reasons for this. The local rural party authorities were engrossed in the procurement campaign, which only drew to an end at the close of 1930, and they tended to ignore their superiors' advice that procurements and collectivisation were integral parts of the same campaign, preferring instead to concentrate on their main concern: procurements. Also many communists were wary of making the mistake of early 1930 by being accused of over-zealousness. Once procurements were completed, with coaxing and encouragement, the local party workers returned to an intensified collectivisation drive. To aid them, hundreds of thousands of outsiders were drafted in. Another spur to activity was the recrudescence of the anti-*kulak* campaign. Party organisations were made wary of 'kulaks destroying kolkhozy from within' and told to remove their 'right-opportunist blinkers' (*pravoopportunisticheskie shory*).[43]

It is worthwhile to cite another *raikom* as a specific example of how the *raion* party worked hand in hand with all those who would assist, and also to convey to the reader the atmosphere of frenzied activity that was an accompaniment of mass collectivisation, as of much else that the party undertook.

In September 1930 the Mordovskii *raikom*, Central Black Earth *oblast*, took the decision to collectivise 50 per cent of peasant households in 1931, in accordance with the party line as laid down in the C.C. resolution of 5 January 1930. The *raikom* started preparations immediatly to co-ordinate the campaign and to this end heard reports from departments of non-party organisations. In this *raion* a month of collectivisation was declared commencing on 8 January 1931, and it serves as an informative presentation of an exercise in mass-work, orchestrated by the party. At the beginning of the month, 160 communists and trade union members were sent to the settlements (*sela*) and ten brigades comprising 85 of the most 'advanced' (enthusiastic) *kolkhozniks* were formed.[44] Other emissaries included 18 *raion* party workers, 20 trade union members, 40 members of the *raion komsomol* and 60 *komsomols* from a nearby sugar combine; 52 *komsomol* brigades were organised in the villages and 27 shock brigades composed of 85 women were deployed over six rural Soviets. These were some of the human resources mobilised for collectivisation, all of whose actions were co-ordinated in large part by the *raikom*. Admittedly some of these groups may have existed only on paper, but it was a substantial assembly none the less. These types of mobilisations were repeated nationwide, particularly in the important grain regions.

In the Mordovskii *raion* a total of 770 meetings of poor peasants, young people, *kolkhozniks* and women were held. The *raion* party assembled shock workers, held production conferences and the *raion*'s first so-called 'congress of mass collectivisation' with 400 people present. The total attendance of all these meetings was estimated at 95 000 peasants.[45] Regular group party meetings were held with the participation of party members from a particular group of cells, members of rural Soviets, trade unionists, *kolkhozniks* and individual peasants. At these meetings the party cell secretaries and Soviet chairmen reported on their work of the previous week. Such meetings were proclaimed great successes. In the Sosnovskii and Lavrovskii rural Soviets evening meetings of *kolkhozniks* and individual peasants were arranged and brigade leaders went the round of the homes of individual peasants to have chats. One can only surmise whether the tenor of these conversations was persuasive, threatening or a combination of the two. In the *raion* as a whole the level of collectivisation rose from 15 per cent on 1 January to 70 per cent on 1 March.[46] These figures were interpreted as a great success, and yet only a few months before such behaviour would have been condemned as a 'left excess' of 'chasing mere percentages'. This testifies to one of the many kinks in the general line during collectivisation in the years 1929–33, and the above picture shows how one *raion* responded to it.

This is in fact a fairly typical example of what was required of rural administrators and activists in this collectivisation drive and other campaigns. As we saw, the *raikom* acted as the initiator by taking the formal decision and setting the target figure; it also deployed *raion* level party workers throughout the *raion*. The cells' involvement would differ from *raion* to *raion* depending on their number in each *raion* – the average varying from approximately 9 to 15 between 1929 and 1932. This average figure meant that most *raikoms* disposed of a nucleus of communists in the cells who could be deployed around the surrounding villages and *kolkhozy* with other state representatives so as to form brigades or to act independently in promoting and propagandising the regime's programmes. At worst, the *raikoms* could spread a thin veneer of cell members over most of the *raion*, concentrating as usual on key points and bottle-necks.

The extent and quality of the local rural party role may well have changed, and most likely improved, between 1929 and 1931. It is, however, extremely difficult to gauge. The goals assigned to the local party – *raikoms* and cells – in early 1931 in collectivisation and dekulakisation differed little from those of the previous year, rather they were a continuation of them. These campaigns in 1931 ran more smoothly than those of 1930. This may well have been due in part to the strengthening of the rural *raikoms* with former *okruzhkom* staff in the autumn 1930, making the *raikom* staffs larger in size and composed of more senior and experienced personnel. The abolition of the *okrug* administrative level stream-lined the rural party organisation, but one has to be most cautious about attributing the successes of early 1931 entirely or mostly to improved party organisation at the *raikom* and expanding rural cell numbers. Other more intangible factors played an equally important part: the increased confidence among rural administrators based on experience gained in previous campaigns – tempered admittedly by wariness of being accused of excesses – and the sense of inevitability which pervaded the whole process of collectivisation among many of the rural population, summed up in the state's slogan 'There is no returning to the past' (*vozrata k staromu – net*). The fact that the rural party increased its size very significantly from 339 201 on 1 January 1930 to 516 897 on 1 January 1931 and 700 000 on the same date in 1932 with the respective cell figures for these years being 29 204, 33 325 and 45 165 meant that the rural party involvement was more widespread than at the beginning of the plan period. This enabled the party to make a considerable turn 'face to production'. However, the biggest test of rural communists was still to come. The more fundamental break with the recent past came in the grain procurement campaigns of 1931 and 1932, when they were asked again to repeat seasonal campaigns, but this time at a much more intensified pitch and in the face of widespread peasant discontent and suffering.

THE RURAL PARTY AND THE GRAIN PROCUREMENT CRISES OF 1931–32

In 1931, to overcome resistance to the extraction of large proportions of the gross harvest, the state mobilised all the forces available to it: the grain procurement campaign of 1931 was in embryo that of the following year. It was during this campaign that the rural party became more enmeshed in economic questions of harvest yields and, most importantly, procurements; its duties being listed in typically general terms in a C.C. resolution of 21 June 1931.[47] As ever in times of crisis, the rural party was fortified with influxes of outsiders. For 'grain procurements and other autumn campaigns' the North Caucasus party organisation mobilised 12 000 party activists from Rostov and other towns, in addition to 15 000 *raion* activists; in September 1931 alone, the Urals *oblast* organisation sent 3000 party workers to the countryside.[48] During the campaign it appears that party members were also co-opted temporarily into the grain procurement agencies.[49]

The campaign made strenuous demands upon the rural institutions and the rural party was at the centre of action. It is important to remember that the grain regions of Ukraine and the North Caucasus were the power bases of the rural party with at the beginning of 1932 party memberships of 112 000 and 100 000 respectively, when the total rural party membership was 700 000.[50] Thus these regions were vital in terms of political forces as well as for the supply of grain. If the rural party in these regions was not up to their tasks, it meant that nearly one-third of the organisation was suspect. One can imagine the methods employed and the tension generated from the fact that S.V. Kosior, first secretary of the Ukrainian party, when making excuses for the slackness and failings of 1932, claimed that the party organisations had been wary of repeating the 'left excesses' of the winter of 1931.[51] The peasants were kept under intense pressure; firm time limits were set for the *kolkhozy* to deliver grain to the silos; specially appointed party workers were dispatched from the *raion* centres to supervise *kolkhoz* plan fulfilment; those *kolkhozy* that lagged behind had special brigades sent to them.[52] The pressure was equally intense on the rural authorities, especially the rural party. Party workers who blamed the weather for bad results were accused of 'Right opportunist' attempts to 'look for loopholes' (*poiski lazeek*).[53] One article in the party press referred to particular shortcomings that were often cited in the following year: party organisations were allowing the *kolkhozy* to set up reserve stores of grain as an insurance fund before meeting all delivery targets to the state. This was interpreted as *kulak* behaviour and those party organisations which permitted this were to be purged of bourgeois-*kulak* tendencies.[54] Similar incidents flared up in a well-publicised scandal in the *sovkhozy* towards the end of 1931.[55] These incidents were early indicators of a potential conflict between the central authorities and the local communists, and reveal the sort of criticism endured by those in the rural party who could or would not obey their orders. The energetic procurement campaign yielded 22.85 million tons, only one and a half million tons short of an optimistic plan. As a consequence grave problems arose in the 1932 spring sowing and harvest campaigns.

Usually excesses were ignored and not censured. The standard party line of the time was that hold-ups in sowing, harvest and procurements were not due to objective factors, even less to the sheer impossible nature of the tasks and plans, but were the fault of weakness and sloth of party and administrative organs. In his address of 8 July to the Third All-Ukrainian party conference, Molotov expressed the authorities' view quite clearly that the Ukraine had been paying too much attention to the demands of industry to the detriment of agriculture, and warned:

> The mistakes in the grain procurement work of the last year create the danger of demobilising tendencies in some layers of the party organisations.[56]

He went on to say that such tendencies were manifested by those party members who felt that the plans of the previous year had been too high, and consequently that the current (1932) procurement plans should be reviewed and reduced; but Molotov merely saw in this the danger of 'deviating from Bolshevik tempos'.[57] In this speech he gave the impression of being adamantly in favour of pushing forward regardless, much as he had been with the rate of collectivisation at the 1929 November C.C. plenum.

With regard to how the 1932 agricultural campaigns were carried out on a week to week basis, the Smolensk archives provide the most intimate insights into how the party functioned.

The precarious state of the countryside in the Western *oblast* was laid out in a circular sent to all *raikom* secretaries on 23 March 1932 by Shatskii, one of the *obkom* secretaries. He informed them that because of the need to supply those regions that had suffered harvest failure in 1931, the Western *oblast* would not be receiving its expected supply of grain in the second quarter of 1932,[58] which would even threaten grain supplies to basic industrial enterprises and parts of the Red Army. The *raikom* secretaries were given their orders: to see that central grain procurement plans were fulfilled; to prevent losses and theft; to ensure that there were no 'dead souls' among those who were on the lists to receive grain.[59] The most far-ranging circular which outlined extreme measures was a top-secret message from Rumyantsev, dated 6 July 1932, in which he called upon the *raikom* secretaries to be aware 'of all the gravity of the situation with grain'.[60] He listed 25 *raions* where party *troikas* had to be set up comprising the *raikom* secretary, the R.I.K. chairman and the head of the *raion* OGPU: in the remaining *raions* the *raikom* secretary was to do the *troika*'s job of overseeing grain procurements. These *troikas* and *raikom* secretaries were to be held personally responsible for the supplies of grain. Any case of theft or unauthorised transfers of supplies was to be dealt with immediately by the OGPU and the courts; those involved were to be dismissed from their posts. The message concluded with a repetition that *raikom* secretaries would be held personally responsible in the event of failure.[61] There can be fewer clearer expositions of how the party's fate was inextricably linked with the success or failure of economic plans. As the autumn months passed by, communications between all levels in the party became more frenetic. Early in October 1932, Sumarev, the Masal'skii *raikom* secretary, received a stinging letter from Rakitov, one of the *obkom* secretaries, which repeated its main point: 'The obkom warns you once again that the grain procurement plan *must be fulfilled no matter what* in the socialist sector' (emphasis in the original).[62]

Complaints about the local rural party performance were not peculiar to the Western *oblast*. One investigation held by the C.C. organisational-instruction department (*orginst*) concluded that many rural *raion* party organisations had been unable to build on the foundations of collectivisation.[63] However, not all local rural communists were willing to accept the centre's analysis. Elements in the Ukrainian rural party refused to be browbeaten. In the autumn 1932, the Orekhovskii *raikom* sent out some of its party workers into the fields to check crops and yields. Armed thus with information, the *raikom* argued with the *obkom* authorities that the plans they were sent were neither realistic nor realisable. This is an interesting example of a *raikom* obtaining detailed verifiable information to support its case: for its efforts and initiative the *raikom* was accused of 'demobilising' the peasantry and of being 'Right opportunist'. An *obkom* secretary was dispatched to mend the ways of the *raikom*, following which the *raikom* made a formal confession of its mistakes, but even then the *raikom* secretary, Golovin, declared that 'the overwhelming majority' of party members recognised their mistakes in word only.[64] This is a singular example of how the superior party organs could make people change what they said, with effort, but could not change what they thought. Nor was the Orekhovskii *raikom* alone. *Raion* party members in the Tsyuryuzhinskii and Gryshkovskii *raions*, Ukraine, were cited as claiming that grain procurement plans were too high.[65] As late as spring 1933, when plans for the party purge were well advanced, the Nagaibaksii *raikom*, Urals, took the initiative to lower quite drastically the sown area of a *sovkhoz* from 29 300 hectares to 15 000 after the *sovkhoz* director had complained of the plan's *nereal'nost'*.[66] Even some of the supposedly tough shock-troops of the political departments, it seems, were not immune from doubts about the effectiveness or desirability of central policy. At the June 1934 C.C. plenum, I.M. Kleiner, head of *Zagotzerno* (the grain procurement agency), revealed that some heads of political departments thought that grain procurement targets were unrealistic and expressed 'reductionist tendencies' (*skidochnye nastroeniya*), as Kleiner put it.[67] At the same plenum, I.M. Vareikis declared that 'several political departments stand completely on the side of the interests of their kolkhozy and M.T.S.'[68]

These examples lead us to a timely consideration of a crucial and problematic question: what was the attitude of those rural communists who criticised or disobeyed their instructions, or, and this is not the same thing, those who failed to fulfil their agricultural plans? The cases cited above seem to include those where party members made conscious decisions about what they thought was physically or humanely possible. These communists decided that either the plans were simply impossible to fulfil or, if fulfilled, would place an intolerable burden on the local population. It is such rural communists as these who were regarded as class alien and politically dangerous by the central authorities; their principal crime was to undermine the regime's legitimacy by stating openly that state plans were unfair on the population. There was another category of rural party workers, perhaps more numerous, who also failed to meet their quotas, even though they exerted all their efforts to do so: these failed in their task either because peasant resistance was too effective, because they themselves were poor administrators, unable to co-ordinate the campaigns or again because the plans set them were well-nigh impossible to fulfil. The authorities bracketed all failures in the same category as subjective resistance to orders, refusing to accept the *nereal'nost'* of any plans. This manifest intolerance at the centre bewildered and frustrated local rural communists.

By the autumn of 1932, news was filtering back to Moscow that despite remonstrations and threats, the 1932 harvest was very bad and the resultant grain procurements were eventually a disappointing 18.8 million tons.

THE CENTRE'S REACTION: PURGING BEGINS

As more peasant clamoured for grain to survive the winter and as procurements dried up completely, the rural party was berated more soundly, particularly in the Ukraine and North Caucasus. From the Central Black Earth *oblast* two cases were cited earlier in the year where *raions* had been lagging behind but had then become successful once the *raion* party leadership had been removed:[69] this was a hint of an exemplary procedure to be followed elsewhere. As the winter weeks went by, the accusations sounded more and more ominous. In the North Caucasus it was claimed that:

> Some settlement [*stanitsa*] party organisations and a few communists have sided with the kulaks and have become themselves perpetrators of kulak sabotage.[70]

This was a most serious charge, followed by the logical conclusion that for passivity and conciliation, in the form of advanced payments in kind to the *kolkhozniks* and communal feeding, 'a certain part of the party organisation of the North Caucasus' needs to 'purge decisively its ranks of degenerate elements'.[71] In the Tikhoretskii *raion*, North Caucasus, one settlement (*stanitsa*) cell secretary named Kotov was expelled from the party and eventually shot for having advanced secretly two to three times the prescribed amounts of grain to peasants.[72] The intense pressure upon the rural party was maintained. Within a fortnight, a *Pravda* editorial, dealing with the problematic grain procurements in the North Caucasus, was commenting that 'a significant part of the rural party organisations' were showing signs of 'weakening class vigilance' and 'conciliation to opportunism' and, as in the early days of mass collectivisation, the cancer seemed to spread upwards in the hierarchy as a 'part of the raion organisations and krai leadership of the North Caucasus' did not notice in time the weakening of party discipline among rural party members.[73] The rural party was faced with a 'no-win situation', chastised as it was for the excesses of 1931 and its slackness of 1932.

The year 1932 was one of a crisis of confidence in the whole rural communist party. This was reflected in the exceptional purge carried out in the southern regions at the end of the year before the full party purge of 1933, and in the high levels of removals, transfers and demotions of rural communists. In the Ukraine between 1 March and 1 November 1932, 922 *raikom* secretaries, heads of organisational departments (*zavorgi*), heads of cultural departments and *raion* control commission chairmen were removed from their posts: in a republic with 400–500 *raions*, this meant that within eight months two leading *raion* party personnel were removed on average from each *raion*.[74] It is useful at this juncture to define what transfers and removals entailed for communists. They often occurred when higher party authorities wanted simply to replace party workers in certain posts with better ones, or to break down any family groups who might seek to safeguard themselves with mutual guarantees; the authorities also responded to requests by local level rural cadres to be removed from less attractive locations after they had finished a reasonable tour of duty there. Here we are trying to identify those transfers and removals that were of a censorious and castigatory nature. In the Lower Volga during 1932 and part of 1933, among those R.I.K. chairmen removed, 11.9 per cent were replaced for deviation from the general line, especially in the matter of grain deliveries, and 19.1 per cent as incapable in the job;[75] among directors of sheep *sovkhozy* replaced, 40 per cent were ousted for their 'uneconomic approach' (*bezkhozyaistvennost'*) and expelled from the party.[76] The point here is that many were removed for a poor showing in the economic field. The extent to which the use of transfers was a response to shortcomings by rural communists in 1932–33 is revealed in information pertaining to a sample of some 30 000 leading *raion* personnel.[77] Of all transfers, a significant number were of a censorious nature: 20 per cent were downgraded to lower work, 4.5 per cent were expelled from the party and a further 3.7 per cent removed from their posts to be brought before the courts.[78] It seems that those who committed the most serious failings of a poor showing in the vital procurements, or gross inefficiency or corruption on a large scale in other economic sectors, were liable to some degree of demotion, and 8.2 per cent of transfers were as a consequence of shortcomings so grievous in the eyes of superiors to merit expulsion from the party or arraignment before the courts.

In order to combat cases of 'weakness', which often implied a certain sensitivity to the suffering of the rural inhabitants by rural party members, and to combat cases of party members stealing grain to survive or to line their own pockets, as happened in the Novo-Pashkovskii settlement, Kaganovich and Molotov were dispatched to the North Caucasus and Ukraine to head special commissions sent to Kharkov, Rostov-on-Don and Saratov.[79] It is hardly surprising that these two trouble-shooters were dispatched to these areas, since it appears that they were bordering on chaotic anarchy and revolt. Of further interest in our discussion is the retribution directed at the rural party for having allowed such a situation to develop.

The Kaganovich delegation, probably in joint sitting with the North Caucasus *kraikom* plenum,[80] resolved to instigate a purge of local communists 'who carry out kulak policy' and who were reluctant to implement the grain collections and sowing campaigns; to this end, a special committee, headed by Shkiryatov, was appointed by the C.C. and Central Control Commission (C.C.C.).[81] This extraordinary purge conducted in the winter 1932–33 in the North Caucasus and some *raions* of the Ukraine and Lower Volga should not be confused with the general party purge announced on 11 December 1932 and carried out from April

1933. The special purge committee organised 56 sub-committees which set about their work investigating the North Caucasian party membership. Within a month (by 5 December 1932) 1278 communists living in 17 inhabited points of the Kuban had been checked and 393 expelled (30.8 per cent); 68.5 per cent of these were expelled for various economic-wrecking activities, relations with the class enemy or passivity and conciliation towards *kulaks*.[82] In a sample of 205 of those expelled, 144 had only one or two years' party membership, and party cells were accused of paying inadequate attention to new recruits. Many communists who held responsible posts in the Kuban were ousted from the party and their posts in this first sweep of the purge: of 113 cell secretaries, 55 were expelled (48.7 per cent) and a further 23 (20.4 per cent) faced party disciplinary measures; of 23 communists who were rural Soviet chairmen 11 (47.8 per cent) were expelled and two received censures; of 77 communist *kolkhoz* chairmen, 37 (48 per cent) were expelled and 22 more disciplined (28.6 per cent).[83] Eventually the purge in the Kuban swept away 43 per cent of all those investigated,[84] including 358 (50 per cent) of 716 secretaries of *stankoms* and *kolkhoz* cells.[85] Some 23 per cent of those checked in the Ukraine were expelled, including the party leadership in a number of *raions* and three *oblasts*.[86] *Raikom* secretaries were not immune from censure: the *raikom* secretaries of the Armavir-skii, Leon-Kaitvenskii and Eiskii *raions* in the North Caucasus were accused of being pro-*kulak*.[87] Despite heavy purging in November in the North Caucasus and Ukraine, it was felt in early December that for several *raions* the purge in essence was 'only just beginning to develop'.[88] The purge also swept its net wider with regard to geographical area. Indeed, menacing observations were made of rural communists far afield. In the Gordevskii *raion*, Western *oblast*, *kulaks* and class aliens were said to be gaining control of lower party organisations.[89] Several party organisations in the Urals were unable to ensure plan fulfilment.[90] With reference to several non-grain regions it was stated that:

We have a few rural cells working in a good, exemplary fashion. However, we cannot say this about rural oganisations in general.[91]

The rural party was to be judged on its performance in the economy. Those who commented on the general party purge were well aware of the rationale behind it:

The party purge will expel from our ranks cheats, double-dealers, kulak degenerates and opportunists of all types, all unsteady and chance elements, all those masking themselves from the party. Spineless whimperers and sceptics, *heros of free-flow* [*samotek*], *conciliators to the advances of the class enemy, those who wreck the grain procurements and other economic-political campaigns* will find themselves out of the party ranks.[92] [my emphasis]

Amid the abuse lies the *raison d'être* behind the purge of the rural ranks. It is very significant that during the purges in the North Caucasus and Ukraine little mention was made of the usual faults and lapses of communists for which they were punished such as drunkenness, moral turpitude, embezzlement and so on; much greater prominence was given to the non-fulfilment of grain procurement plans, failure of assorted economic-political campaigns and failure to implement party policy in the countryside – this latter reference being another veiled allusion to procurements. More general sins were alluded to more frequently only when the purge went nationwide in 1933–34.

Yet the purge was not without alternatives. P.P. Postyshev made an interesting assessment of the rural economy and party in the midst of the Ukrainian and North Caucasian purges (November 1932), in which he emphasised a more careful approach to the training and selection of party members.[93] Nor does it seem that Postyshev was arguing in isolation. During the autumn 1932, there had been much talk of improving the party's middle link – *raikom* secretaries, *raikom* department heads, secretaries of large rural cells – by educating them politically and academically.[94] Some responsible party members, the more naïve or optimistic perhaps, were not thinking in terms of a wide-scale purge even when the economic crisis was brewing and boiling in the autumn and winter 1932. One comment in the party's organisational journal, written in August 1932, was well off the mark with the prediction that 'We are on the eve of a huge new intake into the party'.[95] In fact just the opposite occurred.

The dramatic upheaval in rural economic life, caused in the main by over-ambitious procurement plans in 1931 and 1932, proved a turning point in rural party fortunes and was a traumatic experience for communists and non-party peasants alike. The procurement plans put increasing pressure on rural communists to fulfil policies with harsh consequences for the local population. By the end of 1932, the pressure reached a climax. Very unfairly much blame for the economic débâcle was attributed to the local rural party by the central authorities.

Recruitment to the party was halted; purges were undertaken in the rural party of the southern regions followed by the first part of a national purge in April 1933.

The venom and extent of the purges made them into a process quite different from any routine review, and evidently resulted from the tensions between the rural party and the central authorities which emerged during the bitter struggles of the procurement campaign. In the Ukraine and North Caucasus, on many occasions rural party cadres and rank and file communists were unable and/or unwilling to follow orders and implement policies passed down by their superiors. Some of these communists consciously chose to disobey instructions in what they thought was the best interests of the local population, and ultimately of the regime. The central authorities refused to understand such motivation and responded with a severe purge of the southern rural party organisation at the end of 1932. This crisis in agriculture and the rural party organisation most probably acted as a catalyst in the decision to purge the whole party: this is an important point which has tended to be overlooked, one which we will elaborate in a later discussion of the 1933–34 purge years.

7 The Party and Policy towards the Countryside 1933–39

ECONOMICS

In response to the rural economic débâcle of 1932, the authorities reacted quickly with a series of reforms of the rural-economic administration. The party-political organisation in the countryside was radically reshaped by the introduction of the political departments, which lasted until the end of 1934. On the legislative side, the whole procurement procedure was markedly altered in a series of resolutions, in particular by that of 19 January 1933, which made procurements less arbitrary and based on a known sown area.[1] *Kolkhoz* markets were closed for the duration of the procurements but reopened once a region had completed its procurements. It was stressed that in the new system targets were to be obligatory but fixed and there do seem to have been genuine attempts made to prevent 'counter-plans', that is additional targets, from being slapped on *kolkhozy* which had completed their plans by the local authorities. These were not, however, the only payments that the *kolkhozy* were obliged to make. In 1933, in order to make the MTS more responsible in the work they carried out for *kolkhozy*, they were to receive a percentage of the crop (*naturplata*), rather than a fixed rate in money for every hectare they ploughed. Combined with the introduction of political departments at most MTS, this made the MTS the key centre of economic and political control in the countryside in the early years of the second Five Year Plan. Another category of 'collections', introduced in January 1934, were the *zakupki*, whereby, after deliveries to the state and MTS, peasants could sell more grain to the government at higher prices than those of normal procurements. Later in the year a large degree of compulsion was added to these supposedly voluntary sales.

The results of these measures in terms of harvest production and procurements were an improvement on the previous poor years of 1931–32, but not wholly satisfactory. With regard to harvest size during the years of the second Five Year Plan, nearly all commentators are agreed that the 1933 harvest (68/74 million tons)[2] was an improvement on that of 1932 (62/68) and the 1934 harvest (68/75) maintained this improved standard. By comparative criteria, the 1935 harvest (75/80) was very good, but followed by the very poor one of 1936 (60/66). Thanks in large part to climatic factors, 1937 saw a hugely successful harvest (95/100), easily the best of the inter-war years.

The question to be asked now is, how was the produce distributed and how did the peasantry respond? There is no doubt that procurements in the second Five Year Plan were considerably higher than in previous years, both absolutely and as a percentage of the gross harvest. From 22.8 million tons in 1931 and 18–19 million tons in 1932, procurements rose to 23.6 in 1933, 26.9 in 1934, 28.3 in 1935 and 31.9 million tons in the exceptional year 1937. As a share of the total crop, procurements were 32.9 per cent in 1931, 26.9 per cent in 1932, 34.1 per cent in 1933, 38.1 per cent in 1934 and 37.8 per cent in 1935.[3] The procurement crisis in the Ukraine had evidently been solved during the second Plan period. Postyshev, speaking to a plenum of the Kiev *obkom* on 3 November 1935, noted that grain procurements from the region in 1934 had been 14 million puds, but had nearly doubled in 1935 to total 25 million puds.[4] In addition to regular procurements, the peasantry supplied the state with more grain in the form of *zakupki* at slightly higher prices: grain *zakupki*, in 1932 about 15.5 million puds, rose to 28.9 million in the following year and in 1934–35 amounted to more than 200 million puds of deliveries.[5]

Against the background of famine that was raging in 1933–34, the harvest results with the exception of 1935 are not especially good and there was no easing off in the amount of grain deliveries demanded by and made to the state. One wonders why there was not a repetition of the crisis of 1932 with reported incidents of local peasant risings. There are several possible answers to this query. With the very heavy livestock losses of the early 1930s, there was as a consequence less feed required for animals. Much less grain was exported in 1932–33 than had been the case in the previous two years. Also, with several extra million deaths in the famine years and a sharp drop in the birth rate, there were fewer mouths to feed than otherwise would have been the case. Another mitigating factor was that, whereas 1932 had been a bad year generally for agriculture, later years saw noticeable improvements in potato and vegetable production, much of which was already produced on the peasants' private plots. A useful comparison can be drawn between the worst harvest year of the first Five Year Plan with that of the second plan period. 1932 was generally a bad year agriculturally; the very poor 1936 harvest, on the other hand, followed the relatively good one of 1935 and was accompanied by a much higher level of livestock production and by a relatively good potato and vegetable harvest, and any strains suffered were soon effaced by the abundant produce from the 1937 harvest. Furthermore, the peasantry had less cause or wish to manifest their discontent than they had in 1932. Certainly the suppression of local peasant rebellions would have made most peasants well aware that they could not redress their grievances through violence against the combined forces of the militia, the party and the Red Army. Nor did the *kolkhozniks* have as much cause to resort to violence when they could rely more on their private plots in the second Five Year Plan and have recourse to the *kolkhoz* markets and black markets to sell their private plot produce. At the beginning of the second Five Year Plan, it has been claimed that peasants earned about 60 per cent of their monetary income from their plots.[6] The *kolkhozniks'* right to their private plots was confirmed in the *Artel* Model Statute of 17 February 1935, where it was elaborated in greater detail than in the original Model Statute of 1 March 1930:

After a comparative lull in the collectivisation of the peasantry in the years 1932–33, there was a notable increase in later years: from 15.25 million peasant households (65.6 per cent) in *kolkhozy* on 1 July 1933 to 17.33 million (83.2 per cent) on 1 July 1935 and 18.44 million (93.0 per cent) two years later in 1937.[7] The significant rise in the levels of collectivisation in the three-year period, summer 1933–summer 1936, was achieved mainly by measures adopted after the July 1934 C.C. plenum. Those remaining individual peasants were pressurised into the *kolkhozy* by what Stalin termed the 'strengthening of the taxation press',[8] which included an extraordinary levy on the cash of individual peasants in October 1934 and an increase in their delivery quotas. During the second Five Year Plan it became more evident that there would be neither respite nor alternative for the peasantry, and it was during these years that the process was completed.

POLITICS

The authorities' attitude to the peasantry was not consistently harsh; their attitude seems to have been ambivalent, especially in 1933–34, before the countryside settled down to a comparatively quiet and neglected period. 1933 opened with Stalin's harsh speech '*Rabota v derevne*' (Work in the Countryside), in which he perceived the danger and root of the problem in rural affairs as encapsulated in the form of *kulaks* and White Guards: 'There is no need to look for them [*kulaks* and *kulak* agents] far from the collective farms; they are inside the collective farms, occupying posts as store-keepers, managers, accountants'.[9] He continued in the same vein to speak against neutrality in the struggle to crush *kulaks*. Procurements were the main priority; nothing was to stand in their way. But Stalin's simple hard line was not advocated unequivocally by all. There may well have been a split in the political leadership about what course to adopt. The Soviet historian I.E. Zelenin suggests such a scenario, when he cites archive material on the January 1933 joint plenum. He quotes P.P. Postyshev as saying at the plenum:

> Now we are dealing with economies on a large scale, it is necessary to know how to administer them. It is no good hiding behind the back of the kulak, even more so when his back is not as wide as formerly. No matter how much we squawk that kulaks, wreckers and officers . . . and other elements undermine the harvest or sabotage the grain procurements, we will not change the situation like that. Where does it get us?[10]

This is an exceptionally interesting and perceptive statement. It contradicts the public persona of Postyshev, who in the same month of January was dispatched, with Balitskii, the OGPU chief, to the Ukraine to act as a trouble-shooter to sort out the multifarious problems of the region, and who normally in published speeches adopted a much more standard interpretation of blame laid at the door of the rural party and *kulaks*. The statement shows an awareness of the complexity of the issues such as finance and technology, which could not be overcome by organisational–administrative measures alone; moreover, it conflicts with Stalin's remarks on the crisis delivered at the same plenum. Postyshev, in company with others such as Kirov, may well have supported a programme of limited, moderate, 'liberal' reforms towards the countryside which have become known as the 'thaw' of 1933–34.[11] Even Stalin and Molotov were affected by the new 'liberalism', or were forced to compromise, in their secret circular letter of 8 May 1933, in which they instructed that mass repressions 'be stopped immediately'.[12] This is not to say that the authorities had 'gone soft' since, as we have already noted, pressure was exerted or even intensified to push the remaining individual peasants into the *kolkhozy* and grain procurements did not drop, on the contrary; but the Stalin and Molotov *'Instrukstiya'* of spring 1933 form part of a package of wide-ranging laws and measures, introduced in 1933 and increasing in number in 1934, aimed at bringing some normalisation and stability to state–peasant relationships. The brand of 'revolutionary legality' in vogue in the press in 1934 tended to emphasise the defence of citizens' rights, and rural inhabitants particularly, against infringements by the state. This trend was further underlined by the reorganisation of the OGPU by re-absorbing it into the NKVD, a reform which at the time seemed to deprive the political police of its former juridicial role and to confine its functions largely to preliminary investigations.

Evidently the regime's approach towards the rural population was by no means clear-cut; it was ambiguous, at times seemingly contradictory. This may have been on account of two reasons: the authorities could have consciously adopted a policy of carrot and stick to coax and threaten simultaneously the peasantry; or perhaps the superficial ambiguity between hard and soft policy statements reflected underlying disagreement or differences of emphasis among the party leadership. This would fit in with the debate on the purpose of the political departments and whether they were to be phased out.[13]

Many of the contradictions in policies during 1933–34 and in the regime's attitude towards the countryside were resolved and the debate terminated by the elimination during 1935–38 of any opposition within the party and society as a whole to Stalin's personal hegemony. The party purges of 1933 and 1934, begun in large part as a response to the crisis in the party over agriculture, were predominantly a review of the rank and file to remove those who were unwilling or unable to fulfil the centre's commands, and those who were politically passive and corrupt. The two screenings of party cards conducted during 1935 and 1936 were designed to bring much needed order into the party's house-keeping. The result of these various purges and screenings was to diminish greatly the party's membership, especially that of the rural party, and to alter its role in the countryside. No doubt they contributed to subduing any potential rebelliousness and discord, and information supplied during the verification and exchange of party cards no doubt facilitated the later work of Ezhov and his subordinates during 1937.

These more spectacular and infamous events of the 1937–38 *Ezhovsh-china* have much less direct bearing on the major concerns in this work. As has been suggested, opponents to Stalin on agricultural policies were more likely to have been removed and physically eliminated in 1937–41 for imagined misdemeanours committed in 1932–34 rather than for any more recent slurs against the *vozhd*. This is because the debate on the countryside had become much less heated by about 1935 when the regime's approach had already settled down to some sort of comparative normality well before the *Ezhovshchina*. On the whole a consensus seems to have arisen among the authorities to promote a modified continuation of the policies of restraint towards the countryside, adumbrated and then encouraged in 1933–34. Fewer repressive measures were aimed at the peasantry in 1935–38, and on paper their rights were reasserted in the 1936 Constitution and in such resolutions as that of 19 April 1938 by the *Sovnarkom* and C.C. which imposed sanctions against improper expulsions from *kolkhozy*.[14]

Whilst in the latter half of the 1930s Stalin set out to destroy those he perceived as his enemies, the countryside settled down into a modified *modus vivendi*, which was something quite different from the seemingly tranquil years of NEP and from the trauma-filled years of 1929–33. This modified *modus vivendi* was more to the state's benefit than the peasantry's. The state was assured of receiving its high quotas of agricultural produce at prices (low ones) of its choosing. By force of habit, the peasantry became accustomed to the *kolkhoz* system, avoiding the severest rigours by resorting more to their private plots, the produce from which could be used for personal consumption or sale on the market. For the state, the minimum aims of collectivisation had been achieved – peasants into the *kolkhozy* and produce to the state on its own terms – but at considerable cost to the authorities' and their cadres' nerves and to the life style of most peasants.

8 The Political Departments 1933–34

At the end of 1932, the political departments were introduced to rectify a deteriorating situation in the countryside. The party had always prided itself on its ability to create organisational forms fitting for each economic and political epoch, and Kaganovich, the C.C. secretary responsible for party organisation, made special reference to this in his speech to the joint C.C. and C.C.C. plenum of January 1933.[1] The political departments were also seen in this light, as the organisational response to a problem which was primarily economic. The party authorities were not blind to this fact and hoped to alleviate the problem in January 1933 by replacing the contract system of grain procurements with fixed grain deliveries that were assessed on sown areas, after which the peasantry would be allowed to sell their surpluses on the open market. But it remains typical of the party in the years 1929–34 that to overcome socio-economic problems it introduced either various organisational reforms which tampered with the design, or complete reorganisations which revamped the organisation and its approach to its activities; this has remained characteristic of the party's post-war history to the present day. Given the alleged infallibility of the central authorities, and the lack of initiative in lower bodies, major shifts in policy could not be recognised openly, although logic was often stood on its head and a U-turn depicted as a continuation of a former policy. To avoid open contradictions, the authorities were obliged on occasion to resort to adjustments of organisational forms and to the perpetual turnover of low level party and non-party cadres: this gave the impression that changes were being implemented and sought to pre-empt the need for personnel changes at the very top or a fundamental change in the direction of the general line, such as a move away from collectivisation. Our argument seeks to explain the underlying rationale of frequent activity in the field of party organisation, and throws some light on interesting ideas of the same kind, which merit lengthy quotation:

> The effort to fashion an efficient, centrally directed economic system out of a technologically and culturally backward peasant society was attended by costly failures, in administration as well as policy. Thus,

administrative reorganisations were to be expected. At the same time, the nature and frequency of the reorganisation process suggest that something more than mere growing pains was involved. Reorganisation achieved the status of an administrative technique in its own right . . . a cynical realization appears to have developed fairly early that the only way to get vigorous action out of the burgeoning administrative apparatus, especially in times of crisis, was to shake it up periodically.[2]

THE POLITICAL DEPARTMENTS: ESTABLISHMENT AND COMPOSITION

In December 1932 the first 3000 chosen for the political departments were selected by a high-powered C.C. commission under the chairmanship of P.P. Postyshev.[3] But it was at the joint C.C. and C.C.C. plenum of January 1933 that the political departments were grafted on to the territorial administrative framework. The political departments were established at MTS and *sovkhozy*, but not at large *kolkhozy*, unlike their embyro predecessors, the support points. The major tasks facing the political departments were enumerated in a plenum resolution. Listing some of the priorities of the political departments pin-points what were seen in the eyes of the party leadership as the previous weak areas of work in the countryside.

In his speech to the plenum Kaganovich commented that 'We must state bluntly that the political role of the MTS and sovkhozy in no way corresponds to their economic role'.[4] To rectify this, the resolution on political departments called for 'the development of mass-political work in the kolkhozy and sovkhozy'.[5] These political duties were, however, almost submerged beneath a host of other demands, such as 'the organisational-economic strengthening of the kolkhozy and sovkhozy . . . in order to supplement the economic-technical work of the MTS and sovkhozy'.[6] Perhaps beneath the political verbiage the real primary task of the departments in the MTS was to 'ensure the prompt fulfilment by the kolkhozy and kolkhozniks of their obligation before the state'.[7] This latter duty was underlined by the fact that the heads of departments, although by no means supposed to usurp the MTS director's authority nor to damage the principle of one-man management, were to be held responsible with the MTS director for the fulfilment of production and procurement plans. Such instructions were manifestly contradictory and seem to suggest that the departments were conceived hastily in response to an unforeseen crisis. One would expect that the quest for success would have formed a close bond between the department head and the MTS director but, although this does appear to have occurred in many instances, there was not so much insufficient demarcation lines of authority between them, as too much temptation, especially for the department head, to impinge on the other's authority and to bustle him into hasty action in search of quick results. The chances for the department head to boss the MTS director increased by the fact that not all MTS directors were party members, and thus the political departments could try to use this as a psychological card in their arguments; of course, with each year the percentage of MTS directors in the party ranks grew. Where the department heads, who were officially recognised as deputy directors of the MTS for political work, had a relatively free hand was in the purging of MTS and *kolkhoz* personnel and rank and file communists, although relations between the department director, his OGPU assistant and the MTS director could become fraught with demands for leniency or severity.

By 15 June 1933, some 10 139 party workers had been sent to the political departments,[8] including 8000 to MTS and 2000 to *sovkhozy*: as the MTS political departments had jurisdiction over surrounding *kolkhozy*, they were given priority. Of department workers 53.6 per cent had more than three years' experience of leading work and among department heads 40 per cent more than five years' such experience. They came from a variety of backgrounds, which in percentage terms were as follows: People's Commissariats and central organisations – 6.1 per cent; republic, *krai* and *oblast* organisations – 19.4 per cent; city and *raion* organisations – 36.9 per cent; enterprises – 12.4 per cent; leading work in education institutions – 11.0 per cent.[9] The length of party membership (*stazh*) of the political department staff was impressive with 82.6 per cent of department heads having joined the party prior to 1920 and over 50 per cent of first deputies prior to 1923.[10] This means that the large majority of staff had Civil War experience and probably vivid memories of Civil War techniques of administration for achieving manifest results. The geographical origins of these staff were equally revealing in that they testify to the solid background in party terms of these workers, and also to the nature of the political departments' people as 'outsiders' brought in to do a job in which the locals had failed ignominiously: 33 per cent were from Moscow, about 10 per cent from Leningrad, 18.4 per cent from the Ukraine and 7.2 per cent from the Central Black Earth.[11] Interestingly it was felt that department workers who came from the urban cities of Moscow and Leningrad and were sent to the Ukraine and Central Black Earth were more effective in their work than locally recruited department staff, that is a political department worker recruited in the Central Black Earth to work in the same *oblast*.[12] Once again, this underlines the party's faith in and preference for outsiders to do a job properly. It is therefore not surprising to discover that the best quality personnel, that is those originating from the Political Administration of the Red Army, from Moscow and from Leningrad were concentrated in the most sensitive trouble-spots, in particular the North Caucasus, Lower Volga and Mid-Volga.[13]

A further manifestation which helps to explain the purpose of the departments is their deployment. The C.C. planned to install them in three phases: firstly, they would be concentrated in the Ukraine, North Caucasus and Lower Volga between January and 1 April 1933; second came the Mid-Volga, Siberia, Kazakhstan and the Trans-Caucasus, which were to be operating in the main by 1 July, and the third stage was to cover most other areas by 1 August 1933.[14] On the whole this plan was carried out and by April 1933 there were political departments in two-thirds of the MTS in the Ukraine, three-quarters of those in the Lower Volga and four-fifths of those to be found in perhaps the most sensitive area, the North Caucasus. In terms of saturation, on 1 April 1933 50.4 per cent of MTS had a political department, a figure which rose to 92.9 per cent on 1 January 1934.[15] The significance of the departments' position in the MTS of the all-important southern grain regions ensured that they were in control of the key-points of agriculture, since in 1934 the MTS served and controlled 45.8 per cent of *kolkhozy* in the country, whose sown area represented 63.9 per cent of the sown area of all *kolkhozy*.[16] Thus the political departments were in charge of the most sensitive areas politically and economically the most essential.

THE ACTIVITIES OF THE POLITICAL DEPARTMENTS

As the first departments came into operation in the grain regions of the south, their primary task was to prepare the MTS and subordinate *kolkhozy* for the spring sowing. The departments were part and parcel of a widespread influx of urban cadres dispatched from Moscow and the C.C., as well as from many urban centres.[17] In a resolution of the joint plenum of the Kharkov *obkom* and *gorkom*, based on a speech by Postyshev, it was noted that 'It is necessary to throw into the preparation and implementation of the spring sowing all the best forces from the urban, industrial organisations'.[18] This involved ensuring that a correct approach was adopted by all concerned in the repair of machinery, especially tractors, and that they were provided with the necessary spare parts and fuel. The department staff were expected to tour the MTS and *kolkhozy* frequently, propagandising, coaxing and threatening as they went, and it seems that they were out and about more regularly than the ordinary rural party workers from the *raikom* level, although the *raikom* staffs were entrusted with considerably more varied tasks and general duties than the department staff, who were to concentrate their attention on a smaller number of priorities. On the matter of the spring sowing, it is worth remembering the general environment into which the departments had been thrust. During 1933 the food difficulties of the rural population intensified and the full effects of the previous two years' grain procurements were only experienced in 1933. The Political Sector of the MTS at the *oblast* level of the Central Black Earth noted the lamentable situation in all preparations for the spring sowing as the departments began their work, and mentioned that there were mass cases of death by starvation.[19] As the activities of the political departments are surveyed, one should not underestimate the difficulties faced by them in the implementation of their duties.

Created as they were at the MTS, the departments were also to tighten up the contract system between *kolkhozy* and the MTS, under which the MTS carried out work for the *kolkhozy* in return for payment in crops under the new 1933 model contract. The *kolkhozy* were often reluctant to pay the MTS because the latter conducted their work haphazardly or even not at all; matters were improved in June 1933 when the MTS were given the incentive for working for a higher quality crop by receiving a percentage share of it rather than fixed payments. In addition to involvement in the payments to MTS for services rendered, the departments were also trouble-shooters in seeing that the *kolkhozy* fulfilled their quota deliveries as laid down in the stipulations of the 19 January 1933 legislation. The political departments with their experienced staff were also directed to engage in mass-party work among the MTS workers and *kolkhozniks*. Work with non-party activists took on increasing importance with the resolution on the curtailment of recruitment into the party.

As well as working with non-party activists with a view to encouraging them in production and political activity, the departments made similar efforts with communists. During the one-and-a-half years of their active existence, the departments were involved in the selection and promotion of 200 000 to leading *kolkhoz* work, of whom 30 000 took up posts as *kolkhoz* chairmen.[20] However, these promotions did not expand the size of this body of personnel because they merely replaced a mass of leading *kolkhoz* and MTS personnel who were removed at this time, as well as party members who were purged in large numbers during 1933–34. During 1933 alone the following were removed from the *kolkhozy* of 24 *oblasts*, *krais* and republics: 47.3 per cent of head agricultural workers (*zavkhoz*), 34.4 per cent of store keepers, 25.0 per cent of book keepers (*schetovod*), 23.7 per cent of accountants (*uchetnik*), 14.2 per cent of *kolkhoz* chairmen.[21] A striking example of the political departments' efficiency and assiduity in such work relates to the *kolkhoz* named '*Zavet Il'icha*' (Lenin's Banner) in the Western *oblast*. Here, it was claimed, '*kulaks*' had endeavoured to confuse and distort the accounts of work days in order to discourage shock workers, and even when the shock workers complained the court and investigation organs were hood-winked by the *kulaks*. It was only with the direct intervention of the political department into the affair that the *kulaks* were brought to trial.[22] Nor was it only the leading cadres of MTS and *kolkhozy* who were expelled and brought before the courts; many ordinary *kolkhozniks* were expelled, which in most cases, at a time of famine, had very grave consequences for them.

With regard to the party cells and party members within their scope of activity, the departments also assisted in fulfilling the persistent call for communists to move closer to production tasks, and helped to reorganise the rural party cell system when an intense effort was made in June 1933 to transform inter-*kolkhoz* cells. Superficially all seemed to go very well, but although, as in the past, success was claimed for the departments' efforts in reorientating the rural communist's role in production, a similar success had been proclaimed in previous years and yet the demand continued. It seems that there was an inexorable route out of production into 'cushy' administrative posts once someone had acquired the status of party member, thereby acquiring the knowledge of how and when to pull which strings, and the protection of what were often close-knit 'family' circles. The *raikoms* had tried to tackle these problems, and in their own way at their own level perpetuated them, but now it was the turn of the political departments to struggle to overcome these difficulties.

THE RELATIONSHIPS OF THE POLITICAL DEPARTMENTS WITH OTHER RURAL PARTY ADMINISTRATORS

The departments were faced with a major problem of fitting into the local setting and asserting themselves, whilst securing good relations with the already firmly established rural party units, particularly the *raikoms*. The intrusion of the departments represented a typical case of an 'outsider' being imposed upon local authorities, who took this to be, and correctly so, a censure of their past efforts: not unnaturally, the *raikoms* resented the political departments.[23] It is interesting to note that the *raikoms* were more insistent on controlling the political departments than they had been with their precursors, the support points, seeing in the departments a greater threat to their position. It is therefore surprising that the expert and C.C. secretary for party organisation, Lasar Kaganovich, should have adopted such a naïve and careless approach to this intricate question of the disposition of party forces in his speech to the January 1933 joint plenum. After criticising the *raikoms* for not supervising their cells properly, Kaganovich warned them against too formal an approach towards the political departments: 'the raikom secretaries must now occupy themselves less with questions of legal interrelations between the political departments and the raikoms, and instead help the new people'.[24] Kaganovich only compounded his error when, on speaking of contacts between MTS directors and the political department heads, he expressed the ingenuous wish that: 'Good Bolsheviks ... will always find a common language, will always agree with each other in solving those most difficult problems, which stand before them'.[25] Despite being held equally responsible for the success and failure of the MTS, the political department head and MTS director by no means always banded together, especially when things were going badly, and less frequently were the *raikoms* and departments to get together to solve what were supposed to be mutual problems.

The political departments were a hybrid creation, superimposed on the regular, territorial rural party administration. The departments by-passed the regular system in being subordinated directly to the newly formed political sectors of the land administration of *Narkomzem*, established at *oblast* and *krai* level. Thus they were exceptional in being an independent force within the boundaries of the *raion* and the *raikom*'s normal jurisdiction. They were further unusual in that the political sector at *oblast* and *krai* level was also a party-state unit. The political sector head at the *oblast* centre held the post of deputy chief of the *oblast* land administration, as well as being a member of the *obkom* or *kraikom*; similarly, the political department head was a member of the *raikom*, reporting periodically to it on his work, but members of the political departments and political sectors did not take their orders from, nor were they responsible to the party committees.[26] At the apex of the MTS political department structure was the Chief of the Political Administration of the MTS, working in the All-Union Commissariat of

Agriculture. He was formally designated Deputy Commissar for political work and was under the dual subordination of the Commissar and the C.C.: this post was held by A.I. Krinitskii.

Although administratively independent of the *raikoms*, the political departments did have to rely on them for assistance in such matters as accommodation, rations, supplies and such important matters as local knowledge of people and agriculture in the *raion*, just as they had to rely on the MTS director and his workers for technical knowledge about tractors and other technical details. The early indicators for any close understanding between *raikom* and political department were not promising. The *raikoms* had not been provided with any detailed instructions on how to work with the departments, only with mere vague exhortations and demands, and it is not surprising that many *raikoms* failed to respond. A further factor, which no doubt exacerbated an unpropitious beginning, was that the MTS, and consequently their political departments, tended to be located in or near the administrative centres and/or on the main lines of communication, such as railways. Thus the departments tended to supervise those *kolkhozy* which were conveniently placed, as well as being in the most important grain producing regions, whilst the *raikoms* were relegated to supervising the activities of the smaller *kolkhozy* in the more remote regions.

Throughout the first half of 1933, more and more reports came in of the recalcitrance, passive and open resistance of the *raikoms* to what they regarded as outside visitors. Some *raikoms* withheld rations from department staff, which at a time of severe shortages could have grave consequences for these staff and their families.[27] In April there was news of the Balashovskii *raikom*, Lower Volga, which refused to provide accommodation for the MTS political department staff, and where, after repeated complaints by the department and no response from the *raikom*, Krinitskii himself became involved in bringing the incident to the attention of the Lower Volga *kraikom*, who in turn chastened the head of the *raion* militia for using the quarters allocated to the political department, and ordered the *raikom* to ensure quarters were provided within five days.[28] This is an interesting case in that it displays clearly how the channels of communication operated between the interlocking state-party body of the Political Administration. Krinitskii, officially the deputy commissar for agriculture (state body), had to go via the *kraikom* (party body) in order to have influence over a *raikom*. Similarly the *raikoms* and political departments were unable to pull rank on one another in a dispute and could only resort to taking up the point with their own superiors, who could if they thought fit, take the issue further with their opposite numbers.[29] It is not likely that such an administrative system was designed purposely to provide dual authority in a single geographical area, for each unit to verify that policies were implemented, whilst checking on the other. Although this was one accidental result in the 1930s, it seems to have matured as a system only in later years, and in these early stages there appear more negative aspects than positive ones. It is more probable that the political departments were an un-tested experiment to meet an emergency crisis, in which formal relationships could only be formulated and regularised in the midst of activity. It was a costly method by which to administer the countryside. This view is supported by the fact that the C.C. was forced to define and clarify the respective roles and duties of the *raikoms* and political departments in an important resolution dated 15 June 1933.

As a prelude to the publication of the resolution and shortly after, a host of incidents were narrated in the press, describing how the political department staffs had been harshly treated or ignored by the *raikoms*. The front page *Pravda* article of 12 June 1933 called for 'All possible help to the political departments of the MTS and sovkhozy'. It adopted a far harsher tone than any other previous remonstrations, which seems to testify to a loss of patience on the part of the central party authorities and a realisation that what may have appeared to have been initial teething problems were in fact something more serious. Grave charges were directed at the *raikoms* who resisted the departments, and their actions were termed 'opportunism', even worse 'anti-party' and 'anti-Bolshevik'. A particularly infamous incident was cited of the Urvanskii *raikom* secretary in Karbardino-Balkarskii *oblast*, who, during an argument with the department chief over the removal of a communist in a *kolkhoz*, declared 'If we have to, then we'll arrest the political department head'.[30] A further manifestation of how seriously this matter was considered is that this *raikom* secretary and one other were shortly afterwards expelled from the party for their resistance to the departments.[31] This was the final sanction against unrepentant *raikom* secretaries, and had been employed against those who refused to endorse Stalin's retreat of March 1930 and those okrug workers who had tried to hinder the raionisation process of the autumn 1930. Another damning accusation was that the *raikoms* were resisting the departments' involvement in party work because they had something to hide, and in the same tone was the following insinuation: 'It is characteristic that most of the misunderstandings with political departments are happening in such krais as the North Caucasus and Lower Volga, which have not liquidated the lag in the leadership of agriculture'.[32]

The most common cause of friction was the question of who had jurisdiction over whom or what. There were perpetual arguments over *raikoms* moving personnel and communists from the MTS and *kolkhozy* under the departments' control. Few people seemed to know whether the *raikoms* retained any responsibility for the cells in *kolkhozy* under the MTS supervision, in such matters as cultural work and relations with the Soviets. The Gavrilo-Yamskii *raikom* forbade cell secretaries from attending meetings convened by the political departments.[33] Some *raikoms* simply carried on as before, ignoring the presence of the departments; others sought to discredit the departments by hindering any progress in the areas under the jurisdiction of the departments.[34]

There was an obvious need for clarification on administrative relations within the countryside and to this end the C.C. resolution of 15 June 1933 was a belated attempt to go further than the basic instructions of the January 1933 plenum. In the *kolkhoz* cells and candidate groups served by the MTS, party members were to obey the directives of the MTS political departments in questions which related to the MTS, whereas the *raikoms* were to retain charge in these same cells of matters such as finance, education and relations with the Soviets. The *raikoms* were to remain in complete control of all territorial cells, based at Soviets and co-operatives, and of all *kolkhoz* cells not served by the MTS. The political department was entitled to supervise its *kolkhoz* cells, conduct removals and transfers of *kolkhoz* cell secretaries, hold elections of cell bureaux and meetings of cell and *komsomol* secretaries; it was recommended that the department inform the *raikom* of all such actions, and if there were any disagreement, which seems to suggest that the *raikom* retained some say even in what were clearly department matters, then the argument was to be resolved by a decision of the *obkom* and *oblast* level political sector—another example of how superiors in this dual hierarchy acted as referee and mediator of lower level disputes. The fact that the *raikoms* retained a say in purely department affairs is paradoxical in the context of a resolution designed to curb the excesses of power by the *raikoms*. But the resolution did return to its more expected course when it declared that, in order to prevent the *raikoms* from circumventing the departments by sending plenipotentiaries into the departments' territory, all such party workers from *raion* or *oblast* were to come under the orders of the political department.[35]

The resolution of 15 June 1933 was quite a detailed document. Unfortunately for the central party authorities and for the success of work generally in the countryside, it appears to have arrived too late. Fairly distinct battle lines had been drawn up between the protagonists and they were reluctant to accept meekly what each side saw as rebukes. P.P. Postyshev, speaking at a plenum of the Ukrainian C.C. on 10 June 1933, may have struck the nail on the head when he stated quite bluntly that some *raion* staff looked upon the political departments as 'pretenders for power in the raion'.[36] In any case, some *raikoms* persisted in their errors and made a mockery of some of the stipulations in the resolution. It must be remembered that with hindsight one can appreciate that the political departments were a temporary phenomenon, and although the departments were classified as extraordinary organs, which implied their removal at some later stage, the *raikoms* could never be certain that, if the departments proved successful, they would not become permanent fixtures. This helps to explain a little the *raikoms'* stubborn hostility. However, by the final months of 1933 the climate had changed quite appreciably and the *raikoms* were no longer chastened so frequently. The decline of the political departments had begun.

Before discussing the reasons for this decline, it should be noted that, as well as conflicts with the *raikoms*, department heads often had little peace 'at home'. Although the political department was a small organisation with its head, three assistants for mass-party work, *komsomol* and OGPU work, an editor for its newspaper and a women's organiser, plus one or two technical staff, at the MTS itself was created a complex web of interrelationships between the department head, his special deputy for the OGPU and the MTS director. Just as the department head was independent of the *raikom* and regular party controls, so the OGPU deputy was independent of the political department, certainly in 'agent-operative' work, and responsible for his work to his own boss at the *oblast* level;[37] he was to carry out the general orders of the department head and to report to him on the general economic and political condition of the *kolkhozy* and *sovkhozy*. But, as so often, what seemed reasonably clear could soon turn quite opaque. Just as clarification had been necessary to redefine the relationship between *raikom* and political department, so it was with the department head and OGPU deputy, in the form of a top-secret order of 10 July 1933, which rebuked OGPU deputies for not following the orders of department heads when asked to conduct investigations of impropriety in various *kolkhozy*; on the other hand, the department heads were criticised for using OGPU deputies on work which had nothing to do with normal secret police duties.[38] The 'agent-operative' work of the OGPU deputies was re-emphasised, and department heads were forbidden to require any reports dealing with the 'agent-informer network' of the OGPU;[39] in this way the OGPU deputy was allowed to 'keep tabs' on everybody, including the department head himself. None the less, despite this redefinition of responsibilities, the former transgressions continued and the departments and their superiors tended to view warily, and sometimes disapprovingly, the work of the OGPU deputies.[40]

Although designated as extraordinary organs, in many ways the political departments, like the party as a whole, may be depicted as a tapestry of human relationships, in which people were particularly concerned with and enmeshed in human conflicts over questions of authority, leadership, responsibility and, perhaps more importantly, reward and censure.

WHY WERE THE POLITICAL DEPARTMENTS PHASED OUT?

The political departments were judged in large part on the success of agricultural campaigns, since after all they had been introduced to improve on the débâcle of 1932. Significantly it was during the autumn 1933 that early signs of disillusion and dissatisfaction with the departments appeared, by which time initial results of the harvest and procurement campaign would have filtered back to Moscow.[41] Commencing in 1933 the real size of harvests as a barn yield was distorted and exaggerated by the introduction of the use of biological figures, that is, the size of the harvest in the fields. None the less, the 1933 harvest was a disappointment and reflected badly on the departments. At best, in comparison with the previous year, 1933 saw an increase in gross production of 3.7 million tons; this increase in production was more than taken up by an increase in grain procurements of 4.5 million tons. From the point of view of the peasantry, this was not a success in that it left them with less residual than the previous bad year. Despite some success in procurements, which surely must have reflected well on them, the departments could not claim to have promoted a successful sowing campaign with a subsequent good harvest. But one should not be surprised that the political departments repeated to some extent the failure of the rural party in 1932, since they were quite small organisations, mere oases in the Soviet countryside. Furthermore, one may argue that they too were set tasks beyond their means, which were well-nigh impossible objectively to fulfil. One commentator has noted well this fact: 'Particularly after the technology of Soviet agriculture had risen above the primitive levels, it became less and less feasible to substitute brute political pressure for rational management'.[42] Brute force and ignorance were no longer sufficient, just as Postyshev had implied at the January 1933 plenum.[43]

Judging from the above discussion, another reason for the political departments' demise springs to mind: the conflict between the regular party structure, especially the *raikoms*, and the departments. This is supported by the fact that the political departments in *sovkhozy*, which had no reason to come into conflict with the *raikoms* as they did not supervise surrounding *kolkhozy*, were not abolished at the same time as the MTS political departments, and continued to exist until March 1940. R.F. Miller distinguishes in terms of personality the rival interests of the regular territorially structured party, as defended by regional secretaries Postyshev (Kharkov), Eikhe (Western Siberia), Vareikis (Central Black Earth) and Sheboldaev (Azov-Black Sea), and the political department leadership, as championed by Krinitskii.[44] Miller suggests that these regional secretaries, defending their regular party structure with a view to preventing any further by-passing by the departments, combined this with a preference to reduce the abrasive characteristics of the departments' work. He states: 'By the end of 1933 there were already strong sentiments that the coercive practices of the political departments had passed the point of diminishing returns'.[45] However, considerable confusion arises when other sources reveal that these same personalities could defend a contradictory argument, which was that the political departments were too lenient and for this reason ought to be phased out. At the June 1934 C.C. plenum, I.M. Kleiner, head of Zagotzerno, revealed that some local party workers, and even heads of political departments, thought that grain procurement targets were unrealistic and expressed 'reductionist tendencies' (*skidochnye nastroeniya*), as Kleiner put it. It appears that Kosior, Postyshev and Vareikis agreed in substance with this and put the blame squarely on the political departments.[46] S.V. Kosior was quoted as saying at this plenum that the political departments did not appreciate how the *kolkhozy* tried to reduce their grain procurement quotas, and that 'Now many political departments have already become united with local people'.[47] He was supported by Vareikis, who declared that 'several political departments stand completely on the side of the interests of their kolkhozy and MTS'.[48] Local interests were, of course, juxtaposed to the more important requirements of the centralised state.

If one accepts the above argument that the political departments were not vigorous enough, then one opposes the generally accepted interpretation that they were martinets, phased out as part of the package of reforms in the 'thaw' of 1933–34.[49] Unfortunately the issue is not so clear-cut, and at times it is difficult to distinguish when a thaw is not in fact a frost and vice versa. The Soviet historian I.E. Zelenin adopts a middle position when he depicts the political departments as being firm but fair, in that they insisted on no unlawful distributions among *kolkhozniks* until state deliveries had been made in full, but once this had been achieved, they followed the law to the letter and prevented the *raikoms* from slapping 'counter-plans', that is extra ones, on those *kolkhozy* which had succeeded in completing their quota.[50]

By the beginning of 1934 the die was cast. Views on the departments were crystallised at the seventeenth party congress of January–February 1934. By the opening of the congress attention was once again, after an interval of more than one year, focused on the *raikoms*. It is possible that the departments were not phased out early in 1934 because the spring sowing campaign, with its reliance on the tractor power of the MTS, would have been immeasurably disrupted by any sudden transformation in the status of the political department. Kaganovich, in his speech to the congress, hoped unrealistically that 'An atmosphere of abolition should not be created around the political departments'.[51] In fact this is indeed what happened. During 1934 more derogatory and critical observations were made about them.[52] For some ten months the departments continued a zombie-like existence with everyone awaiting the *coup de grâce*: just like the support points before them, after one year's heady and well-publicised existence, the departments faded away and much less was heard of them during 1934.

It was the C.C. plenum of 25–28 November 1934 that reshaped the rural party organisation. The political departments were to be blended into the existing *raikom* network, with smaller *raikoms* created from larger ones to absorb the departments' staff. Agricultural departments were to be organised within the *raikoms* with the *raikom* secretary or his deputy at the head of this new department – such departments were probably created to reassert the *raikom*'s position in agriculture and to fill the void left by the MTS political department. A new post was created within the MTS, that of deputy director of political affairs, which would represent the remnant of the once powerful political departments. The new MTS deputy had no jurisdiction over any *kolkhoz* cells and was to confine himself to activities within the MTS, and thereby a former source of contention was removed.[53] The phasing out of the departments was interpreted as another step on the path of 'completing raionisation which had begun with the abolition of the okrugs', and as ever it was intended that the reform would bring the administrative organs closer to the village (*selo*).[54] The hurt feelings of the *raikoms* were soothed when their final victory was announced with the words: 'The leadership of all primary party organisations in the raion is entrusted to the party raikoms'.[55]

The following posts were recommended for former staff of political departments: *raikom* secretaries of new or existing *raions*, deputy *raikom* secretaries and heads of *raikom* agricultural departments, MTS deputy directors for political affairs, and finally, and less prestigiously, posts within the *raikom* apparatus or *komsomol raikom*.[56] It was stressed that such well-qualified personnel as the political department staff must in all circumstances remain within the bounds of *raion* work and not drift away or be poached by the *obkoms*, *kraikoms* and republic party organisations. The November plenum resolution on political departments noted that in the previous two years 3368 MTS political departments had been established,[57] but only some 500–800 new *raions* were to be created as a result of the breaking down in size of the larger *raions*.[58] This meant that not all former political department heads would walk into the post of *raikom* secretary of a new *raion*, even though some would remove *raikom* secretaries in existing *raions*. By the end of 1934 there were 2535 *raions* in the USSR.[59] Of the 2604 former heads of political departments, as many as 2534 were kept on in leading work in the *raions* and only 70 were moved to leading work in the *oblast* organisations: 1506 of these former heads of political departments were confirmed as *raikom* secretaries.[60] This latter figure means that, with 800 new *raions* created, some 700 *raikoms* secretaries were ousted to make way for the former department heads, although these gains here are compensated by the fact that approximately 1000 political department heads had to content themselves with posts beneath the level of *raikom* secretary. There were both advantages and disadvantages to this new position. Having been selected for special work in the political departments, some may have been deflated at finding themselves in the more mundane posts of the *raikom*; others may have been grateful of the opportunity to work in a less trying environment than that of the former departments.

The stipulations of the resolution on political departments were to be implemented by 1 March 1935, and in the southern regions by 1 February, so as not to interfere with the spring sowing. Kaganovich himself added to this atmosphere of interregnum when he advised that the winter of 1934–35 should be used as a period in which to regroup and prepare for coming tasks ahead.[61]

When the official reasons for the abolition of the political departments were announced, several problems that they had encountered and their own possible deviations were not alluded to. Fortunately for Stalin and Kaganovich, who had been hailed as the instigators for the departments' promotion on to the rural scene, they could always claim that the departments were an extraordinary and temporary phenomenon, due to be phased out in any circumstances: this avoided any embarrassing confessions that the departments had proven too brutal or too lenient or had dislocated the regular rural party system of administration. The November plenum resolution claimed a little unconvincingly that the creation of the political departments had 'completely justified itself' on the fulfilment of shock tasks.[62] It was also stated that the departments were unable to encompass the whole panorama of rural affairs, a capability which was required at this stage of economic and political development, and therefore the normal party and Soviet organisations were to be strengthened.[63] By thus whitewashing some causes behind the removal of the departments, the hard-liners within the party leadership were protecting their reputation of infallibility.

The political departments are worthy of detailed attention principally because such a study permits a further consideration of the gap between theory and practice in party administration. Related to this, they are a further manifestation of the difficulty of the 'outsider' in imposing himself upon and dominating the milieu of the 'insiders', even when the protagonists were members of the same party. Also, they represent the final determined attempt before the war of the Soviet communist party to impose its political leadership on the peasantry and rural economy as a whole in the countryside. The end of the political departments saw the beginning of a new era in rural administration, in which an effort was made at an indirect method of leadership. The party was exhorted to concentrate more on its purely party-political activities, to meddle less in economic matters and to leave the latter to other institutions. This attempt was in sharp contrast to what had been the general trend during 1929–34. Just as the party changed its position over whether to adopt a 'production' or 'function' approach to organisation, so, not untypically, having tried one method, the saturation of the countryside, none too successfully, the party leadership altered course in favour of concentrating on a few key points with smaller resources of personnel. Certainly by the end of 1934 both the party and peasantry manifested signs of exhaustion, brought about by the 1932–34 famine. Tacitly the party leadership seems to have accepted a truce with the peasants, if they accepted certain minimum demands made upon them. The willingness of the authorities for peace in the countryside was influenced by the new atmosphere within society and in the party itself generated by the assassination of Kirov. New enemies were to be found in the future in the party ranks and this was to be almost a full-time occupation for the ever-diminishing number of 'loyal' members. For a number of years the party had to concentrate more on itself, less on the countryside.

9 The Soviet Rural Communist Party and the Purges 1933–39

THE PARTY PURGES OF 1933 AND 1934

The special purges of certain regions of the rural communist party conducted at the end of 1932 dragged on into the early months of 1933; they were soon to be overtaken by larger events. On 11 December 1932 a C.C. resolution appeared in *Pravda* proclaiming the general party purge of 1933.[1] A gestation period of several months followed. A joint resolution of the C.C. and C.C.C., dated 23 April 1933, described the reasons making a purge necessary and outlined the procedures for its implementation.[2] The resolution laid stress on how in the previous two or three years hundreds of thousands had joined the party, most of whom were honestly dedicated to the party but suffered from poor political awareness and/or poor academic-political education. Six categories of communists were listed liable for expulsion: class alien and hostile elements; double dealers who hid their real motivation from the party and in fact sought to undermine the party's policies; careerists who used their party cards for their own purposes; and moral degenerates. This was standard fare of those not fit to remain in the party ranks. The two remaining classifications are of particular interest to our discussion. One hostile grouping contained those:

> Open and hidden infringers of party and state discipline, who do not fulfil party and state decisions, subjecting to doubt and discrediting decisions and plans by the party with nonsense about their 'unreality' and 'unattainability'.[3]

The phraseology of this statement is most revealing, harking back as it does to the events of 1932 and the language used about local rural party cadres. Another grouping of those thought fit for removal also seems to have certain relevance for the rural communist party and included: 'those degenerates, joining with bourgeois elements, who refuse to fight in reality with the class enemy, who in practice do not struggle against kulak elements, idlers, wastrels and . . . thieves of social property'.[4] This was all very reminiscent of the countryside in 1932, of those who sided with the peasants in need and of those who infringed the law of 7 August 1932. It is such remarks as these, bearing in mind the events of 1932, and being aware of the disproportionately severe consequences of these purges for the rural communist party, as we shall see shortly, that makes us stress the part played by the rural party in these affairs.

The resolution on the purge went on to name those ten party organisations where the purge was to be carried out between 1 June and the end of November 1933. They were: Moscow, Leningrad, Urals, Donets, Odessa, Kiev and Vinnitsa *oblasts*, Eastern and Far Eastern *krais* and the White Russian Republic.[5] From this it can be seen that the 1933 purge was a separate, limited operation, not to be confused with or run into other events. The processing of party members continued throughout 1933 and at the beginning of 1934, when the seventeenth party congress convened, Rudzutak could inform the assembled delegates that 1 149 000 communists had been investigated, of whom 17 per cent had been expelled and 6.3 per cent reduced to sympathiser status.[6]

Results published later in the year showed that the purge levels in the four Ukrainian *oblasts* were not below average; the purge in these areas must have bitten deep, coming so soon after that of 1932. Those regions which were identified as major rural regions (Vinnitsa and Kiev *oblasts* and the East Siberian *krai*) had some of the highest expulsion levels (26.5 per cent, 29.6 per cent and 33.5 per cent respectively, including those reduced to sympathiser status).[7] Other sources of information suggest that the rural communist party was hit disproportionately severely by the 1933 and 1934 purges. For example, the national level of purges was 17 per cent but in samples from rural *raions* in several areas it was appreciably higher: in the rural *raions* of Kiev 34.2 per cent, in Odessa 25 per cent and in East Siberia 25.4 per cent.[8] From this it is evident that the rural communist party was bearing the brunt of a purge once again, especially in the rural areas of the Ukraine, and that when one includes those reduced to sympathiser status between one third and two fifths of rural communists were being effectively expelled. Although these particular samples are perhaps not large enough to make solid assertions, they are, as we shall see, reinforced by some extensive findings concerning the 1934 purge.

During the 1933 purge 195 330 communists were expelled and 72 387 reduced to the level of sympathiser.[9] When one realises that sympathiser status was often a long-term or permanent exclusion from the party, then a total of 265 000 had been effectively removed from the party ranks.[10] When looked at like this the 1933 purge takes on greater significance in party life. It has been argued by others that the 1933 purge was a normal, procedural review of the party ranks because with a 17 per cent expulsion level it was not very different from previous party purges.[11] But in absolute terms no previous party purge could match expulsions of over a quarter of a million.

With the results of the 1933 purge announced, a second purge began of nine other party organisations: the Gorky, Western Siberian, Azov-Black Sea and North Caucasus *krais*, the Crimea, Kharkov, Dnepropetrovsk and Chernigov *oblasts* and Uzbekistan.[12] This second purge was conducted between 15 May 1934 and the spring 1935. Those party organisations not touched by either the 1933 or 1934 purge, which numbered 17, were left to be attended by the 1935 verification of party cards.[13] Although there is less information on the 1934 purge than its predecessor, knowing the number of those checked in 1933 and that the total checked for the two years 1933–34 was 1 916 500, it is possible to calculate that 767 000 communists were verified in the 1934 purge.[14] To discover how many communists were purged, reference is made to two modern sources which note that 312 000 communists were expelled (not including those reduced to sympathiser level) in the 1933–34 purges taken together, and that this represented 16.3 per cent of those examined.[15] With these data, and knowing that 195 330 were expelled in the 1933 purge out of 1 149 000 investigated, we can estimate that 117 470 communists were expelled in the 1934 purge out of 767 000, giving an expulsion level of 15.3 per cent.[16]

Having established these facts, it is possible to highlight the process underway in the rural party. Of all rural party organisations checked in 1934 (for which we do not know the absolute figure) a massive 33 per cent were expelled or reduced to sympathisers, and amongst the *kolkhoz* party organisations this reached 38 per cent.[17] Very little like this had happened before in the party's history, except perhaps the expulsion rates in the partial purges of the rural organisations in the Ukraine and North Caucasus at the end of 1932. Table 9.1 gives the expulsion levels in *kolkhoz* party organisations in some regions during the 1934 purge.

This was quite devastating. Precious little could have been left of the rural party in North Caucasian *kolkhozy*, when it is remembered that already during 1932–33 some 26 000 out of 120 000 rural communists had been purged, 13 000 ousted from office and another 30 000 departed without being registered.[18] Similarly in these national republics with the verification and exchange of party cards to follow there would be little left of the communist party in the collective farms within a few years.

This evidence that the rural communist party was most severely hit in the 1933–34 purges finds support in other discriminatory measures against the rural party adopted in 1934. The number of recommendations required for prospective candidates to the party and their quality were altered at the seventeenth party congress. Compared with the categories operative until 1934, as outlined at the fourteenth party congress (1925), these new regulations made peasant entry considerably more difficult by increasing the number of necessary recommendations from two to five and the length of party membership (*stazh*) of the proposers from two years to five.[19] Potential peasant applicants when recruitment would be resumed were thus discriminated against indirectly. At a time of dwindling numbers, a decline especially steep in rural areas, there were far fewer communists on hand who could act conveniently as proposers: in many *raions* a peasant would be hard pressed to find five communists willing to support his application.

The importance of the events in the countryside of 1932 and their consequences for the party as a whole in subsequent years is further substantiated by reviewing the reasons given for expulsions in the two purges of 1933 and 1934. Unfortunately the data on reasons given for purge expulsions are sparse and patchy and can only play a subsidiary part in our argument. The rural party had been expected, incorrectly and unjustly, to be able to solve the agricultural crisis by organisational methods and basic mobilisation techniques, which proved inadequate. More communists were expelled for alleged failures in the implementation of economic policy than has been thought hitherto, and more relative emphasis needs to be given to this than to considerations such as moral degeneracy, other personal failings and inactivity and passivity in party duties.[20] Several sources in fact show that in the 1933 and 1934 purges only between one fifth and one quarter were removed because of their so-called passivity.[21] Within the rural party the proportion was even smaller. During the 1934 purge the proportion of all *kolkhozniks* expelled for passivity was only 8.1 per cent.[22] In the rural *raions* of White Russia, the category of 'ballast' and passivity was ignored entirely by the purge commissions, and it is relevant to remember that this category had not been included in the relevant C.C. resolution of April 1933. The classification of expellees as passive seems to have been a vague one. Categories of expulsion other than passivity and ballast deserve close attention, and suggest that many communists were expelled for recalcitrance, disobedience and resistance to orders from above. Information on violators of party – state discipline indicates that about one-fifth of expellees were in this category,[23] and this reaches almost one third in the rural *raions* of White Russia.[24] The further categories of 'double dealers' and 'degenerates' siding with class aliens were said to undermine party and state policies. Thus it seems possible that a significant proportion of communists, especially rural ones, were expelled for not fulfilling instructions, for disobeying orders and related failings.

The most candid comment on the rationale of the purges and a pointer to its probable effects on the rural party appeared in the C.C. resolution of 22 March 1933 on the *kolkhoz* cells '*Iskra*' and '*Vpered*':

> The C.C. underlines especially that just as in the Civil War period the work of the communists and cells was judged by the state of their fighting discipline, just as the work of factory cells is judged on the basis of the fulfilment of the industrial financial plan, so too the C.C. will judge the work of kolkhoz cells, particularly with regard to the forthcoming purge, by how the cells as a whole and by how each communist ... are able to master kolkhoz production, questions of work organisations, work rates and norms, by how the struggle for ... the successful completion of sowing, by how the kolkhoz commitments towards the state are fulfilled.[25]

Simply put, communists had to make a success of the rural economy, and if 'commitments', specifically grain procurements, were not fulfilled, the communists were warned that they would be punished in the purge. This was most likely to be the case for rural communists in the southern grain regions, where the spirit of 1932 lingered on.

This interpretation, approaching the subject from the perspective of the rural party and bearing in mind the 1932 crisis, differs from that advocated by other scholars in that it emphasises economic and political shortcomings, real or imagined, of communists for which they were disciplined. But this is a question of emphasis. Many communists were indeed expelled and reduced in status because of their inadequacies, inexperience and need for self improvement.[26] Our argument seeks to highlight more the relative significance of previous failings in the economic field by a party involved in and held responsible for economic affairs. Incidentally, the implications of this argument may not be confined to the rural party.

Summing up the Purges of 1933–34

There appears to be no precise information available in absolute terms for the whole USSR on the decline of the rural communist party in these years. With regard to the 1933–34 party purges, it has been generally

Table 9.1   Expulsion levels in some regional *kolkhoz* party organisations in the
1934 purge

Tadzhikistan	49.1%	North Caucasus	25.0%
Turkmeniya	43.9%	Moldavia	39.1%
West Siberian *krai*	41.3%	Chernigov *oblast*	43.9%
Dnepropetrovsk *oblast*	21.2%		

Source: *Partiinoe stroitel'stvo*, No. 7, April 1935, p. 33.

accepted in western studies that more than three-quarters of a million communists were expelled in these purges.[27] However, it seems certain that the various expulsion rates cited refer not to total party membership but to the substantially lower figure of *those who actually underwent the purge process.* It was always stated explicitly or implicitly in the literature of the 1930s that the expulsion percentage and absolute figure of the expelled referred to those who had undergone the purge, and recent sources state quite clearly that the 1933–34 purges were not carried out in 17 party organisations.[28]

If the percentages expelled refer to the number undergoing the purge (1 916 500) then it follows that only 312 800 (16.3 per cent) were expelled and 111 157 (5.8 per cent) were reduced to sympathiser status during the two official purges of 1933 and 1934. This is a much lower figure than has generally been accepted to date by western scholars. One Soviet source provides the following detailed information: 14 per cent of full members and 22.2 per cent of candidate members were expelled, 8.8 per cent of all communists 'undergoing the purge' reduced to candidate status and 1.5 per cent of full members and 16.5 per cent of candidates investigated were reduced to sympathiser status.[29] The following results as displayed in Table 9.2 can be derived from the above.

As the party membership dropped by 1.2 million in the two years 1933–34, we are left with the extremely high figure of 775 000 for losses from the party due to other reasons such as voluntary or mechanical withdrawal, natural deaths and any expulsions not included in the two official purge processes.[30] Normal disciplinary proceedings are distinct from the two offical purge processes. There are to my knowledge no available sources to allow an estimate of such ordinary proceedings on a nationwide scale.[31] Thus it is extremely difficult, if not impossible, to discriminate accurately any sub-groups within this 775 000 total.[32]

To summarise this discussion on the 1933–34 purges, a number of major points have been made. It has been suggested that 'passivity' was

Table 9.2 Expulsions and reductions to sympathiser level in the 1933 and 1934 purges

	Expelled	Reduced to sympathiser
1933[a]		
(1 149 000* investigated)	195 330	72 387
	(17.0%)	(6.3%)
1934[b]		
(767 000 investigated)	117 470	39 778
	(15.3%)	(5.2%)
Totals		
(1 916 500 investigated)	312 800[c]	112 165[d]
	(16.3%)	(5.8%)

Sources: (a) *XVII s''ezd Vsesoyuznoi Kommunisticheskoi Partii(b): stenograficheskii otchet*, p. 287. * If Yaroslavsky's figure of 1 075 943 had been preferred, the resulting change in Table 9.2 would have been only marginal; (b) derived from information for 1933 and total figures; (c) I.N. Yudin, *Sotsial'naya baza rosta KPSS*, p. 126; (d) Derived from information in N.A. Zolotarev, *Vazhnyi etap organisatsionnogo ukrepleniya kommunisticheskoi partii (1929–1937 gg.)*, p. 127. See note 32 for further explanation.

not the only major reason for expulsions, but one equal to others. A clear distinction was drawn between the 1933 and 1934 purges as separate processes and doubts were cast on generally accepted calculations, while at the same time questions were raised about the accuracy with which the quantitative effects can be gauged of the various processes going on in this two-year period. It was argued that the two official purges of 1933 and 1934 actually purged fewer people than generally imagined. The high residual of losses due to other reasons was explained in part by those expelled from the party in proceedings other than offical purges.

THE DECLINE IN RURAL PARTY MEMBERSHIP 1933–37

Although we are unable to calculate any meaningful absolute figures for the whole rural party for 1933–34, we are able to do this for the period 1933–37.

The party purges of 1933 and 1934 were promptly followed by other checks of the party ranks: the verification of party cards in 1935 and the exchange of party cards in 1936. These operations formed part of much needed reorganisation in the party book-keeping. The maintenance of party records was generally chaotic and as of 1 January 1934 there were 56 000 'dead souls', persons listed in party documents but who were nowhere to be found. Much of the reason why such a condition had arisen was because Soviet society in the 1930s was exceptionally fluid. People moved from place to place, job to job, looking for better conditions; party members were transferred to and fro and moved on their own initiative in search of a better paid, more cushy administrative assignment. In the mid-1930s, when the party was disengaging from the economy, it was only fitting that the authorities should seek 'to bring Bolshevik order into . . . their own party home'.[33]

The operation of the verification, announced in May 1935, was not efficient and dragged on until, still incomplete, results were published at the C.C. plenum of 21–25 December 1935. Some 81.1 per cent of the party's membership was checked, of whom 9.1 per cent were expelled, equalling approximately 170 000 communists.[34] Materials on the reasons given for expulsion are rare and the information regarding the class composition of those expelled is slight or not reliable. Some scattered information suggests that the rural party was once again more heavily purged than other sectors of the party's membership.[35] It was towards the end of 1935 that a particularly tense atmosphere was created within the party ranks, foreshadowing the ferocity of the *Ezhovshchina*.[36] In this prevailing atmosphere the 1936 exchange of party cards was announced at the December 1935 C.C. plenum.[37] This exchange dragged on through most of 1936 during which year the total party membership declined by 95 000 (4.6 per cent).[38] In the standard western historiography of the 1930s these processes in 1935–36 are viewed as consciously planned stages escalating in intensity and paving the way for the 'Great Terror', but recently seemingly sound arguments have questioned this interpretation and suggested that these processes should be seen more as necessary events for the party's effective internal administration and management.[39]

Despite the spectacular nature of the 1937–38 'Great Purge', the real decline in total membership in 1937 was only 101 695.[40] What did happen in 1937 was a very large turnover in one sweep of primary party organisations (ppo) committees and ppo secretaries. In a sample of 54 000 ppos surveyed nationally in 1937, 55 per cent of party committees were removed and 36 per cent of ppo secretaries.[41] This represented a massive influx of new blood into junior cadre positions. Coming in the wake as it did of the various purges and screenings in the previous years, this meant that there could have been very few local level party cadres occupying the same posts or even the same level posts that they had occupied at the beginning of mass collectivisation or even at the end of the first Five Year Plan. Since it was regular procedure to transfer personnel to and fro in normal times, those party cadres who could avoid expulsion were liable to quick promotion through the hierarchy. Inevitably in the circumstances, the face of the party had changed.

We will now address ourselves to the crucial question of how the rural communist party membership changed numerically during the years of the second Five Year Plan and compare this with trends in other sectors of the party. Table 9.3 sets out our available knowledge on the decline in the various sectors of the rural party.

Table 9.3 shows that the membership of the whole party at no time fell below 50 per cent of its mid-1932 figure, whereas rural party membership dropped to less than a third of the mid-1932 level at the beginning of

Table 9.3 Comparisons of party membership 1932–41: whole party, *kolkhoz* and *sovkhoz* cells

Date	Total party membership[a]	Total rural party membership	kolkhoz cell membership	sovkhoz cell membership
mid-1932	3 400 000 (100)	832 000 (100)[b]	569 000 (100)[b]	122 070 (100)[b]
January 1933	3 555 338 (105)	—	—	—
October 1933	848 000 (102)[c]	—	—	—
January 1937	1 981 697 (59)	296 900 (36)[d]	187 000 (33)[d]	52 000 (43)[e]
January 1938	1 920 002 (56)	255 852 (31)[f]	c.137 000 (24)[g]	—
January 1939	2 306 973 (68)	315 699 (38)[f]	153 000 (27)[h]	—
January 1940	3 399 975 (100)	534 448 (64)[f]	343 000 (60)[i]	—
January 1941	3 872 465 (114)	623 419 (75)[f]	>350 000 (>61)[h]	—

Sources: (a) T.H. Rigby, *Communist Party Membership in the USSR, 1917–1967*, p. 52; (b) *Partiinoe stroitel'stvo*, No. 21, November 1932, p. 46; (c) based on information in Kaganovich speech in *XVII s''ezd Vsesoyuznoi Kommunisticheskoi Partii(b): stenograficheskii otchet* (1934), p. 557; (d) *Istoriya KPSS*, vol. 4, book 2, p. 507; (e) T.H. Rigby, op. cit., p. 223; (f) *Istoriya KPSS*, vol. 5, book 1, p. 49; (g) My estimate based on speech made by Andreev at the eighteenth party congress, *XVIII s''ezd Vsesoyuznoi Kommunisticheskoi Partii(b): stenograficheskii otchet* (1939), p. 109, who states that in the last year, that is 1938, there had been some growth in the number of party members in the *kolkhozy;* (h) G.A. Chigrinov, *Bor'ba KPSS za organizatsonno-khozyaistvennoe ukreplenie kolkhozov v dovoennye gody*, p. 163. The original source for this 1939 figure is Andreev, *XVIII s''ezd;* (j) V.K. Palishko, *Rost i ukreplenie partiinykh ryadov v usloviyakh stroitel'stva i uprocheniya sotsializma*, p. 60.

1938. Most striking is the elimination of the *kolkhoz* party membership, which at the beginning of 1938 had shrunk to a mere quarter of its mid-1932 size. As a proportion of the rural party membership, the *kolkhoz* cell communists declined significantly from about 70 per cent in mid-1932 to just over 50 per cent in January 1983. This paucity of rural communists was bound to have a profound effect on the way the party and state approached the collective farm sector; the rural party would have to adopt new methods of working in the countryside.

The regional figures fit in with the general pattern. In White Russia the party numbers fell from 59 175 in January 1932 to 33 828 in January 1937 and the rural component in this was 32 768 and 10 305 respectively.[42] Thus the White Russian communist party in 1937 remained at over half the 1932 figure, whereas the rural party element was less than one third. In the predominantly urban *oblast* of Leningrad the party's strength at its lowest point at the end of 1937 hovered at about 60 per cent of its 1932 size.[43] It was the party organisation in the North Caucasus *krai*, that part remaining so designated after a portion had been incorporated into the newly created Azov–Black Sea *krai* in 1934, which suffered the most dramatic decline: by 1937, it was less than one quarter its 1934 size, falling from 61 870 to 15 000.[44] These losses of 75 per cent in the North Caucasus, with more having occurred in the larger *krai* size of the pre-1934 days, are reminiscent of the losses sustained by all *kolkhoz* organisations in 1932–37. Similarly, the rural *raions* of the Azov–Black Sea *krai* sustained greater proportional losses than the urban *raions* in the same *krai*, as is shown in Table 9.4

Several points arise from Table 9.4. Firstly, major losses were incurred in the urban and rural *raions* in the years 1933, 1934 and the first quarter of 1935, that is during the purges of these years before the verification of party cards came underway in spring 1935. Secondly, there is the obvious distinction between what happened to the party membership in rural and urban areas. Both sectors declined sharply in numbers, but whereas the urban *raions* lost over half their membership in the period 1933–first quarter 1935, rural ones sustained huge losses of over two-thirds in the same period, and by January 1937 were reduced to less than one quarter of their size five years previously. This is nothing short of the devastation of the rural party organisation in the North Caucasus, and one can assume that the position was little different in the Ukraine and Volga regions. Nor does the time-scale of our figures portray the full picture of losses: the January 1932 membership figure was certainly not a maximum for that year, nor was the January 1937 figure the minimum during that year. A further interesting point on the urban *raions* is

Table 9.4   A comparison of party membership in six urban* *raions* and thirteen rural *raions* of the Azov–Black Sea *krai* in January 1932, April 1935 and January 1937

	1 January 1932	1 April 1935	1 January 1937
party membership of 6 urban *raions* and index	51 847 (100)	21 849 (42.1)	23 565 (45.5)
party membership of 13 rural *raions* and index	13 340 (100)	3 903 (29.3)	3 249 (24.4)

Source: *Rostovskaya oblastnaya organizatsiya KPSS v tsifrakh 1917–1975*, pp. 60–61 and 67–69.
*Urban is defined as those *raions* where over 80 per cent of all recruits to the party were workers by occupation in 1931. Rural is defined as those *raions* where over 50 per cent of all recruits were peasants by occupation in 1931. In fact, of our sample of 13 rural *raions*, nine have such a percentage over 75 per cent.

noticeable in Table 9.4. Here, between 1935 and 1937, the number of communists actually rose, thanks no doubt either to imports from other areas or to new recruitment at the end of 1936. This did not happen in the rural *raions*, and serious replenishment of rural party ranks nationally did not get underway until the beginning of 1939.

The above findings support our view that the rural party, and especially collective farm organisations, and the southern regions generally, were more severely hit by the various purges, purges which no doubt stimulated many of the voluntary and mechanical withdrawals. Another phenomenon which also explains some of the rural party losses during the 1930s is the migration of rural communists to the towns and cities. We are unable to quantify this movement with any precision. Such migration was, however, compensated by temporary and permanent transfers of urban communists to the countryside.

A CHANGE IN COURSE

Beginning at the end of 1932 and continuing into 1938 the rural communist party was ravaged. The huge reduction in rural party membership was bound to have serious effect on the party's operational role. Throughout the period under discussion, the leading party figures seem to have been in favour of a shrunken party organisation.[45] But some people apparently had doubts about where all this was leading and expressed reservations about the impact of the rural party purges. This is indicated by remarks uttered by Kaganovich at the seventeenth party congress: 'Must we force recruitment into the party in the rural party organisations? Some say once there are no party organisations or communists in the kolkhozy, let's start recruiting into the party. This is a mistake . . . '.[46] It is significant that, according to Kaganovich, renewed recruitment was called for in the rural party especially and not in the non-rural sectors, and that particular mention was made of the shortage of communists in *kolkhozy*, where party organisations suffered most in 1933 and in 1934 after the congress. Those who thought that recruitment should be resumed were not identified. It is likely that cadres in the *raikoms* and *obkoms* complained of supervising so many rural Soviets and *kolkhozy* without a sufficient number of subordinates to fulfil routine and arduous tasks. Perhaps some of the most authoritative appeals came from the political department staffs who were expected to produce quick, successful results with very little manpower resources. For example, the Western *oblast* political sector of MTS, in a report of 15 July 1934 to the Political Administration of the USSR, complained bitterly that the *kolkhozy* and MTS of this *oblast* were 'extremely poor in party forces' and that 'without fresh deployments you will not improve anything'.[47]

The C.C. declared recruitment open again as from 1 November 1936.[48] But recruitment in the last two months of 1936 and throughout 1937, at the height of the *Ezhovshchina*, was not surprisingly very sluggish. Membership rose in 1938 when a number of C.C. resolutions were published encouraging accelerated recruitment procedures, and following this increased still further during 1939. Recruitment promptly slowed down again after a C.C. resolution issued on 16 November 1939 warned against the rapid intake of new members.

How did the resurrection of the rural party proceed in comparison with the rest of the party? Table 9.5 is useful in showing the increase of various sectors in the party for purposes of comparison.

Table 9.5 shows that the rural party outpaced non-rural sectors. Of course the use of 1938 as a base year is deceptive: the rural party was more depleted than the rest of the party during 1933–37. The growth in rural party and *kolkhoz* membership remains significant: almost in compensation for the disproportionately heavy losses they had suffered, the rural party ranks were being quickly replenished. The rural party rate of growth merely kept pace with that of the party as a whole until the

Table 9.5 Size of total party membership and various sectors of party, 1938–41

Date	Total party[a]	Industrial party[b] organisations	Transport[b] party organisations	Total rural party[b]	kolkhoz party organisations
Jan. 1938	1 920 002 (100)	536 000 (100)	170 926 (100)	255 852 (100)	137 000 (100)[c]
Jan. 1939	2 306 973 (120)	647 541 (121)	210 313 (123)	315 699 (123)	153 000 (112)[d]
Jan. 1940	3 399 975 (177)	837 387 (156)	277 272 (162)	534 448 (209)	343 000 (250)[e]
Jan. 1941	3 872 465 (202)	903 552 (168)	289 279 (169)	623 419 (244)	> 350 000 (255)[f]

Sources: (a) T.H. Rigby, *Communist Party Membership in the USSR, 1917–1967*, p. 52; (b) *Istoriya KPSS*, vol. 5, book 1, pp. 45 and 49; (c) My estimate based on remarks by Andreev in *XVIII s''ezd Vsesoyuznoi Kommunisticheskoi Partii (b): stenograficheskii otchet* (1939), p. 109; (d) ibid; (e) V.K. Palishko, *Rost i ukreplenie partiinykh ryadov v usloviyakh stroitel'stva i uprocheniya sotsializma*, p. 162; (f) G.A. Chigrinov, *Bor'ba KPSS za organizatsionno-khozyaistvennoe ukreplenie kolkhozov v dovoennye gody*, p. 163.

beginning of 1939, but overtook it appreciably thereafter. This may well be due in large part to the impact of Andreev's speech at the eighteenth party congress of March 1939, in which he catalogued manifestations of the rural party's woeful condition, especially in the collective farms.[49] The figures for the rural party and *kolkhoz* organisations also reveal the extent to which non-*kolkhoznik* categories must have been recruited to the rural party ranks, presumably representatives of the rural intelligentsia and those working in the Soviets, trading organisations and other administrative posts.

The significance of the recrudescence of the rural party should not be over-emphasised. Between 1 January 1938 and 1 January 1941 the net growth in the rural party was 367 567, but this was only 18.9 per cent of the net growth of the entire party in the same period. The effect of the purges had been to downgrade the rural party in relative importance. The rural party as a proportion of the whole party had represented 20.2 per cent in January 1930, 23.3 per cent in January 1931, 22.4 per cent in January 1932 and this rose to 24.5 per cent in July 1932. By January 1937 this had declined to 15.0 per cent and remained low in the years immediate to the out-break of the war: 13.3 per cent in 1938, 13.7 per cent in 1939, 15.7 per cent in 1940 and 16.1 per cent in 1941. In January 1941 total rural party membership was still considerably smaller than in 1932.

In this chapter the decline in the rural party ranks during the second Five Year Plan period has been illustrated, a decline proportionally more pronounced than that of the party as a whole. A number of reasons for these losses were suggested; some were due to purging, some to other causes. Amongst those purged, emphasis has been laid on the element of punishment for real and alleged failings in economic campaigns. The decline in rural party size had very profound effects on the rural party's organisation and operational role, as we shall see in subsequent chapters.

10 The Rural Party Cell 1933–39: Structure, Numbers and Deployment

An earlier chapter described how the rural party network was radically transformed during the years of the first Five Year Plan, how at a time of massive expansion in party membership figures the cell numbers augmented to accommodate the new recruits, at the same time as many changed their location from Soviet and village bases to be deployed in *kolkhozy*, *sovkhozy* and MTS. The 27 039 cells and a rural party membership of 358 936 in July 1929 increased to 63 135 with a membership over 800 000 in July 1932. The environment in which the rural cells existed in the years of the second Five Year Plan was to be entirely different. The rural party membership shrank drastically during the purges with a consequential fall in cell numbers, whilst at the same time the rural cells' operational role was reassessed. This chapter discusses the effect on the rural cell network of the major reorganisation of June 1933, the decline in cell numbers resulting from the purges and the new system designed to accommodate a shrinking and scattered rural party membership.

THE 1933 REORGANISATION: THE BEGINNING OF THE END

Introduction: the Debate on *razukrupnenie*

The objective of establishing cells and groups in all collective farms and even in their brigades was not always taken for granted. In this section we consider the doubts expressed and examine *razukrupnenie* (the breaking down in size of party units) in comparison with developments in the urban party.

Superficially it may appear that there was little *razukrupnenie* of the rural party cells during 1929–32. The number of communists in the average size rural party cell was fairly constant at 13 and 14 in 1929 and

1930 and 15 in 1931 and 1932. The huge number of new recruits enabled an equally large increase in the number of cells. The appearance of inter-*kolkhoz* cells and support points resulted in a complex hierarchy of party committees, cells, 'shop' cells, party groups and party organisers. A similar trend occurred in the party organisations of urban enterprises during the first Five Year Plan, which has been noted already by one researcher:

> The years 1930–1932 saw a proliferation of organisational forms which reflected the vagueness of the instructions to restructure the form of party work according to production principles and the enormity of tasks imposed on party organisations which created a tendency to establish complex committee or cell like apparati in ever smaller units of production so that organisations, especially in the largest enterprises often ended up with a four or five-tiered structure.[1]

These complex systems of inter-*kolkhoz* cell and support point in the countryside were designed to co-ordinate the activity of the various tiers.

At about the same time as internal sub-division within the cells was accentuated in the spring of 1932, some authoritative misgivings were expressed. When one writer in the party's organisational journal supported the creation of party cells at every *kolkhoz* in the West Siberian krai, the journal editor thought this to be a contentious view.[2] The peril of over-extending party forces was most immediate in those regions with a weak party base. A. Shil'man, second secretary of the Western *obkom*, warned of the danger of creating 'dwarf cells' (*karlikovye yacheiki*).[3] Even in the grain regions, where the rural party was comparatively more consolidated thanks to the large size of *kolkhozy* and the higher party membership per household, similar difficulties arose. On 3 April 1932, the Kursavskii *raikom*, North Caucasus, resolved that all its *kolkhozy* and brigades should contain a cell or group. But in view of the inadequate recruitment to the party, this resolution was criticised for its distorted emphasis on a mechanical expansion which exceeded the rural party's abilities.[4] This was one of the most categorical expressions of concern that the rural party might be going too far in the breaking down process and overstretching itself.

The reasons for this concern are not far to seek. When the party units were sub-divided into ever smaller units, frequently composed of inexperienced candidate members, they quickly became isolated from the party-state, political and economic centres, and were liable to be neglected and forgotten by their party superiors. Without the guidance, prompting and coaxing of party committee secretaries close at hand, the more junior members of rural cells often could not cope in the wilderness of the Soviet countryside. However, this presents us with a conundrum. In June 1932 the units of the industrial party organisations were revamped and enlarged, thereby reversing the trend to *razukrupnenie* of the previous years. A. Sadler suggests that this was due chiefly to a shortage of adequately qualified party members capable of administering so many small party units.[5] If this was the case, one would expect the central party authorities to have discovered the same shortcoming in the rural party organisation. Instead, having faced a shortage of qualified cadres to man the numerous small industrial party units, the authorities persisted in the pronounced *razukrupnenie* of the far less reliable rural party in June 1933. Not only was this contradictory to trends in the party in the factories, but it took place even more illogically when the 1933 party purge was underway and beginning to decimate rural party ranks. As a result, a declining number of rural communists were scattered over a growing number of small, isolated party units. Indeed the *razukrupnenie* plus the purge proved especially counter-productive by producing the phenomenon of the single communist on a greater scale than ever before. The *razukrupnenie* of the rural party in early 1932, whilst membership was comparatively large and still expanding and before its efficiency and loyalty were called into question during the autumn and winter of 1932, is perhaps comprehensible. But the sub-division of the rural party organisation carried out in the summer of 1933 was paradoxically more fundamental and radical.

The 1933 Reorganisation

In endless official announcements the rural party, and the party as a whole, was congratulated and prided itself on its major achievement of turning its organisational face to production. This had been the organisational linch-pin of the first Five Year Plan and had apparently been successfully accomplished. It was repeatedly proclaimed that the rural party had been transformed from a small, predominantly territorially organised body into a large organisation centred on the production process. Between July 1929 and spring 1932, the proportion of all rural cells at production centres such as *kolkhozy*, *sovkhozy* and MTS had risen from 10.3 per cent to 82.1 per cent, whilst that of territorial cells had declined from 89.7 per cent to 17.9 per cent.[6] Therefore it came as a revelation when the C.C. resolution of 15 June 1933 declared that 'the construction of party organisations in the countryside is predominantly on a territorial basis', and went on to complain that most production-based rural cells were artificial creations concealing a hotch-potch of communists originating from a variety of institutions and geographical areas merely joined together under the title of production cell. The C.C. resolution demanded that these large amalgams be broken down into genuine, independent *kolkhoz* cells.[7] How can one explain this apparent anomaly and was it really such a surprise? Initial misgivings were obviously expressed in the C.C. resolution of 15 May 1932, which urged that more rural communists be involved directly in production activities. One could assume from this that much of the face to production drive had been formalistic in merely basing the cells at production centres, whilst the cell members themselves shirked participation in agricultural production. Amid the panegyrics about 'face to production' other discordant notes are faintly discernible. In the spring of 1932 it was casually mentioned in the party press that the majority of inter-*kolkhoz* cells, promoted enthusiastically in 1930–31, were in reality based on a territorial principle at the local Soviet, thereby contravening the plan for them to be centred at the strongest *kolkhoz* in a group of *kolkhozy*.[8] The production principle was undermined more fundamentally when party members belonged officially to a particular type of production cell, say at the MTS, but in fact worked at a local Soviet, co-operative or elsewhere, and thus had very little to do with the production cycle of the MTS or any other MTS activities. Towards the end of 1932, of 32 658 communists belonging to MTS cells, only 67.3 per cent (21 658) genuinely worked full-time in the MTS while the other 11 000 really ought to have come under the jurisdiction of Soviet and *kolkhoz* cells where they spent most of their time.[9] It was already thought in 1932 that large cells could be broken up into smaller units established in places where the communists actually worked. Just as there was a move towards the establishment of one *kolkhoz* cell in every *kolkhoz*, there was a parallel argument in favour of one Soviet cell to focus its attention on a single Soviet. In grain production areas, the inter-*kolkhoz* cell could be broken down into viable, smaller, independent *kolkhoz* cells, comprising usually between three and eight members and candidates.[10]

Such proposals as these were mooted before the June 1933 resolution and are relevant background to it, and resurfaced in the C.C. resolution. This noted that communists working in *kolkhozy* belonged to territorial cells even when the opportunities existed to establish independent kolkhoz cells based at a single *kolkhoz*. In an effort to bring this about, the resolution required that in *kolkhozy* with the requisite number of three full members, a party cell shoud be formed, and a candidate group should be formed wherever there were one or two members plus candidates. New provisions stipulated that those communists belonging to a territorial cell who worked in a *kolkhoz* which did not have sufficient party members to justify a full cell or candidate group were to detach themselves organisationally from the territorial cell in order to establish the innovatory party-*komsomol* 'nucleus' composed of the party member(s), any *komsomols* in the *kolkhoz* and even non-party sympathisers (*sochuvstvuyushchie*).[11] This especially represented a considerable shift from previous procedure, and indicated the extremes to which the authorities were willing to go in pursuance of their aim to spread the diminishing rural party forces as extensively as possible. The resolution also required that in *kolkhozy* without any communists at all, and without any communist in a nearby territorial cell who could transfer to live and work permanently in the *kolkhoz*, sympathiser groups should be formed with a special party organiser attached to them. Presumably the *raikoms* nominated the party organisers, who were supposed to visit the groups and encourage them in mass-party work: this sounds familiar and not very promising. Demarcation between production and territorial type cells was made more distinct; overlapping of the two, as in the inter-*kolkhoz* or inter-Soviet cells, was forbidden. Communists not in kolkhozy, working in Soviets, co operatives, schools and other organisations should set up their own territorial based cell.[12] When there were no other communists, *komsomols* or sympathisers to accompany an isolated communist at a *kolkhoz* or Soviet, then the party member remained alone organisationally as a single communist; such isolated communists were no longer allowed to be attached to the nearest cell when one was available.

When these stipulations were implemented in practice the number of units proliferated and their size diminished. Although there were no comprehensive figures available for the whole country of the results of the reorganisation, many partial, regional surveys confirm that this is what occurred. The number of rural party units increased from 63 135 on 1 July 1932 to 80 000 cells and candidate groups, plus 22 000 party-*komsomol* nuclei in October 1933.[13] Information for 1933 from 814 MTS and the *kolkhozy* they served indicate an increase from 5290 party units before to 12 510 after the reorganisation: the number of party cells rose by over one thousand; the number of candidate groups almost quadrupled; the number of party-*komsomol* groups rose from 450 to 3770.[14] In the Chernigov *oblast* of the Ukraine *kolkhoz* cells increased from 450 to 3770.[15] The greatest proliferation seems to have occurred in party-*komsomol* groups, followed by the candidate groups; the increase in the number of full party cells was smaller. In the Ukraine, thanks to the breaking down of party organisations, the percentage of *kolkhozy* encompassed by party units increased from 34 per cent on 1 May 1933 to 78 per cent on 1 November 1933.[16] Here lay some of the reorganisation's rationale. The rural party in a region like the Western *oblast*, with so many small, diverse economic units, might well be expected to have benefited particularly from the reorganisation. It also had a negative impact. Before the summer 1933, each *raikom* in this *oblast* supervised on average 20–25 cells and groups, but later this number rose to between 50–150.[17] This may well have put too much strain on the new, small party units and the *raikoms* who were supposed to supervise them.

The reorganisation was thus a national one, affecting grain regions, non-grain regions and national republics alike. However, there was a fundamental, constraining factor which prevented the reorganisation's ultimate or long-term success: this was the party purge. The severe contraction in rural party numbers meant that the reorganisation led to small units each with comparatively few members, and above all to the phenomenon of the single communist. The effects of the party purge soon cancelled out the expansion in the number of party units, which declined dramatically at the end of 1933 and continued to decline during the purge years which followed. To buttress the flagging network, and perhaps to conceal the full extent of self-inflicted destruction, pseudo-party bodies were created such as the party-*komsomol* nucleus and the sympathiser group.

In brief, the 1933 reorganisation remains an enigma. One can only suggest tentative answers by way of explanation. It certainly extended the rural party forces over greater numbers of production units and spread them thinly over larger geographical areas. Perhaps the reform is best seen in this light, as a response to the devastating effects of the party purge, a last ditch attempt to make a lot less go a lot further.

THE RURAL PARTY NETWORK

In mid-1932 there were 63 135 rural party cells and candidate groups, of which 44 045 (69.8 per cent) were located in *kolkhozy*. Until some time in the autumn of 1932, when the gravity of the grain collections began to dawn on the central authorities, rural party membership grew and cell numbers followed upwards in their wake. Whatever increase occurred from the base figure of 63 135 in mid-1932 until the end of the year, this was more than compensated by the effects of the party purge on the rural ranks in key concentrations of the rural party membership in the Ukraine and North Caucasus. Beginning in December 1932 recruitment to the party was curtailed and there was no reported reorganisation in party units until summer 1933, so one can presume confidently that cell numbers would have stagnated in normal circumstances, but in fact must have fallen at a time of purges in the southern regions during the winter months of 1932–33 and commenced to decline on a nationwide scale in April–May 1933. This line of reasoning is supported by a rare reference to rural party cell numbers for the beginning of 1933 made in *Pravda*, which stated that on 1 January 1933 there were 61 100 rural party cells with near parity between party units and rural Soviets.[18] In June 1933 the rural party reorganisation was announced and, judging from our foregoing examples, produced an increase in cell and candidate group numbers of at least 50 per cent. The number of cells and candidate groups alone probably increased to in excess of 100 000 for a very brief period in June–August 1933. However, one cannot be too confident about such an estimate, as this was a time of great flux both in the party membership figures and in the number of party organisations. Table 10.1 presents the available information on the number of party units over the period 1932–39.

The most authoritative statement on rural party unit numbers, often quoted since, was made by Kaganovich at the seventeenth party congress. Kaganovich revealed that on 1 October 1933 there were 80 000 rural primary party organisations (ppos) and candidate groups containing 790 000 communists in addition to which there were 22 000 party-*komsomol* groups and a further 38 000 single communists in *kolkhozy*.[19] This makes for a steady progression in party unit numbers when compared with the published figure of 61 000 for January 1933. Indeed this was just the impression Kaganovich sought to create by contrasting the October 1933 data with that for 1930. This hid or distorted the true picture of what was in the process of happening and what was about to happen. In retrospect Kaganovich managed to make his revelations both precise and ambiguous. In addition to his information for October 1933, he informed the assembled delegates that 'at the present time', which presumably meant January–February 1934, there were 30 000 *kolkhoz* ppos. Most commentators have ignored the underlying significance of Kaganovich's figures, possibly because they did not connect them with information from another source that in October 1933 there were over 36 000 *kolkhoz* ppos: in other words, between October 1933 and January 1934 some 6000 *kolkhoz* ppos had disappeared.[20] Kaganovich's subterfuge, if that is what it was, could not mask the

Table 10.1　Rural party unit numbers, 1932–39

	July 1932	October 1933	February 1934	January 1935	January 1938	March 1939
All cells/ ppos and candidate groups	63 135[a]	80 000[b]	—	61 700[c]	—	—
All cells/ ppos	—	—	—	36 396[c]	—	40 000[d] (Jan.?)
of which kolkhoz ppos	44 045[ai]	36 196[c]	30 000[b] 24 333[c] (November)	18 000[c]	<12 000[ei]	12 000[e]
All candidate groups	—	—	—	25 381[c]	—	—
of which kolkhoz candidate groups	—	—	20 000[b]	—	—	—
territorial based ppos	—	—	—	c.9000[f]	—	c.20 000[f]
party-komsomol groups	—	22 000[b]	22 000[b]	15 131[c]	—	—
single communists	5–15 000[g]	38 000[b]	38 000[b]	101 583[c]	—	—

Sources: (a) *Partiinoe stroitel'stvo*, No. 21, November 1932, p. 46; (ai) This figure includes candidate groups in *kolkhozy*. An approximate estimate would be that of this total of 44 045, candidate groups represented less than a quarter, that is 9–10 000, as they had done on 1 January 1932, see *Istoriya KPSS*, vol. 4, book 2, pp. 154–5. Although candidate groups certainly existed after the seventeenth party congress of 1934, where their separate identity from full cells was confirmed, there are very few statistics available for them. One presumes reasonably safely that statistics referring to ppos are precise in their definition and do not include any candidate groups; (b) *XVII s″ ezd Vsesoyuznoi Kommunisticheskoi Partii (b): stenograficheskii otchet* (1934), p. 57; (c) F. Chivirev, in *Partiinoe stroitel'stvo*, No. 14, July 1935, pp. 30–4; (d) derived from V.K. Palishko, *Rost i ukreplenie partiinykh ryadov v usloviyakh stroitel'stva i uprocheniya sotsializma*, p. 162, who states that rural party organisations doubled from 1939 to 1941, using a base figure of 82 956 for 1941 provided in D. Bakhshiev, *Partiinoe stroitel'stvo v usloviyakh pobedy sotsializma v SSSR*,

p. 87; (e) *XVIII s'ezd Vsesoyuznoi Kommunisticheskoi Partii (b): stenografi-cheskii otchet* (1939), p. 109 (Andreev); (ei) This figure is an estimate based on Andreev's statement that 'the last year', that is 1938, had seen 'some growth in the number of party members in kolkhozy', *XVIII s''ezd*. This means that there were fewer than 153 000 communists in the collective farms in 1938, and presumably fewer ppos required to accommodate them. (f) Estimate based on total number of ppos given in the same columns and assuming the number of MTS and *sovkhoz* ppos to be between 7–10 000 in these years; (g) V.P. Danilov in *Istoricheskie zapiski*, No. 79, 1966, p. 13.

decline for long. During the second Five Year Plan, the number of rural party units, specifically cells/ppos and candidate groups, declined substantially from a peak of probably more than 90 000 in the summer–autumn 1933 to approximately 40 000 (ppos only) at the beginning of 1939. There is strong evidence that the large majority of party units which disappeared had been located in collective farms. For example, between October 1933 and January 1935 the total number of rural ppos and candidate groups fell by 20 000 and *kolkhoz* ppos alone accounted for 18 000 of this loss. In the last eight weeks of 1934 6333 *kolkhoz* ppos were dissolved, equivalent to a daily loss of 113. In July 1932 *kolkhoz* cells represented 69.8 per cent of all rural cells, but this proportion fell to 50 per cent by January 1935.[21] This was due to the high losses of communist-*kolkhozniks* during the 1933–34 purges, who were held directly responsible for many of the economic failures of the collective farm sector. Those communists who worked in the rural Soviets, co-operatives and other institutions would have been comparatively less liable to purging. The extent of the damage is reflected in information relating to the White Russian republic which underlines the dispropor-tionately steep decline of rural as compared with industrial cells, and of *kolkhoz* cells as compared with all others. In the White Russian republic from a point in mid-1932 when *kolkhoz* cell numbers almost equalled those of industry, transport and construction, they declined as a proportion of these latter cells to less than one sixth in 1936 and one tenth in 1938. Proportionately the decline in the average size of *kolkhoz* and urban cells was similar, but in 1934–36 *kolkhoz* cell sizes were pitifully small, barely exceeding the minimum requirement of three full members to constitute a cell/ppo.[22]

Information on what happened to the rural party cell network in the purge years is very sparse, but thanks to data supplied by Andreev at the eighteenth party congress in March 1939 and other scattered references, one is able to build up a reasonably full picture of the effects of the purges on the party's collective farm network.[23] Andreev's report to the congress is revealing in that it shows how retrograde the movement had been in *kolkhoz* party organisations. Only five per cent of *kolkhozy* contained a ppo, which equalled approximately the proportion at the beginning of mass collectivisation: in a decade the rural party organisations in the collective farms had come full circle. The size of the average *kolkhoz* ppo had also fallen to slightly less than 13 communists, when it had stood at 15.6 in 1931. Furthermore, one can conclude from his information that many areas must have been as badly provided with *kolkhoz* ppos as White Russia because a surprisingly large proportion of the total number of remaining *kolkhoz* ppos in 1939 were located in the national republic regions of Azerbaidjan, Kazakhstan and Uzbekistan – 21.2 per cent in fact. One tentative explanation of this concentration is that, as comparatively less important grain regions, they were less severely affected by the grain procurement crisis of 1932–33.[24]

As *kolkhoz* ppos felt the brunt of the purges and withdrawals from the party, so the proportion of non-*kolkhoz* ppos grew. With the resumption of recruitment in 1936, greater attention was paid to non-production ppos based at Soviets as more of the rural intelligentsia and administrators were brought into the party. An additional feature readily detectable is that other production based ppos at *sovkhozy* and MTS were able to remain relatively stable. In the White Russian republic between 1933 and 1939, when all types of cells were being dissolved in large quantities (industrial cells during these years declined from 683 to 502 and *sovkhoz* cells from 287 to 47), the MTS actually managed to quadruple their numbers.[25] This same trend is visible in Uzbekistan where MTS and *sovkhoz* ppos taken together grew in numbers between 1932 and 1939 whilst losing only one-third of their membership, considerably less than their fellow rural party cell/ppos based territorially and in the *kolkhozy*.[26] Comparatively then, the MTS ppos were doing well. Our partial findings tend to suggest that the MTS party organisations and, to a lesser extent, those of the *sovkhozy*, where political departments were retained, were spared the harshest rigours of the purge years and stood as some of the last bastions of the rural communist party when much else of the network lay in ruins. This was one means by which to retain some party supervision over the large number of collective farms left without a party organisation.

The generally weak state of the rural party units in these years is also exemplified by the status of those communists who headed them. In 1933 more than two-thirds of *kolkhoz* cell secretaries in a grain region like the Mid Volga worked *po sovmestitel'stvu*, very often combining their party duties with the post of chairman of a *kolkhoz* or rural Soviet; only 15–20 per cent of these *kolkhoz* cell secretaries were paid, full-time party workers.[27] At a time of diminishing manpower resources, the rural party concentrated its limited forces in key positions and tended to work them hard. New party statutes introduced in 1934 noted that ppos with less than 100 communists were to be headed by party workers not freed from other work, and since rural party units were invariably small at this time, this had the effect that few rural ppo secretaries were full-time, paid party workers during the second Five Year Plan.

The dispersal of rural communists owing to the purges and the June 1933 reorganisation was emphasised by the growing phenomenon of single communists. Whenever a territorial or *kolkhoz* cell was broken up to form a variety of new cells and other units, a number of single communists working in isolated villages, institutions or *kolkhozy* were left over and prohibited from attaching themselves to the nearest cell which would have only resurrected the heretical inter-*kolkhoz* or inter-Soviet cell structure. In more normal circumstances, as before and after the purge years 1933–37, these communists would have been members of cells or candidate groups. The number of single communists rose dramatically from 15 000 at the beginning of 1933 to 38 000 one year later and to a huge 101 583 twelve months later at the beginning of 1935. By this time they probably included about a quarter of rural party membership.[28]

These isolated communists acted as the party's sole representatives in many parts of the countryside. Many were of only candidate status and therefore less likely to be experienced propagandists; without supervision there was the danger that these relatively inexperienced communists would become totally neglected and of little value in promoting the party's goals. On the other hand, by no means all single communists were hopeless, helpless individuals; in fact a high proportion of them occupied influential positions in rural society. In several regions as many as 75 per cent occupied posts as local level functionaries: *kolkhoz* administrators, accountants, Soviet chairmen, teachers and the like.[29] This is another example, like that of the MTS, of how the party retained a small but important presence in a number of key positions. If single communists had to exist, all the better for the party if they played central roles in the economic, administrative functioning of the Soviet countryside. The fact that many single communists occupied prestigious posts need not invalidate our earlier remarks: since many single communists were inexperienced candidate party members and many were *kolkhoz* chairmen and so forth, there must have been some correspondence between politically immature communists and rural functionaries.[30]

But reliance on single communists was only an attempt to make the best of a bad job. The rural party was reduced by stages to concentrating on even fewer and smaller clusters of isolated communists: first single communists generally, and then only a special élite of these. This was not a decent alternative to an extensive network of party organisations in the Soviets, collective farms and other production centres. The party did not lose entirely its grip on the countryside because it adopted more flexible, less total approaches to work methods.[31] But for those who had to supervise and control the rural party's operations, and for those who thought in hitherto traditional terms of a large, pervasive rural party organisation, its state in the mid-1930s was not a satisfying one. How the party authorities responded eventually to this state of affairs is the subject of subsequent chapters.

COMING FULL CIRCLE

We have already noted that there were misgivings about over-extending the rural party cell network even prior to the 1933 reorganisation. It was to be expected then that these concerns would resurface after the years 1933–34. Doubts were raised very early on in some quarters about the advisability of the 1933 reorganisation itself. Unfortunately we are unable to gauge how widespread was this discontent with the 1933 reorganisation, but suffice it to say that several criticisms were cited in the party's organisational journal. As early as June 1933 'some party members' were said to have resisted the breakdown of territorial cells on a production basis for fear that this would scatter excessively the party's manpower resources.[32] Despite such apprehensions, the June 1933 reorganisation went ahead. The smaller, dissipated version of the rural party which emerged did not correspond well with operational requirements as formulated at the beginning of the first Five Year Plan, when the rallying cry had been 'face to production'. But in the years 1934–37 the central authorities, whilst espousing the theme that the party had to lessen its direct involvement in economic processes, did not redefine its objectives clearly. This vagueness in operational methods engendered uncertainty in the debate on the party organisational structure: if discussants were not clear about the purposes of the party in the countryside, they could hardly make appropriate proposals. Furthermore, since some of the commentators sought to modify or reverse C.C. instructions, the debate was often muted and contained various circumlocutions to disguise the full intent of certain proposals.

Local party cadres obviously found difficulty in organising and monitoring the large number of single communists and small party units, and it was this problem which first led to suggestions for change. Citing the example of *raions* in the Vinnitsa *oblast*, Ukraine, M.Meksina, a regular contributor to several party journals, noted the neglect of single communists by *raikoms* and their instructors, and went beyond the bounds and against the spirit of C.C. instructions by recommending that three or four single communists working in institutions such as Soviets, schools, co-operatives and so forth in several different settlements should create a ppo; the C.C. had envisaged that single communists from separate settlements would remain such under *raikom* subordination.[33] Meksina's suggestion displayed a realisation that the rural communist party was reverting to an earlier stage of its evolution in the 1920s with many scattered individuals who, when not working in *kolkhozy*, ought to have been united in inter-settlement and perhaps eventually inter-Soviet ppos to create a sense of unity and to allow the *raikoms* to work through a smaller number of subordinate units.

Following quickly on the heels of Meksina's proposals, which were confined to territorial based ppos, another commentator, F. Chivirev, went one step further by advocating a mixture of *kolkhoznik* and non-*kolkhoznik* workers in one ppo or candidate group. Chivirev baulked at the idea of suggesting openly the reintroduction of inter-*kolkhoz* cells, which had been anathema in official pronouncements on party organisations since the summer of 1933. He complained firstly that the reduction in numbers of rural ppos was due to the purges, and sought to open the gates to *kolkhoz* cell membership by permitting 'single communists who work in the same territory as the kolkhoz' (and had no other connection) as well as *kolkhoz* household members who worked outside the *kolkhoz* to join existing *kolkhoz* ppos.[34] This still stopped short of reintroducing inter-*kolkhoz* cells joining together communists from more than one *kolkhoz*, but did suggest the creation of stronger, larger party units centred on a single *kolkhoz*, uniting a number of communists from within the *kolkhoz* and the surrounding area. Despite Chivirev's assertion to the contrary, this type of ppo infringed the production principle of cell organisation as laid down by the C.C.

Quite authoritative party commentators like Meksina and Chivirev were arguing in favour of a type of rural cell network that would consolidate and make better use of the dissipated manpower resources available and ensure greater solidarity among the rank and file rural communists. Was any attention paid to them and like-minded thinkers? Not until 1938, and then for different reasons. After recruitment was resumed towards the end of 1936 new ppos were essential to accommodate new recruits, rather than to consolidate isolated communists as had been the case in 1935–37. But the new ppos also incorporated many of these isolated communists. The results were the same, but the intent was different; and even the results came four or five years later than Meksina and Chivirev would have wished.

Renewed Expansion

As the rural party replenished its ranks at an almost identical rate to the whole party between January 1938 and January 1941, that is almost doubling in size, so too the number of rural ppos leapt upwards. In the two-year period 1939–41 the number of rural ppos rose from 40 000 to reach 82 956 by January 1941. This was quite spectacular growth. An important portion of these rural ppos were located in the *kolkhozy*: from the spring of 1939 to that of 1940, the number of *kolkhoz* ppos almost doubled from 12 000 to 22 000 and rose to 29 723 on 1 January 1941.[35] However, this increase in *kolkhoz* ppo numbers marked only a slight reversal of the trend during the second Five Year Plan for the number of *kolkhoz* ppos to decline very significantly as a proportion of all rural cells/ppos. Numerically at least, non-production based ppos had increased dramatically: as a proportion of all rural party cells/ppos they rose from 13.8 per cent in July 1932 to 24.7 per cent in January 1935 and approximately 50 per cent in March 1939. It would seem from this, and with at the beginning of 1941 only 29 723 ppos out of 82 723 located at *kolkhozy*, that the rural party's network had undergone a considerable transformation in the deployment of its organisations and in this sense, that of numbers deployed, was reverting to a large extent to a pre-collectivisation arrangement. However, *kolkhoz* and production ppos generally were larger in size (containing between 12 and 16 communists during 1939–41) than the territorial ppos. At the beginning of 1941, some 450 000 rural communists belonged to production based ppos, or 72 per cent of the membership, and yet production based ppos represented less than 50 per cent of rural ppos. The territorial based ppos contained then in 1941 approximately 170 000 communists in 53 000 units, giving them an average size of only three communists.[36] This is remarkably small and explains how the number of party units leapt so dramatically during 1939–41. These new territorial ppos contained the bare minimum of communists necessary to constitute a ppo under the party statutes. These territorial ppos were no doubt manned by the non-*kolkhoznik* recruits who joined the party in 1939. The fewer but comparatively much larger *kolkhoz* ppos managed to retain their importance in the rural party's network.

In the years immediately prior to the war, the rural party organisation was beginning to regain its hold on Soviet rural life. More rural Soviets and settlements than ever before contained a party organisation, albeit a very small one. The party's collective farm network was repairing the damage inflicted upon it during the second Five Year Plan years and rising from its pitiable position of 1937–39. By the beginning of 1941, the collective farms contained 30 000 ppos, just as they had done at the start of 1932: as then, they were quite decent-sized organisations with between 10–15 communists in each. The party in regard to its rural cells was reverting in many ways to the state of affairs that had existed during the first Five Year Plan.

11 The *raikom* 1933–39: Adapting to Change

Overshadowed by the political departments in 1933–34, the *raikoms* emerged as victors from the administrative-jurisdictional conflicts in the autumn of 1934. Prior to this the *raikom* internal structure had been transformed more fundamentally. This change – the replacement of *raikom* functional departments by a number of *raikom* instructors – was announced at the seventeenth party congress early in 1934 as part of a package of organisational innovations and modifications, the primary objective of which was to move the party's and state's organisational basis from a functional one to a production one. As a matter of fact, the gist of the reshaping of the *raikom* was contrary to the trend of the 1934 reorganisation. The following analysis seeks to explain why this was so.

RAIKOM INSTRUCTORS

Although not publicised at the seventeenth party congress, several variations on the theme of *raikom* instructors had been introduced before 1934. The localities which introduced the instructors felt the need to justify this initiative and their comments help to explain why this administrative reform came about. As a result of the June 1933 party cell reorganisation and purges, smaller party units and single communists proliferated. This made the *raikom* task of supervising its party subordinates more complex. In Bryansk *raion*, Western *oblast*, 27 cells had multiplied into 92 party units. The Bryansk town *raikom* responded by deploying seven group instructors (*kustovye instrucktory*), each allocated three-four rural Soviets, in order to ensure day-to-day supervision over the party network.[1] The proliferation of party units and single communists was rarely, if ever, mentioned in official announcements emanating from the C.C., but this was the major reason for the introduction of *raikom* instructors. Trends in the rural party membership and deployment were overtaking the normal organisational structure of the *raikom* and led some local party organisations to introduce spontaneously their own *raikom* instructors.

The abolition of the *raikom* functional departments was incorporated in the relevant C.C. resolution on organisational questions issuing from

170

the seventeenth party congress. It is worth quoting this document at length to bring out important points. After describing the orientation of party organisation on a production basis at the C.C. and *kraikom/obkom* levels, the resolution discussed the *raikom* in the following terms:

> To reorganise the raikoms' work *by drawing closer to production questions*, . . . To abolish in raikoms and gorkoms . . . all departments, and to have in their place roving [*raz"ezdnye*] responsible instructors – members of the raikoms and gorkoms with each of them attached to a specific group of primary (party) organisations, *in which they are responsible for organising all branches of party work: cultural-political-agitational-mass and organisational*. Supervision of the instructors' work, the deployment of cadres and verification of implementation lies with the [*raikom*] secretary and his deputy.[2] [My emphasis.]

There is an apparent contradiction here between the emphasis in the *raikom*'s operational role, which concentrates on 'production questions', and that of the instructors, which focuses on party-political questions; in fact the contradiction was to prove a real one. During the second Five Year Plan period the central authorities failed to articulate clearly what the local rural communist party's operational role was to be: whether it was to focus on economics or politics. This ambiguity persisted more or less until the Second World War. Instead of participating directly in the economy, the local party organisations were exhorted to turn inward in self-examination. The official line of argument was that the party had been too involved in economic management in 1929–32 and as a result had tended to neglect inner-party work. The *raikom* instructors' restricted brief, so orientated to party affairs, was one indication of this inward-looking direction. To summarise, the *raikom* instructors replaced the former functional departments because they were better suited to keep contact with the dispersed rural party network and because they could be adapted easily to concentrate on internal party affairs.

For the *apparatchiks* of the former *raikom* departments, most of whom were expected to transform themselves into roving instructors, the new job held few attractions. Instead of sitting in the relative comfort of the *raikom* centre, having people come to him, a former *raikom* department worker was expected to roam about the countryside, often on foot, in an effort to galvanise local primary party organisations and scattered single communists. In the Ukraine some former heads of *raikom* departments thought instruction work was 'beneath their dignity', and the posts attracted less well qualified people.[3] On 19 April 1934 the Ukrainian C.C. pointed out that *raikom* department heads had moved out of *raion* party work when they ought to have been actively encouraged to become *raikom* instructors.[4] By the spring of 1934, of a sample of 559 former *raikom* department heads in the Ukraine, only 295 had taken up posts as *raikom* instructors.[5] Among heads of organisational departments (*zavorgi*), a large proportion (123 out of 171) were selected to occupy the new post of deputy *raikom* secretary; this indicates that in practice they had already performed this role.[6] However, this again meant that many of the best qualified *raikom* party personnel and those most closely acquainted with internal party affairs remained in the *raikom* centre.

The changeover to a system of *raikom* instructors to co-ordinate party work disrupted the *raikom* functioning for several months in 1934. It coincided with a period of turmoil and uncertainty during the second of the major party purges, when the MTS political departments still existed but were visibly in decline.

A major reason for the confusion caused by introducing *raikom* instructors was the vagueness of the instructions emanating from the C.C. The relevant part of the C.C. resolution based on the report at the seventeenth party congress has already been cited, and it is unlikely that the C.C. elaborated on this before hitches arose. The resolution did emphasise the instructors' role in inner-party work but failed to clarify how extensively they were to be involved in and responsible for local economic affairs. It specified that each instructor was to be responsible for a certain number of ppos, but did not stress this nor forbid them to base themselves in *kolkhozy*, Soviets or settlements. This was in fact how most instructors chose to be deployed. The instructors centred themselves on *kolkhozy* and Soviets to be better able to supervise rural life generally and economic activities in particular. The *raikom* staff, secretaries and instructors alike, found great difficulty in breaking old habits. This is quite understandable, for while the central authorities were urging the local cadres to dissociate themselves from direct participation in day-to-day economic management, there was no hint that the *raikoms* had been released from their responsibilities for economic success. The *raikom* staff refused to disabuse themselves of the probably well-founded notion that they would be called to account for economic failure and they were therefore most reluctant to cease meddling in economic details in favour of a more general, overall, indirect supervision. By insisting that instructors concentrate on party work, this increasingly left only the *raikom* secretary, his deputy and technical staff to attend to all other matters of *raion* life; the burden of non-party institutions had to be, and was, increased.

The *raikoms*, somewhat bemused by the reorganisation, were not always sure how to relate to their instructors, whose work was also hindered by logistical problems. Some *raikoms* kept their instructors under too strict control, ordering them to return frequently to the *raion* centre with written reports; others allowed their instructors to roam loose.[7] The instructors were further hampered in their work by problems relating to transport, housing and wages.

Despite these problems and the tumultuous times in which they were inaugurated, the *raikom* instructors survived and flourished. They became a major concern of the newly formed departments of leading party organs (ORPOs – *otdely rukovodyashchikh partiinykh organov*).[8] Given the circumstances of a more dispersed rural party membership and the authorities' expressed desire of focusing on inner-party work, the *raikom* instructor system was quite suitable. One wonders whether it was stumbled upon by accident after some spontaneous regional experimentation in 1933; certainly many *ad hoc* measures were employed in the organisation of *gorkoms* and *raikoms* in 1934–35.

In the towns during 1934–35 a reassessment of the middle level party organisation (*gorkom* – the equivalent of the rural *raikom*) was made to ensure that these party units were well equipped and prepared to focus on party work. This did not happen in the rural *raikoms*. With regard to party work, the rural *raikom* was reasonably satisfactory: the *raikom* instructors supervised the rank and file rural communists, while the ORPOs at the *obkoms* paid close attention to the *raikom* staffs, secretaries as well as instructors. Instead, the rural *raikom*'s organisation was thought to require modification because it had swung too quickly and too far from facilitating the supervision of economic affairs. In these years when the objective seemed to be only general and indirect economic supervision, it was still felt more beneficial for the *raikoms* to have some sort of department to assimilate and co-ordinate agricultural information and campaigns, rather than leave these matters to loose *ad hoc* arrangements. The C.C. recognised this at the end of 1934, at the same time as the *raikom*'s importance was reasserted with the abolition of the MTS political departments. In the November 1934 C.C. resolution on political departments in agriculture, the post of second *raikom* secretary was created in the 'largest agricultural raions' and new agricultural departments were inaugurated in all *raikoms*, headed by the *raikom* secretary or his new deputy, a point which underlines the new departments' importance.[9] This was not a complete reversal to concentrating on production, as had happened in the first Five Year Plan period, and the *raikoms* were exhorted repeatedly not to neglect inner-party work by devoting all their time and energies to economic matters. Some balance had returned to the distribution of the *raikom* organisation and personnel between inner party and economic questions. A useful division of labour had been created: the *raikom* secretary or his deputy and some assistants oversaw general economic policy, plans and campaigns within the *raion*, working in conjunction with other institutions – the rural Soviets, *kolkhoz* administrations, the MTS and *sovkhoz* directors, the grain procurement agencies. The *raikom* instructors roamed the countryside looking after the *raion*'s often small number of communists, busying themselves with party education and propaganda among the non-party masses and often acted as *raikom* plenipotentiaries or messengers in economic campaigns.

THE CREATION OF NEW *RAIKOMS* IN 1935

The position of the *raikoms* in the party structure was from 1929 onwards a vitally important one and recognised as such except briefly in 1933 when, to cope with an emergency, the political departments superseded them. With the abolition of the MTS political departments at the end of 1934 the *raikoms* were greatly strengthened, not simply by the fact that the departments had gone but because their staffs were incorporated into existing and newly created *raikoms*.

As a consequence of the abolition of MTS political departments and the attempt to incorporate a large proportion of their staff into the *raikom* network, some 800–900 new *raions* were established by dividing existing units. Between January 1933 and June 1936 the number of rural *raions* rose from 2466 to 3269. Where possible, the new *raion* centres were to be constructed around convenient MTS. The breaking up in size of *raions* meant that when the new *raikoms* were fully staffed, their workload was lessened in comparison with the former larger *raions*: *raikom* instructors had fewer ppos to supervise; the *raikom* was responsible for fewer economic units and a smaller population and was regarded as more capable of keeping a closer watch over all aspects of rural life. This breaking down process also facilitated internal *raion* control. But *obkoms* and *kraikoms* now had to cope with a larger number of sub-units.

It has already been noted that transfer of party personnel in large numbers was usually attended by difficulties.[10] Their transfer to new *raions* was no exception. However, on this occasion the problems arose less from recalcitrance on the part of the political department personnel who were being transferred, than from the inability of the *obkom* to co-ordinate a complex administrative operation and the reluctance of existing *raikom* personnel to be moved about and make way for outsiders. The Orenburg *obkom* and *oblast* institutions nominated workers for the new *raions* but 'almost nobody arrived'.[11] This was reminiscent of the transfer of *okrug* personnel to the *raions* in 1930, as was the language employed by the authorities: 'Party organisations must decisively put a stop to similar occurrences of a non-party, anti-state attitude of some communists to the organisation of new raions'.[12] The reasons behind some of this were in large part similar to those of 1930. 'Specialists' to be sent to one *raion* refused to go because of poor 'living social conditions'.[13] It was a lack of basic amenities which deterred the less hardy from leaving their home ground. Life was by no means luxurious in the established *raions*; it was less likely to be so in the new *raions*. Some of the latter were without reading huts, hospitals, libraries, cinemas, radios or telephones.[14] Not all the former MTS political department staff were transferred to the *raikoms*; some remained in the MTS to become their directors, others took up the newly created post of deputy director of the MTS for political affairs. This one man post was a mere shadow of the former prestigious political departments. These MTS deputies worked very much in the shadow of the *raikoms* and did not encroach on their jurisdiction, thereby avoiding former wrangling.

As the average size of *raions* was reduced, simultaneously most *raion* party organisations experienced sharply declining membership figures as a result of the purges. Concurrently the rural party was disengaging itself from direct involvement in economic affairs. For all these reasons it was decided in a resolution of 20 March 1936 to downgrade the rights and responsibilities of those *raikom* bureaux in *raions* where party membership was less than 100. A significant number of *raikoms* was affected: 795 out of 3269.[15] The *raion* committees, composed mostly ex officio of the *raion*'s leading party and state personalities, were reduced in number, and the number of *raikom* staff size was diminished. In 1936 the Lazorskii *raikom* staff of 12 full-time party workers for a member-ship of 120 communists was criticised as being excessively large.[16] In the Moscow *oblast* the move to reducing the number of *raikom* staff had already begun in 1934 when full-time staff were reduced by 40 per cent leaving on average 8–12 full-time party workers.[17] In comparison, the full-time staff of *raikoms* during the first Five Year Plan, after the abolition of the *okrugs*, depending on the size of *raions*, varied between

10–15 for smaller ones and 20–25 for larger ones.[18]

Although some of the *raion* party committees and their staffs were reduced in size, the *raikom* as a party unit did not decline in importance. The impact of the transfer of 1500 former heads of MTS political departments to *raikom* secretaryships was considerable and elevated the average quality of those occupying the post in terms of party *stazh* and party work experience: moreover, from the point of view of social origin more were now from an urban background. In recognition of the *raikom* secretary's status and pivotal position in the party hierarchy, the C.C. included this post in its *nomenklatura* along with that of the MTS deputy director for political affairs.[19] This was stipulated in the November 1934 plenum resolution; prior to this at the seventeenth party congress the necessary minimum party *stazh* for a *raikom* secretary was raised from five years to seven.[20]

Inclusion of the *raikom* first secretary in the C.C. *nomenklatura* was also aimed at reducing the level of turnover. This may have been because the high level of turnover had not abated significantly during the relatively calm year of 1934.[21] Among the reasons given for removals in 1934 a comparative novelty was the category of those removed for suppressing self criticism. This may have indicated the beginnings of a campaign to subject the middle link party cadres to greater scrutiny and accountability from their subordinates, a campaign which culminated in the *Ezhovshchina*. Those removed for excesses fell foul of the 'thaw' of 1934 when unreasonable actions against the *kolkhoznik* population were frowned upon. This did not mean that party cadres had to reject harsh methods in fulfilling economic goals, only that they were to eschew them when they did not conflict with economic objectives and to seek a *modus vivendi* with the rural population, a new approach which was given much publicity in later years.[22]

Little precise information is available on the composition of the *raikom* personnel in 1935–37, but a campaign to improve the educational qualifications of *raikom* secretaries received prominence in 1936. This was another element in the 'face to the party' movement, with its emphasis on party education and ideology. *Raikom* secretaries were urged to study more; the consensus was that middle level education was a basic requirement. If this was the case, there was room for improvement. In mid-1936 in the Saratov *krai*, of a sample of 69 *raikom* secretaries, 11 had higher education, 26 middle education, but as many as 32 had only lower education; at the same time in the Northern *krai* only 12 per cent of *raikom* secretaries had middle education.[23] As the level of technology rose, as more 'Red experts' were recruited and promoted to state, trade and agricultural organisations, so too the *raikom* secretaries were obliged to buckle down to serious study to equip themselves for the rapidly modernising Soviet countryside. The *raikoms* and their staffs were adapting to a changing environment.

This adaptation to a changing environment was the theme for the *raikoms* in the second Five Year Plan period. The *raikom*'s internal organisation and size were altered to cope better and to correspond with a dwindling rural party membership: the *raikom* instructors were better suited to supervise and visit scattered ppos and communists than the former *raikom* departments; with smaller *raion* party memberships the *raikom* staff size and administrative structure could be rationalised; as the *raikom*'s responsibilities and duties became more wide-ranging, complex and technically orientated, so the calibre of *raikom* secretaries had to be improved by drafting in the experienced former heads of MTS political departments and by improving educational standards generally.

REORGANISATION IN THE *OBKOMS, KRAIKOMS* AND CENTRAL COMMITTEE

The seventeenth party congress convening early in 1934 proved a convenient juncture at which to introduce broad organisational reforms. The 1934 reorganisation entailed basing the party at C.C. and *oblast/krai* level, but not in the *raions*, on production orientated branches. The 'integral production branch departments' established at C.C. level were those for agriculture, industry, transport, planning-finance-trade, political-administrative, leading party organs (ORPOs), the Institute for Marx, Engels, Lenin and two sectors, one for administration and the other a special sector. These were less extensive at the *obkom/kraikom* level and included departments for agriculture, industry-transport, Soviet-trade, culture and propaganda of Leninism, an ORPO and a special sector. Each department was responsible for all work connected to its branch of production: for example, in the C.C. agricultural department this encompassed organisational party work, deployment and training of cadres, agitational-mass work, production propaganda, supervision over the fulfilling of party decisions by the relevant Soviet, economic and party organisation.[24]

At the seventeenth congress, the Central Control Commission (C.C.C.), hitherto responsible for party disciplinary matters, was replaced by a Commission of Party Supervision (KPK), which acquired all the C.C.C.'s apparatus.[25] The responsibilities of the KPKs were defined as supervising the fulfilment of party decisions, and bringing to account those who infringed party discipline or party 'etiquette'. The work of the KPKs overlapped that of the ORPOs in the sphere of checking the implementation by local party committees of congress and C.C. decisions. These departments of leading party organs (ORPOs) were created at the same time as the KPKs. The ORPOs, which existed from 1934 to 1939, dealt with the selection and deployment of party cadres in the *obkoms* and *raikoms*, whilst the various production-branch departments handled personnel matters, both party and non-party, within their own production sectors. The authorities were seeking greater control over party personnel who could quite easily become 'lost' when stationed hundreds or thousands of miles away from Moscow. Nor, does it seem, were the ORPOs an immediate solution to this problem for in a top-secret circular dated August 1935 Ezhov admitted: 'It is necessary to say that in the C.C. apparat we are presently beginning only now to find out the composition of the leading party workers in the oblasts and raions'.[26] The C.C.'s cadre selection was limited to intervention in the posting of high level personnel. Beneath this the *obkoms/kraikoms* supervised the *raikoms* and *gorkoms* who in turn supervised their ppos; there was considerable local autonomy. This has led one scholar to conclude that 'Moscow's writ was by no means law everywhere in the 1930s'.[27] This was especially true in the countryside.

The ORPOs, and to a lesser extent the KPKs, should be seen as devices to put this right. Kaganovich, speaking at the 1934 party congress, noted that the *obkoms* and *kraikoms* had been working badly in their supervision and control of the raions in the 'last two or three years', and he hoped that the ORPOs would improve supervision and verification of decision implementation.[28] Along these lines the ORPOs were instructed to compile details on some 800 responsible *raion* party workers in each *krai* or *oblast* and to create a reserve of about 100–150 to replace those *raikom* cadres not up to scratch.[29] It is unlikely that the ORPOs were constructed consciously as a tool to be used in the *Ezhovshchina*, but the results of their work, the data collated by them, did in fact supply future purgers with valuable information on party personnel and facilitated the purge operation, as it did the promotion of those thought suitable to step into new posts.

The ORPOs comprised a chief, a deputy, two instructors, two information workers, two accountants and two technical workers, making a staff of ten. This was not large nor a great number of instructors to supervise anything between 50–150 *raions*, and therefore to supplement their ranks they could employ non-staff instructors.[30] Their workload was a heavy one, especially when attention was being focused on inner-party work, personnel selection questions and the increase in technical-educational qualifications. Nor could the ORPOs rid themselves entirely of economic concerns. On one occasion, as a helpful hint, the ORPOs were advised to economise their time by conducting time-consuming complete surveys of a *raikom*'s operations only when its political-*economic* results warranted it. This suggests that the *raikoms* were still being judged on the economic performance of their *raions* and that the ORPOs were not to dedicate themselves solely to party affairs, inextricably linked as they were to the economy. None the less, in comparison with the former organisational-instruction departments (*orginst*) in the *obkoms*, the ORPOs distinguished themselves by restricting their duties to monitoring party workers' performance; they were much less general in their approach and less economy orientated.

12 The Role of the Rural Communist Party 1933–39 and in Perspective

INTRODUCTION

Over the years the role of the rural communist party changed; there is a vivid contrast between the first and second Five Year Plan periods. During the first Five Year Plan the party's priorities were the supervision and control of the economy and direct participation in economic processes by party members; in the period 1934–37 this system of operation was downgraded as party cadres were instructed insistently to focus more attention on party affairs and inner-party work.

Before continuing further we should clarify our understanding of party work and economic supervision and control. 'Party work' is not difficult to define. It refers to the recruitment, placement and education of party personnel including cadres and the rank and file, the development of effective party organisation aided by improved intra-party communications and the monitoring of performance of various party units and individuals; 'inner-party work' also includes all operations to do with party purges, and verification and exchange of party cards. 'Mass-party work' involved the dissemination of the regime's values and objectives among the population by means of meetings, speeches and courses. The meaning of 'economic work' changed in emphasis with time and could mean the direction, supervision, control of and involvement in economic affairs by communists. We seek here to distinguish between the two stages of party involvement in economic matters in the years 1929–39. During the 1920s the rural communist party's concern with agricultural production had been marginal. At the beginning of the first Five Year Plan and until 1934, the rural party was turned 'face to production', its operational model was one in which it was supposed to maintain general supervision over all aspects of economic affairs and in addition sought to deploy large numbers of communists directly in the production processes in the *holkhozy*, *sovkhozy* and MTS. The rank and file rural communists, the cells and party committees were held responsible for economic success and failure

180

in their area. From the end of 1929 to 1934 the rural party, owing to the precariousness of the newly established socialised agricultural sector, was obliged to experiment in taking control of rural economic activity. But towards the end of 1932 the rural economy had almost collapsed and parts of the rural population were on the verge of open revolt. The political departments managed to stabilise the situation but could not initiate marked production success. A change of course was called for. Beginning in 1934 the policy became to confine the rural party's role to a supervisory, co-ordinating one. This is a most important distinction which needs to be made clear from the outset.

As the rural party modified its involvement in the economy, more emphasis was placed on party work. There are several reasons to explain this shift. Firstly, the party's direct participation in and administration of the economy had not brought resounding success, producing few material results in return for considerable time and energy. This point is linked to our second reason, the party purges. These required that the party examine closely its personnel. Thirdly, the effects of the purges, resulting in a huge diminution of party forces, particularly in the rural party, meant that it was no longer physically possible to maintain large numbers of communists working in production or even for them to retain a controlling influence; more and more settlements and *kolkhozy* were without communists or had only a minimal presence. The 'face to the party' movement, in contrast to the rallying cry 'face to production', was brought about in large part because the party no longer disposed of manpower resources in adequate numbers to attempt to delve into economic processes; the rural party had little choice but to become more inward-looking. The party's move away from the economy was facilitated and indeed made possible by the fact that other individuals and organisations were able to step into its shoes and take on some, but not necessarily all, of its duties.

In this chapter a discussion of the timing and the method of the party's disengagement from the economy is followed by an examination of the important question of why the central party authorities felt the regime secure enough to do away with close party control in the countryside.

PARTY AND ECONOMIC WORK: THE CAMPAIGN TO EXTRICATE THE PARTY FROM ECONOMIC INVOLVEMENT

The policy of disengaging the party from economic involvement was first authoritatively articulated at the seventeenth party congress in early

1934 and was repeated *ad nauseam* for the next three or four years. This repetition was necessary: old habits died hard among local communists who experienced difficulty in breaking the routine of earlier years. Furthermore, party members were most reluctant to desist from their direct involvement in economic management as long as they were still held responsible for economic failure and did not feel confident enough to leave crucial affairs in the hands of others. Gradually, and by about 1937, a certain ambiguity set into policy articulation with emphasis placed on balance between party and economic work. There were those who advocated reverting to close participation in the economy, especially in the years immediately prior to the war. This was particularly the case with the rural economy.

An examination follows of how the party was asked to make these adaptations, what problems were encountered and why a distinction was made between the rural and urban economies.

It is possible to estimate fairly precisely to within a few months when the shift in the party's operational role occurred. The C.C. resolution of 22 March 1933 dealing with the activities of two *kolkhoz* cells focused entirely on the participation of party forces in economic processes.[1] The resolution spoke in the language of the first Five Year Plan and its gist was that the *kolkhoz* party cells must concentrate on the *kolkhoz* economy; communists were criticised for not delving into details. It was most striking that internal party work was not mentioned once in a resolution five large printed pages in length. When 'party-political' work was referred to, it was connected directly to the 'kolkhoz production life'.[2] This resolution's recommendations and its underlying theme soon became outmoded. It is remarkable how only a few months later the severest criticism was reserved for those who did 'meddle' in economic detail; this became a grave error. The resolution itself warned communists that they would be judged on the basis of their performance in economic activities and by how well the *kolkhoz* fulfilled its grain procurement plans; this would be borne in mind 'particularly in connection with the forthcoming purge'.[3] Once large numbers of rural communists were purged or drifted from the party, it no longer disposed of sufficient communists to control *kolkhoz* and brigade activities.

In 1933 it was still somewhat early to talk of disengaging party forces from economic involvement when the political departments and many thousands of urban communists had been mobilised for this very purpose. But the 1933 harvest period was the rural communist party's 'last hurrah' in this type of large-scale, grass-roots participation for several years to come. Within a couple of months of the 22 March 1933

C.C. resolution, there were calls for more balance between economic and party work.[4] Towards the end of 1933 political departments were advised to focus more on party matters rather than discussing endlessly and solely topics such as the spring sowing and fulfilment of milk and meat plans.[5] This shift in policy was adumbrated in 1933 for the reasons enumerated earlier and because, after the comparatively successful 1933 grain procurement campaign, the regime in the countryside was stabilised.

It was at the seventeenth party congress that the policy change in the party's operational role was elucidated. Kaganovich argued in his report that during the first Five Year Plan the party had immersed itself in the day-to-day running of agriculture with meagre results and to the detriment of inner-party work.[6] He gave notice that the authorities would no longer support direct interference in production activities by local party officials; instead much more reliance on the regular administrative organs was required. In a speech eight months later Kaganovich was more emphatic that the *raion* party organisations were not to become bogged down in economic questions and he specified the party's major preoccupations henceforth with the phrase 'It is necessary to love party work'.[7]

Beginning in spring 1935 the favouring of a redirection in the rural party's operational role was articulated more frequently. *Raikoms* were told to make a sensible distinction: they were not to dissociate themselves completely from economic questions but to avoid meddling in day-to-day management. This latter duty was in the purview of the other bodies: 'It is time . . . for the growing cadres of Soviet and economic workers to conduct independently their operational work'.[8] The *raikoms* had now to delegate operational work more and content themselves with a co-ordinating, supervisory role. This view persisted, not without shifts of emphasis and various nuances, into 1937. In the early months of 1937 and throughout the year this line of argument was used as a weapon against party *apparatchiks*. With regard to the Kiev party organisation under the secretaryship of Postyshev, it was stated that the party had been carried away by economic details to the detriment of political leadership. Not infrequently the *obkom* and *raikoms* had discussed heatedly economic minutiae and neglected the party membership. The *obkom* agricultural department was accused of merging into the land department and usurping the role of *Narkomzem* at the *oblast* level:

party organisations must not replace the Soviet and economic apparatus, must not take over [*podmenyat'*] their work, but with the political mobilisation of the masses they must achieve the implementation of the party line in all sectors of socialist construction.[9]

This was the standard proposal to secure economic success by indirect methods and it was a criticism of past failings used against party officials to undermine their position during the *Ezhovshchina*.

The years 1934–36 marked the peak in agitation for disengaging the party from participation in economic management, although it was not always clear what was required. It seems that beginning in 1936 fears were nurtured that the party was going to the opposite extreme of overemphasising party work; calls were voiced in favour of greater balance between party and economic work. To complicate matters, the local rural party cadres were unwilling to make the distinction between leading economic activities from above by indirect methods of supervision and co-ordination and leading by direct administering and interference. This was because they were still held responsible for economic success, and as far as they were concerned, the authorities' instructions were ambiguous, changeable, confusing and placed them in a vulnerable position of relying on others, whose performance would determine their own fate. Therefore, the 'majority of local party officials ... usually interpreted these conflicting instructions to mean that overinterference would be considered less of a sin than underinterference'.[10]

Certainly the policy line on the rural party's operational role seems to vary or change emphasis during the second Five Year Plan: in 1933 production success and direct involvement is still the key; in 1934–36 the emphasis shifts back to party work and in 1936–37 the consensus seems to favour neither party or economic work to the detriment of the other. The emphasis of articles published in the press may have depended on the outlook, mood or responsibilities of the individual authors concerned. M. Khataevich, first *obkom* secretary in the Dnepropetrovsk *oblast*, in an article six columns long published in *Pravda* on the forthcoming tasks in the 1936 harvest, made the briefest mention of the party (a mere two lines).[11] Conversely, at about the same time as Khataevich's writing, D. Gurevich, the deputy head of the C.C.'s agricultural department, supported the party's return to involvement in the economy. He urged party organisations to participate actively at all levels in the harvest, to extend socialist competition and to promote the Stakhanovite movement in agriculture.[12] Gurevich and his colleagues in the agricultural department obviously had a vested interest in seeing that the party cadres took their responsibilities for agricultural performance as seriously as possible and did not relegate them in favour of party work. The article's timing (August 1936) is significant, a time when early harvest results would be arriving in Moscow, whereupon the authorities would have drawn the conclusion that the 1936 harvest was about to prove abysmally low.

The involvement in the economy was a question of degree. Although in 1937 regional party secretaries such as Postyshev were accused of excessive meddling in economic activities, it was in this year, perhaps as a partial response to the very poor 1936 harvest, that a return to economic involvement was more frequently publicised and advocated more insistently than at any other time since 1933. *Raikom* secretaries in the West Siberian *krai* were rebuked for detaching themselves from agricultural campaigns: secretaries were quoted reprovingly as saying 'I don't take part in economic or sowing questions' and 'raion party committees are not involved now in such [economic] matters'.[13] These particular local party cadres had responded enthusiastically to appeals to disengage from the economy, but as far as the authorities were now concerned, they had reacted excessively and gone to an extreme. A *Pravda* editorial of the spring 1937 explained what was expected of local party organisations, in this case in the important southern grain regions, and disabused them of any misconceptions they might have harboured on the subject:

It is necessary to warn again the party and Soviet organisations of the southern regions that any further delay in sowing is a crime against the state's interests . . . Again and again it is necessary to explain to party organisations that nobody released them from leadership over agriculture and in particular of sowing.[14]

A very interesting commentary appeared in another *Pravda* editorial at about the same time. It drew a clear distinction between agriculture and the rest of the economy. It proposed that agriculture be made an exception, one in which the party organisations could still 'concern themselves with even the details of economic construction' because in agricultural organisations 'the cadres were weaker and less well trained' than their counterparts in industry, who were to be allowed a freer hand.[15] In this post-1936 period the rural party was distinguished from the party working in industry. The need for more constant party supervision in agriculture arose from the comparative weakness of agriculture and state organisations in the countryside. The difficulties of agriculture loomed larger than those of industry. In the attempt to harness agriculture all human resources were employed, few could be regarded as superfluous. Even the rural party's partial detachment from agriculture was no longer sponsored.

This policy became feasible when the rural party began to replenish its ranks in 1938. Once again the rural party disposed of relatively large manpower resources and was able to revert to direct participation at the grass-roots level of production, something it had been unable to do in 1934–38 on account of purge losses. The culmination of this reversal to the methods of the first Five Year Plan era was expressed thus in the summer of 1939: 'The party, if it wishes to direct the kolkhoz movement, must enter into all details of kolkhoz management. From this it follows that the party must not decrease but multiply its links with the kolkhozy.'[16] The party's exceptionally high profile in agriculture was highlighted in organisational terms when the C.C. agricultural department was retained in spite of the reintroduction of functionalism at the eighteenth party congress in March 1939. There are grounds, it seems, to relate the rural party's involvement in the economy to its size. Simultaneously with the 'face to production' drive, rural party membership figures leapt up, as did those of the entire party. When the authorities blamed the local party organisations for the rural economic débâcle of 1932, an extensive purge, which drastically reduced rural party size, ensured that it would disengage from the economy: this was an objective consequence of the purge and at the same time, since close rural party involvement in the economy had shown so few successful results, one probably consciously desired by the authorities. With the major resumption of rural party recruitment taking place in 1938 and 1939, the rural party was encouraged again to adopt a larger, more immediate profile in production.

With the rural communist party a shrinking organisation and playing a lesser role in rural life in 1933–37, one wonders how the regime could dispense in large part with the party's services and what took its place. The question can best be answered by first stating that the rural party in the past had never approached ubiquitousness. Furthermore, the rural party was dispensed with in large part but not entirely; important outposts remained. The *raikoms* retained their pivotal position in co-ordinating and supervising the life of the *raion*. A high proportion of single communists worked in key economic, administrative posts as *kolkhoz* or rural Soviet chairmen. The rural party also retained a considerable presence at the other key points of MTS and *sovkhoz*. Notwithstanding these vestiges, the rural communist party existed in a very emasculated form. A major reason why the party's role could be downgraded in this period was that the peasantry has been pacified after the experiences of 1932–34. The bulk of the peasantry realised that they would henceforth lose any test of strength with the regime. In this pacification the authorities did not solely employ terror. In spring 1932 *kolkhoz* markets were introduced, followed by a more equitable system of assigning procurement quotas in January 1933. Another notable factor in placating peasant discontent was the private plot. Reassured of this safety net, the peasants' discontent became less manifest; whether underlying dissatisfaction had evaporated is another matter. After the trauma of 1932–34 the *kolkhozy* were consolidated, the countryside stabilised, and there was less need for tight party control. The regime was also fortunate that the very bad 1936 harvest was followed by the excellent one of 1937 which prevented a repetition of the harrowing effects of the two poor harvests in 1931 and 1932, combined as they were with harsh procurement plans. Close party control and a pervasive party network could be dispensed with as other non-party organisations came into their own, such as the rural Soviets, the *raion* land department (*raizo*), the *kolkhoz* administration, the grain procurement agencies and the *komsomol*: this was perhaps a response to the party's diminution as much as a cause or precondition.

And yet the procedure may not have been as foreseen nor as logical as implied here. Perhaps the consequences of the curtailment in recruitment, in conjunction with severe purging, were not fully realised. It seems that there may well have been conflicting assessments of what type of organisation the rural party was becoming in the purge years.[17] Or perhaps the central party authorities, and Stalin in particular, regarded the turmoil of 1933–37 and the downgrading of the party's role as a necessary concomitant of the major transformation in the party's personnel. There is a case for conjecturing that the whole episode of the small-scale rural communist party in these years was an aberration, quickly rectified in later years and never reverted to since.

Conclusion

Five models for rural party involvement in rural economic affairs have been distinguished. The first existed prior to 1929 and was a very loose arrangement under which the local rural party concerned itself little with any supervisory or participatory role in agriculture; production and deliveries did not figure much in the party's purview.[18] The second model, that of the first Five Year Plan and 1933, entailed the rural party being responsible for economic success and failure, endeavouring to supervise *and* control the rural economy in addition to deploying communists directly in production processes. The third model lasted from 1934 until sometime in 1937 and consisted of the rural party limiting itself to a supervisory, co-ordinating role from the *raikom* with most direct participation in production rejected; at the same time much greater emphasis was laid on party work. The fourth model endured between 1937 and 1939 and represented a transition stage between the third and fifth models. Here the *raikoms* were given more opportunity to dabble and to interfere in production when they identified bottle necks, which had always been their inclination since 1929 in any case. The fifth model took shape in 1939 and saw a return to the second model of the first Five Year Plan, where an expanding rural party took upon itself more economic duties: for the *raikom*, those of supervision, direction and control, and for the ppos that of direct participation. This was interrupted by the war.

The first Five Year Plan period was one of experimentation in rural party organisation and in the degree to which the party sought to control the economy. During 1929–33 the party commanded the rural economy to ensure that agricultural produce was delivered to the towns on the state's terms. After 1933 the party reverted more to the role of prompter and only recommenced direct participation in economic activities in the immediate pre-war years. In the post-war period the rural communist party has grown in size and expanded its organisational network.

Perhaps the most lasting indication that the party had outlived its temporary aberration of almost doing without a rural party network in the mid-1930s was the post-war consolidation, which saw the proportion of *kolkhozy* possessing a party organisation rise from 12.5 per cent in 1941 to 80 per cent in 1953.[19] The rural party's organisational picture from 1946–47 resembled that of 1931–32 with the party in the *kolkhoz* sector blooming and the territorial party organisations diminishing relatively. The party authorities had finally decided to keep faith with the rural party organisation elaborated during the first Five Year Plan period. This resurgence in the rural party's organisational network was necessary as the rural party adapted to its role of direct involvement in the post-war reconstruction of the rural economy. Communist involvement in production was once again equated with economic success. Successful *kolkhozy* were those where the 'party organisation delves into all the details of kolkhoz production, tenders daily assistance to the artel's administration'; it was necessary again 'to raise the communists' role in the kolkhozy'.[20]

The model which has endured after the war period, after the frenetic, immediate post-war reconstruction phase, was one where economic management personnel, of a higher calibre and with better educational qualifications than their pre-war counterparts, have been granted a considerable degree of independence and the principle of one man management perpetuated.[21] This system has developed as the state and economic institutions have matured and as more and more administrative, economic, managerial personnel have joined the party. As better qualified agricultural experts and rural administrators joined the party, there was less cause to doubt their loyalty. There was no longer the same need to have the party acting as an interfering overseer. With a large, pervasive rural communist party and trained, educated administrators, both communist and non-party, there was more opportunity for party and rural society to blend together; certainly more opportunity than there had been in the 1930s.

13 Conclusions

At the end of the 1920s, after several years of comparative stability under the New Economic Policy (NEP), the Soviet leadership embarked upon a programme of massive economic expansion incorporating industrialisation and collectivisation. The greatest shocks and repercussions of this colossal effort to transform society were felt in the countryside, where an attempt was made to socialise the means of production and to transfer millions of peasant households into collective and state farms. Few ground plans for this policy had been laid before 1929 because of the ambiguity over the essence of NEP and, connected with this, because of the splits in the political leadership. The rural communist party, along with other organisations, was caught unaware by the sweep of the collectivisation programme and spent most of the first Five Year Plan adjusting to it. It is important to note, however, that the party's relations with the rural population had already begun to change thanks to the measures adopted during the 1928 grain crisis. The atmosphere of a comparatively relaxed *modus vivendi*, which had reigned for much of the mid-1920s, was dispelled. The showing of the rural party in the 1928 grain crisis was such as to alienate it sufficiently from many elements of the local population without satisfying the demands of the centre (see Chapter 1).

The central party authorities were convinced that the rural party of the 1920s was, by social composition and outlook, unable to cope with the demands of the new policies now being imposed on the countryside. This conviction found striking expression in the party purge. This purge was designed to shape and prepare the rural party for collectivisation. At the same time, rural communists were mobilised ahead of the non-party peasantry to join the collective farms. Several suggestions were proposed why the rural communist party acted in this instance in a vanguard role, one to which it was not accustomed in the 1920s (see Chapter 3).

The purge was accompanied and followed by a major recruitment drive. The major impact of collectivisation upon the rural party membership was seen in recruitment policies adopted towards the end of 1929 and the resultant change in composition. In size the rural communist party increased by as much as 132 per cent, from 358 936 in July 1929 to 832 000 in July 1932. Between January 1930 and July 1932 rural party membership rose from 20.2 per cent to 26.6 per cent of the membership of the party as a whole. The change was not merely a quantitative one; the rural party's composition altered markedly. The proportion of peasant recruits to the whole party rose sharply in the second quarter of the 1930 from 11.9 per cent to 20 per cent. *Kolkhozniks* within the rural party rose from a mere five per cent in 1928 to two-thirds of the membership in mid-1932. Also, in addition to *kolkhozniks*, the proportion of *batraks* and agricultural workers in the rural party rose from 7.6 per cent in July 1928 to 16.2 per cent in January 1932. During mass collectivisation these are features one might expect. This build up in size was necessary to keep pace with the expanding socialised economy. Necessary because it was a *sine qua non* of the face to production drive beginning in 1929 that economic expansion be matched by political-organisational expansion, and the role of monitor and guardian over the socialised economy was allotted to the party. And yet for the duration of the first Five Year Plan, the authorities were frustrated in their aim to mobilise a substantial portion of rural party forces to work directly in production (see Chapters 3 and 8). Nevertheless, the location, occupation and concerns of rural communists had undergone fundamental change since the 1920s; they now lived in collective farms, engaged more were in agriculture, certainly during the major agricultural campaigns, more in production jobs and many in positions of responsibility such as *kolkhoz* chairmen and *kolkhoz* administrators.

In order to supervise and administer this growing number of rural communists working in a changing environment, the party organisation was modified and developed. The district party committee (*raikom*), covering on average 8–10 000 households, became the key administrative unit at the local level in the party's hierarchy. The rural party organisation was stream-lined and the *raikoms* strengthened with the abolition of the *okrug* level and the transfer of their personnel to the *raions* (see Chapter 4). Communists were deployed in an expanded network of rural party cells, which developed their internal organisation and level of sophistication: much thought and energy were expended in trying to establish a satisfactory organisational structure in the countryside. A variety of cell types sprouted in the countryside as the party endeavoured to adapt to local conditions. To co-ordinate the cells' work and to improve contacts with the *raikoms*, experimentation was conducted with the construction of support points, designed to unite several party cells in a developed form of the inter-*kolkhoz* cell, but jurisdictional wrangles occurred about whether the support points were usurping the *raikom*'s position and discussions were initiated about the most desirable level of sophistication at the cell level (see Chapter 5).

This expanded membership and organisation were adapted to the party's new role of supervision and control over production and the delivery of agricultural produce to the state. Rural communists perceived their major function to be concern for agricultural procurements and related economic matters. The complex, hectic relationship between *raikom* and cells in conducting operations was examined in a case-study based on the Smolensk archives of the Monastyrshchi *raikom*. The *raikoms* played generally a more important role than the cells because they were part of a more pervasive, national network and staffed with better trained, more experienced personnel. The cells, on the other hand, often contained no more than a handful of communists, many of only candidate status, and did not exist in many of the important production centres. The machine tractor stations (MTS) and state farms (*sovkhozy*) fared best in possessing a party unit on account of their comparatively small numbers which facilitated party coverage in them. But even when rural party membership was at its peak in 1932, only 20 per cent of *kolkhozy* contained a party unit; without a party presence, there could be no direct party influence (see Chapter 5). The *raikom*'s general supervision of the *raion* and a variety of urban plenipotentiaries mitigated this shortcoming to some degree, but they were an imperfect substitute for a pervasive, mass rural party organisa- tion. Towards the end of the first Five Year Plan, the rural party was on the verge of becoming a mass organisation in rural society with a membership quickly approaching, if recruitment had continued, the one million mark. The party purges, however, intervened.

The dramatic upheaval in rural economic life, caused in the main by over-ambitious procurement plans in 1931 and 1932, proved a turning point in the rural party's fortunes and was a traumatic experience for communists and non-party peasants alike. The procurement plans put increasing pressure on rural communists to fulfil policies with harsh consequences for the local population. By the end of 1932 the pressure reached a climax. Very unfairly, much blame for the economic débàcle was attributed to the local rural party by the central authorities. Recruitment to the party was halted; purges were undertaken in the rural party of the southern regions followed by the first part of a national purge in April 1933. There is more than one reason to explain the rationale of the purges. In recruiting so intensively during the first Five Year Plan, questions were raised about the quality of the new recruits. This is an important question, one which, with available sources, it is not easy to answer, for if quality (as defined in the party's terms) could not be maintained as recruitment reached some saturation level, then this makes the national purges of 1933 and 1934 more understandable as regular reviews to improve the party's quality whilst reducing its quantity. But the venom and extent of the purges made them into a process quite different from any routine review, and evidently resulted from the tensions between the rural party and the central authorities which emerged during the bitter struggles of the procurement campaign of 1931 and especially of 1932. In the Ukraine and North Caucasus, on many occasions rural party cadres and rank and file communists were unable and/or unwilling to follow orders and implement policies as passed down by their superiors. Some of these communists consciously chose to disobey instructions in what they thought was the best interests of the local population, and ultimately the regime. The central authorities refused to understand such motivation and responded with a severe purge of the southern rural party organisations at the end of 1932. This crisis in agriculture and the rural party organisation most probably acted as a catalyst in the decision to purge the whole party: this is an important point often overlooked in the past (see Chapters 6 and 9).

Our assessment of what happened in the rural party in 1932–33 helped in an analysis of the results of the national purges of 1933 and 1934. It has been widely believed that these purges can be explained on the whole as processes to rid the party of the inactive members and of those who lacked adequate political training. Our findings, on the other hand, tend to emphasise more that many communists in the rural party, and in the party generally, were expelled or demoted because of their failings and/or lack of vigour in conducting economic campaigns, their suspected lack of belief in the regime's goals and methods. In addition to those communists expelled, several hundred thousand 'dropped out' of the party or left it 'mechanically' by not attending purge meetings: we tend to think that this portion of various drop-outs has been underestimated hitherto. There is no doubt that once again the rural party, and its organisations in the collective farms and southern regions, received the full force of the various purges and screenings of 1933–37. Rural party membership declined from a figure of some 850 000 in October 1933 to 296 000 in January 1937 (see Chapter 9).

Simultaneously with this great decline in rural membership, the party adopted a scheme for the reorganisation of cells which would have been viable only if rural party membership had remained stable, or better still substantially increased. The June 1933 decision proposed to integrate the rural cells with *kolkhoz* production by breaking down existing inter-*kolkhoz* cells in separate, independent units at single *kolkhozy*. This separated out into different party units communists who worked in production centres (such as *kolkhozy*) and those who did not (for example, the staff of Soviet institutions). The result was to create many more party units whilst at the same time reducing their size. But this was a time of biting purges of the rural ranks. In practice, therefore, party units were dissolved and disappeared from party statistics: *kolkhoz* cell/ primary party organisation numbers fell from a near peak figure of 36 196 in October 1933 to a mere 12 000 in March 1939. According to the regulations of June 1933, those communists who were detached from cells recently dissolved were not permitted to attach themselves to the most convenient nearby cell, as had been the rule formerly; instead they were obliged to remain as single communists, scattered about the countryside, many working in key economic-administrative posts. Their number rose from 38 000 in October 1933 (4.5 per cent of the total rural party membership) to 101 583 in January 1935 (approximately 20 per cent). This seems counter-productive at a time when greater consolidation might have been thought preferable. This process of organisational disintegration is in striking contrast to the consolidation of party cell organisations in industry which was already underway in 1932; the contrasting developments in the party in agriculture and industry are anomalous and seem illogical (see Chapter 10).

During 1933-38, therefore, the rural party shrank from prominence and could not perform functions and fulfil objectives designated in 1929 – the face to production drive with the party acting as a close monitor of economic life – goals which, with modification, have remained standard to the present day. The authorities, or sections among the decision makers, in effect renounced for several years the goal of creating a growing, pervasive party acting as instigator and controller. Much about this decision remains enigmatic. The party leadership was made aware by responsible middle-level party commentators in the press, and presumably in private, of the impact of the rural party's dwindling membership and the difficulties resulting from its emasculated cell network, but contented themselves with generalisations about the need for quality rather than quantity (see remarks by Stalin and Kaganovich in Chapter 9). Yet in the vastness of the Soviet countryside there was no avoiding the issue that the rural party required some quantity as well as quality.

The low ebb of the rural party throughout the period 1933-38 seems anomalous when compared with the developments which preceded this period in 1929-33 or followed it, both on the eve of the Second World War in 1939-41 and in the post war period. In terms of the party's goals as promoted during the first Five Year Plan, there was modification in the rural party's role in 1933–38, of which we are well aware. This period of party history is almost completely ignored by Soviet historians, nor are primary sources available that enable us to arrive at satisfactory conclusions about the decision-making process in the highest echelons of the party administration. The decisions taken seem to be neither logical nor well thought out and their consequential results not desirable in the interests of the party's functioning in the countryside. The purge experience was common to the whole party between 1933 and 1937, but the consequences for the rural party membership and organisation were disproportionate and more fundamental. It was only in March 1939 that the rural party's weakened state was publicly admitted by the authorities in Andreev's speech at the eighteenth party congress. The period 1933–38 in the countryside can be judged as one of aberration for internal party policy.

The party membership was rebuilt from 1938 onwards. By 1941 a large scale rural party was once again being assembled along the lines, with some minor modifications, of that first constructed in 1929–32: this had proved to be the most informative and influential period for thinking on relative party size, organisation and role, many aspects of which have been retained until the present day.

In conclusion the major themes of this study are summarised below. Collectivisation was an unprepared, disruptive 'leap in the dark' for the party and Soviet society. In our examination of various operational programmes, it was noted that often throughout the collectivisation process only vague, general instructions were issued from superior authorities to subordinates. Those who passed on instructions to their own subordinates, on account of their inexperience, ignorance of technical methods and the pressure of time, often were obliged to confine themselves to set phraseology of demanding 'measures to be taken'. Confusion also arose when the central authorities did not issue precise, unambiguous instructions on how to introduce various organisational–administrative reforms: for example, in the case of the support point cells in 1931 and relations between political departments and *raikoms* in 1933. This vagueness on the part of the centre was not mere inefficiency. The problems faced by the communist party in the countryside can be judged in large part as one facet of the building of 'socialism in one country', a country that was backward and isolated internationally. The political leadership made mistakes and the personality of Stalin had an influence on events, but more fundamental issues were involved. The Bolshevik regime was operating in the unfavourable circumstances of the aftermath of the devastation of world war and civil war. It had no concrete model on which to base its projects. The party had been initially unable to work out even a medium-term programme towards the countryside, on the contrary it found itself responding to national conditions and events, first with War Communism and then with NEP. With the plans laid for rapid industrialisation, Stalin and his supporters believed it was necessary to harness agriculture to the needs of industry. Mass collectivisation was a sharp break with the past. The party had to adapt quickly. Mistakes and tensions were inherently likely.

   The consequence arising from these circumstances was that the rural communist party was transformed within a few, short years. The central authorities had not built up during the 1920s an internal party infrastructure sophisticated enough to control and manipulate the party cadres at the lower levels of the party hierarchy in the *raikoms* and the rank and file communists in the cells. A central theme of the present study has been the appearance of recalcitrance and resistance in various forms by local level communists to instructions from above. On several occasions when communists thought that policies and plans put forward by their superiors were either unreasonable, unrealistic, counter-productive, or insensitive to their interests or to those of the local population, or plainly impossible, rural communists strove to delay, circumvent or scuttle the authorities' plans. Important occasions when this happened include the campaign to mobilise rural communists to join the collective farms in 1928–29 (see Chapter 3); the reluctance of some rural communists to accept Stalin's infallibility on the issue of the 1930 spring retreat (see Chapter 5); the transfer of the *okrug* staff to the *raions* in the autumn of 1930 (see Chapter 4); the mobilisation of rural communists to work more directly in production (see Chapter 3); the reluctance shown by *raikom* staff in 1933 to accept the political departments (see Chapter 8). The most significant recorded manifestations (which need not have represented the full picture) of rural party recalcitrance on the part of *raikom* cadres and rank and file communists occurred when they argued over and disobeyed orders emanating from the *obkoms* and Moscow on the harvest and grain procurement plans for 1931 and more especially those for 1932. This was a most crucial affair in the history of the Soviet rural communist party during the 1930s: it was a replay in more intensified form of the 1928 grain procurement crisis and like that it was followed by a major reassessment of the rural party's position. Several factors favoured the recalcitrance of rural party members: they could, with good fortune, lose themselves in the wilderness of the Soviet countryside or in the extensive Soviet local rural administration and/or transfer themselves without the knowledge of their superiors and become lost in the party's filing system, always more chaotic in the countryside. We have thus argued that the rural party membership was by no means always a passive, malleable mass to be moulded at the authorities', even less Stalin's, will.

The authorities could not always fulfil their objectives simply by bulldozing local cadres into action. This is not to say that the *raikom* or cell tail wagged the Moscow dog. When the centre believed its authority was being undermined, and it was quick to jump to that assumption, it resorted to threats, individual expulsions, mass purging, arrests and even executions, but this in itself did not guarantee smooth policy fulfilment, rather it often complicated operations and raised tensions. More often than not in the cases we have cited, the centre's will was forced through and reluctantly accepted, but at considerable cost even in terms of the party's own objectives. The centre had not intended originally to employ such a panoply of disciplinary measure. Its attention was distracted, its efforts diverted and its policies sometimes modified or drastically changed (for example, the rural party purges in late 1932), and to this extent its will was frustrated. In these disputes there were no real victors, only more exasperated personnel working at all levels in the party administration.

It was noted in the introduction that we would focus on problems encountered during collectivisation. This was done with the aim both of depicting how the party fared in the transformation process and of questioning some of the more traditional, western interpretations of the communist party and Stalinist society. This task proved productive thanks to a close examination of the party at the grass-roots level (sub-*obkom*). Collectivisation was a limited success in the sense that the state's minimum aims (peasants into collective farms and agricultural produce to the state on its terms) were achieved, but at great economic and human cost. The rural communist party also made very considerable progress in beginning to adapt to the new conditions prevalent in the collectivised countryside; but the party, the vanguard of society, was not a monolithic, blindly obedient and efficient unit. The fact that there were few well-formulated plans for how the party ought to develop during collectivisation and few appraisals of how it might be affected was to have important consequences later. Tinkering and readjustment by various reforms and reorganisations took place in 1929–32, but this did not prevent some rural communists, when under the stress of the 1932 agricultural crisis, refusing to be brow-beaten into passive acceptance of orders, the wisdom of which they doubted, and as a result policy was modified or changed. Nor, as far as the approach towards the countryside and the rural party was concerned, were members of the political leadership clear-headed, rational appliers of a consistent policy. They were buffeted in high office by the 1932 crisis and responded somewhat irrationally in trying to solve it (for example, a mixture of conflicting harsh and soft measures in 1933–34, the June 1933 cell reorganisation and the subsequent excessive running down of the rural party), before re-emerging with a traditional policy to the party after 1938. Thus the traditional picture of the party as a relatively smooth-running monolith is modified from below and above.

The model for party organisation and operations elaborated, at times haphazardly, during the first Five Year Plan was to prove central to thinking on how the party was shaped after 1937. The period 1929–32 saw the rise of the rural communist party, but after the 1932 agricultural crisis, the years 1933–38 were those of decline and fall. At the end of the second Five Year Plan, a re-evaluation of the party's needs and goals was made and efforts begun to reassemble the rural party along lines similar to those of 1929–32; this effort was interrupted by the war, but continued and intensified after 1945. After the aberration of 1933–38, it was reaffirmed in practice that the rural communist party was an essential thread in the fabric of Soviet society.

Appendices

Appendix 1 Size of communist party and rural communist party, 1919–41

Date	Size of rural party	(% increase or decrease on previous year or period) [a]	Size of whole party [b]	(% increase or decrease on previous year or period) [a]	Rural party as percentage of whole party [a]
winter 1919	600 000[c]	—	c.400 000[c]	—	15.0
Sep. 1920	200 000[c]	—	c.700 000[c]	—	28.6
Jan. 1924	136 996[c]	—	472 000	—	29.0
Jan. 1925	154 731[c]	(12.9)	801 804	(69.9)	19.3
Jan. 1926	251 050[d]	(62.2)	1 079 814	(34.7)	23.2
Jan. 1927	264 055[e]	(5.2)	1 212 505	(12.3)	21.8
Jan. 1928	—	—	1 305 854	(7.7)	—
July 1928	317 603[f]	(20.3)	c.1 400 000	(7.2)	22.7
Jan. 1929	—	—	1 535 362	(9.7)	—
July 1929	358 936[f]	(13.0)	—	—	—
Jan. 1930	339 201[g]	(−5.5)	1 677 910	(9.3)	20.2
Jan. 1931	516 897[h]	(52.4)	2 212 225	(31.8)	23.4
Jan. 1932	700 000[j]	(35.4)	3 117 250	(40.9)	22.5
July 1932	832 580[k]	(18.9)	3 130 000	(0.4)	26.6
Jan. 1933	—	—	3 555 338	(13.6)	—
Oct. 1933	c.848 000[l]	(1.8)	—	—	—
Jan. 1934	—	—	2 701 008	(− 24.0)	—
Jan. 1935	—	—	2 358 714	(− 12.7)	—
Jan. 1936	—	—	2 076 842	(− 12.0)	—
Jan. 1937	296 000[m]	(− 65.0)	1 981 697	(− 14.6)	15.0
Jan. 1938	255 852[n]	(− 13.8)	1 920 002	(− 3.1)	13.3
Jan. 1939	315 700[n]	(23.4)	2 306 973	(20.1)	13.7
Jan. 1940	534 448[n]	(69.3)	3 399 975	(47.4)	15.7
Jan. 1941	623 400[n]	(16.6)	3 872 465	(13.9)	16.1

Sources: (a) all percentages are my calculations; (b) T.H. Rigby, *Communist Party Membership in the USSR, 1917–1967*, p. 52; (c) ibid., pp. 77–8, 106 and 134, note 8; (d) I. Glazyrin, *Regulirovanie sostava KPSS v period stroitel'stva sotsializma*, p. 31; (d) E. Smitten, *Sostav Vsesoyuznoi Kommunisticheskoi Partii (bolshevikov), po materialam partiinoi perepisi*, p. 48; (f) *Pravda*, 6 February 1929, p. 6. This source gives a rural party membership of 311 000, but it is not clear whether this refers to mid-1928 or early 1929; (g) *Partiinoe stroitel'stvo*, No. 11–12, June 1930, pp. 9–12; (h) *Partiinoe stroitel'stvo*, No. 17, September 1931, p. 39; (j) *Partiinoe stroitel'stvo*, No. 9, May 1932, p. 48. The January 1931 and January 1932 figures are also given in *Partiinoe stroitel'stvo*, No. 11–12, June 1932, p. 47 as 513 588 and 700 951 respectively; (k) *Partiinoe stroitel'stvo*, No. 21, November 1932, p. 46. These figures are not complete and are explained in this source; (l) my calculation from figures reported by Kaganovich in *XVII s''ezd Vsesoyuznoi Kommunisticheskoi Partii (b): stenograficheskii otchet* (1934), p. 557. My estimate is higher than that of T.H. Rigby, *Communist Party Membership*, p.231, who does not take into account single communists, who were not included in the cell membership figures cited by Kaganovich, and any party members in party *komsomol* groups; (m) *Istoriya KPSS*, vol. 4, book 2, p. 507; (n) *Istoriya KPSS*, vol 5, book 1, p. 49.

Appendix 2   Numbers and size of rural party cells and candidate groups, 1922–32

Year	Party cells	Candidate groups	Totals	Average size [a]
1922	14 983	—	14 983[b]	—
1924	14 630	—	14 630[b]	9.4
1925	13 879	—	13 879[b]	11.1
1926	15 819[b]	1502[c]	17 321[a]	14.5
1927	17 456[b]	3422[a]	20 878[d]	12.6
1928	20 719[e]	3393[e]	24 112[e]	13.2
1929	23 458[b]	3581[a]	27 039[e]	13.3
1930	24 750[f]	4454[a]	29 204[g]	11.6*
1931	27 349[g]	5827[g]	33 325[g]	15.5
1932	35 358[g]	9807[g]	45 165[g]	15.5

Sources: (a) my calculations; (b) A.S. Bubnov, *VKP (b)*, p.619; (c) I. Glazyrin, *Regulirovanie sostava KPSS v period stroitel'stva sotsializma*, p. 32; (d) E.H. Carr, *Foundations of a Planned Economy*, vol. 2, p. 179; (e) V.P. Danilov, '*K kharakteristike obshchestvenno-politicheskoi obstanovki v sovetskoi derevne nakanune kollektivizatsii*', in *Istoricheskie zapiski*, No. 79, 1966, pp. 12–3. The figures of Danilov refer to July of the respective years; (f) S.P.Trapeznikov, *Istoricheskii opyt KPSS v osushchestvlenii leninskogo kooperativnogo plana*, p. 226; (g) *Partiinoe stroitel'stvo*, No. 11–12, June 1932, pp. 46–8. The total figure for 1930 refers to April of that year.
*This temporary reduction in average size was a result of the steady increase in cell numbers during 1929–30, which took place at a time when rural party membership actually declined in the wake of the 1929–30 party purge.

Appendix 3 Party cells in the collective farms: nationally and regionally, 1926–41

Region	1926	1927	1928	1929	1930	1931	1932	1933	1934	1935	1936	1937	1938	1939	1940	1941
Soviet Union	560[a]	501[b]	587[c]	1514[d]	9257[d] (Apr.) 13 132[d] (Oct.)	14 962[d] (Jan.)	29 989[d] (Jan.) 36 000[e]/44 045[f] (April) (July)	36 196[g] (Jan.)	24 333[g] (Nov.)	18 313[g] (Jan.)	—	—	—	12 000[h] (spring)	22 000[j] (spring)	29 723[k]
Ukraine	—	—	—	174[l]	1446[m] (Apr.) 2217[m] (Oct.)	—	5188[n] (Jan.) 5952[o]	—	—	—	—	—	—	—	2944[p]	3156[q]
Lower Volga	—	—	—	—	1355[r] (July)	2016[r] (July)	—	—	—	—	—	—	—	—	—	—
Mid Volga	—	—	—	—	—	1380[s]	2700[s]	—	—	—	—	—	—	—	—	—
Central Black Earth	—	—	—	64[t] (July)	809[u] (July)	1429[u] (July)	2054[v]	—	—	—	—	—	—	—	—	—
Western Siberia	—	—	—	—	1059[v] (Apr.)	—	2829[v] (Apr.) 3000[v]	—	—	—	—	—	—	—	—	—
North Caucasus	—	—	—	105[v] (July)	528[t] (Apr.)	1700[v]	—	—	—	—	—	—	—	—	—	—
Azerbaidjan	—	—	—	56[y] (July)	—	—	380[w] (Jan.) 2228[z] (July)	3000[x] (Nov.)	5306[ai] (Jan.)	—	—	—	882[h]	—	—	—
Moscow oblast	—	—	—	—	—	—	—	—	—	—	—	—	—	304[h]	—	—
Leningrad oblast[ci]	—	—	—	—	—	—	—	—	—	159	98	63	25	—	54	—
White Russia[di]	—	—	15[e] (autumn)	41	161	290	623	608	134	123	64	100	48	44[h]	93	193
Mordovskii oblast[fi]	—	—	—	—	—	—	—	322 (Nov.)	—	—	—	13	77	87	123	178
Stalingrad krai[gi]	—	—	—	—	—	—	—	—	—	—	—	703	512	507	—	—
Western oblast	—	—	—	—	—	—	—	782[hi] (July) 987[ji]	1438[ki]	—	—	—	122[li]	—	—	—

Sources: (a) I. Glazyrin, *Regulirovanie sostava KPSS v period stroitel'stva sotsializma*, p. 32; (b) ibid., p. 51. The 1926 figure is higher than that for 1927 probably because *kolkhozy* were still breaking up in 1926 as a result of which *kolkhoz* cell numbers declined as they were dissolved or transformed into ordinary rural territorial cells; (c) *Derevenskii kommunist*, No. 1, 12 January 1929, p. 22; (d) my estimates based on *Partiinoe stroitel'stvo*, No. 11–12, June 1932, p. 46. *Derevenskii kommunist*, No. 9–10, 30 May 1930, p. 28 gives a figure of 1303 *kolkhoz* cells for 1 July 1929; (e) *Partiinoe stroitel'stvo*, No. 10, May 1932, p. 36; (f) *Partiinoe stroitel'stvo*, No. 21, November 1932, p. 46; (g) *Partiinoe stroitel'stvo*, No. 14, July 1935, p. 30; (h) *XVIII s'' ezd Vsesoyuznoi Kommunisticheskoi Partii* (b): *stenograficheskii otchet* (1939), p. 109 (Andreev speech); (j) my estimates based on V.K. Palishko, *Rost i ukreplenie partiinykh ryadov v usloviyakh stroitel'stva i uprocheniya sotsializma*, p. 162; (k) D. Bakhshiev, *Partiinoe stroitel'stvo v usloviyakh pobedy sotsializma v SSSR (1934–1941 gg)*, p. 87; (l) *Spravochnik partiinogo rabotnika*, vol. 7, part 2, p. 113. There were 1800 communists in these cells; (m) *Partiinoe stroitel'stvo*, No. 3–4, February 1931, p. 18; (n) I.F. Ganzha, I.I. Slin'ko and P.V. Shostak, '*Ukrainskoe selo na puti k sotsializmu*' in V.P. Danilov (ed.), *Ocherki istorii kollektivizatsii sel'skogo khozyaistva v soyuznykh respublikakh*, p. 192; (o) *Ocherki istorii kommunisticheskoi partii Ukrainy*, (Kiev, 1961), p. 393; (p) my estimate based on *Partiinaya zhizn'*, No. 12, June 1958, p. 58; (q) T.H. Rigby, *Communist Party Membership in the U.S.S.R. 1917–1967*, p. 293. This figure refers to 'before the war'; (r) *Saratovskaya partiinaya organizatsiya v period nastupleniya sotsializma po vsemu frontu. Sozdanie kolkhoznogo stroya: dokumenty i materialy 1930–1932 gg*., p. 283; (s) *Kollektivizatsiya sel'skogo khozyaistva v Srednem povol'zhe (1927–1937 gg.)*, p. 285. In these cells in 1931 and 1932 there were 20 000 and 44 000 communists respectively; (t) *Derevenskii kommunist*, No. 9–10, 30 May 1930, p. 28. In April 1930 there were 904 *kolkhoz* cells in the Central Black Earth *oblast*, ibid.; (u) P.N. Sharova, *Kollektivizatsiya sel'skogo khozyaistva Tsentral'no-chernozemnoi oblasti 1928–1932 gg*., p. 185; (v) B.A. Abramov, '*Kollektivizatsiya sel'skogo khozyaistva v RSFSR*', in V.P. Danilov (ed.), *Ocherki istorii*, pp. 122–3; (w) *Partiinoe stroitel'stvo*, No. 3–4, February 1932, p. 26; (x) *Partiinoe stroitel'stvo*, No. 22, November 1933, p. 32; (y) *Pravda*, 2 October 1929, p. 2. There were 565 communists in these cells; (z) *Partiinoe stroitel'stvo*, No. 17–18, September 1932, p. 33, of which 714 were candidate groups; (ai) *Ocherki istorii Moskovskoi organizatsii KPSS, 1883–1965*, p. 518; (bi) D. Bakhshiev, *Partiinoe stroitel'stvo v usloviyakh*, p. 86; (ci) *Leningradskaya organizatsiya KPSS v tsifrakh 1917–1973*, p. 130; (di) *Kommunisticheskaya partiya Belorussii v tsifrakh, 1918–1978*, pp. 172–3; (ei) *Izvestiya TsK VKP (b)*, No. 33 (254), 13 November 1928, p. 14; (fi) *Mordovskaya partiinaya organizatsiya v dokumentakh i tsifrakh, 1918–1972 gg*., pp. 205, 205–9; (gi) *Volgogradskaya oblastnaya organizatsiya KPSS v tsifrakh, 1917–1978*, p. 55; (hi) *Partiinoe stroitel'stvo*, No. 17–18, September 1932, p. 29 and *Partiinoe stroitel'stvo*, No. 22, November 1932, p. 39; (ji) *Partiinoe stroitel'stvo*, No. 17–18, September 1932, p. 26; (ki) *Partiinoe stroitel'stvo*, No. 19, October 1934, pp. 23–4; (li) J. Arch Getty, *The "Great Purges" Reconsidered. The Soviet Communist Party, 1933–1939*', unpublished Ph.D thesis, Boston College, Mass., 1979, p. 81 and *Partiinoe stroitel'stvo*, No. 14, July 1938, p. 23.

204

Appendix 4 Party administrative units, 1926–39

Unit	Jan. 1926[a]	Jan. 1930[a]	Jan. 1933[a]	Jan. 1934[a]	June 1936[b]	March 1939[a]
National C.C.s	7	8[c]	9[c]	} 70	—	—
Kraikoms	4	9	12		—	6
Obkoms	37	—	—		—	104
Gubkoms	40	—	—		—	—
Okruzhkoms	114	228	20	—	36	30
Ukoms	442	26	—	—	—	—
Rural raikoms	1530	3012	2466	} 2559	3269	3479
Gor. raikoms	—	—	93		257	336
Gorkoms	—	—	132	—	176	212
All party cells	28 864	54 000[c]	139 000[c]	110 806	90 181[a]	113 060
			(Oct.)		(Jan.)	

Sources: V.K. Palishko, *Rost i ukreplenie partiinykh ryadov v usloviyakh stroitel'stva i uprocheniya sotsializma*, pp. 90, 120–1, 150 and 153; (b) *Istoriya KPSS*, vol. 4, book 2, p. 279; (c) *XVII s"ezd Vsesoyuznoi Kommunisticheskoi Partii (b): stenograficheskii otchet* (1934), p. 555 (Kaganovich). At the sixteenth party congress, Kaganovich gave a figure of 49 712 'lower party cells' in the summer of 1930 (*XVI s"ezd Vsesoyuznoi Kommunisticheskoi Partii: stenograficheskii otchet* (1930) p. 66).

Notes and References

Introduction

1. Several major studies of the Soviet communist party were influenced by the totalitarian model of the Soviet system, for example, Z. Brzezinski, *The Permanent Purge*; R. Conquest, *The Great Terror;* M. Fainsod, *How Russia is Ruled*; L. Schapiro, *The Communist Party of the Soviet Union*. Other scholars have adopted a different approach and have come to regard the Soviet political system from a historical perspective as more multifaceted than as depicted in the totalitarian model, see for example, E.H. Carr, *The Bolshevik Revolution 1917–1923*, vols 1 and 2; E.H. Carr, *Socialism in One Country*, vols 1 and 2; E.H. Carr, *Foundations of a Planned Economy 1926– 1929*, vol. 2; R.W. Davies, *The Industrialisation of Soviet Russia, vol. 1. The Socialist Offensive. The Collectivisation of Soviet Agriculture*; R. Service, *The Bolshevik Party in Revolution, 1917–1923. A Study in Organisational Change*; J. Arch Getty, *Origins of the Great Purges. The Soviet Communist Party Reconsidered, 1933–1938*. The concept and approach of the present study have more affinities with these latter works.
2. See, for example, J.F. Hough and M. Fainsod, *How the Soviet Union is Governed*; and V.K. Belyakov and N.A. Zolotarev, *Organizatsiya udesyateryaet sily*. Using the Smolensk archives as a source, M. Fainsod provides a pioneering study of central and local party activities in *Smolensk Under Soviet Rule*.
3. The term 'rural party' is used for convenience and is not intended to imply that the communist party in rural areas was formally a separate, independent organisation working apart from the All-Union communist party. We do argue though that the party in rural areas functioned differently from the party in other sectors because of a variety of objective, geographical, social and economic reasons.

1 The 1920s: the Soviet Communist Party and the Rural Scene

1. For a vivid description of peasant life in tsarist Russia in 1860, which was much unchanged during the 1920s, see M. Matossian, 'The Peasant Way of Life', in W.S. Vucinich (ed.), *The Peasant in Nineteenth Century Russia*, pp. 1–40.
2. L. Trotsky, *1905*, p. 52. The poverty and suffering associated with backwardness intensified social antagonisms within tsarist society. The socio-economic characteristics of tsarist Russia with its relatively unimportant bourgeoisie and small proletariat did not fit well the standard Marxist model of a society ready for proletarian revolution. However, in Trotsky's interpretation the structure of Russian society provided the revolutionary movement with certain advantages: in particular Russian industrial workers

were highly concentrated in a few locations and worked in a relatively advanced technical environment which encouraged their social and political awareness. When the proletarian revolution had succeeded, after the formation of a tactical alliance with the poorer strata of the peasantry, the revolutionary regime would be faced with the problem of building socialism on the foundations of backwardness. In order to achieve this, reliance was placed by Trotsky (and other Bolshevik leaders until Stalin's revision of 'Socialism in One Country') on the success of international revolution. For a detailed analysis of Trotsky's theories, see Knei-Paz, *The Social and Political Thought of Leon Trotsky*.

3. The *mir* was a traditional peasant institution that controlled the land and periodically redistributed it among its member households. It was governed by an assembly of heads of households (*skhod*), which chose an elder (*starosta*) through whom the state dealt with the peasants. Peasants could not leave the *mir* without permission and there was collective responsibility for tax payment and military service. After 1905, in the Stolpin reforms, the tsarist government allowed peasants to leave the *mir* to consolidate their holdings in forms such as *khutors* and *otrubs*, but the *mir* was able to retain its authoritative position in the 1920s.

4. For the evolution of the policy, see E.H. Carr, *The Bolshevik Revolution, 1917–1923*, vol. 2, pp. 280–2.

5. A. Nove, *An Economic History of the U.S.S.R.*, p. 96. E.H. Carr pointed to the underlying social–political bias in the state's economic policies when he entitled the relevant part of his history 'The Wager on the Kulak', E.H. Carr, *Socialism in One Country*, vol. 1, pp. 240–82.

6. *KPSS v rezolyutsiyakh i resheniyakh s''ezdov, konferentsii i plenumov TsK*, vol. 3, pp. 189–204.

7. E.H. Carr, *Socialism in One Country*, vol. 1, pp. 189–95. Carr concludes in his inimitable style that: 'The price fixing policy had been defeated. The kulaks had proved victorious. The cities were once more held to ransom', ibid., p. 193.

8. *Sobranie uzakonenii*, 1926, No. 80, article 600. The amendment came into force on 1 January 1927 and in later years was used against hoarders and provided that hoarded grain should be confiscated by the state, with 25 per cent of such grain to be distributed to poor peasants at low prices – no doubt to enlist the poor peasant as an ally of the regime, see E.H. Carr and R.W. Davies, *Foundations of a Planned Economy*, vol. 1, pp. 50–1.

9. See for example, G.A. Konyukhov, *KPSS v bor'be s khlebnymi zatrudneniyami v strane 1928–1929*; E.H. Carr and R.W. Davies, *Foundations of a Planned Economy*, vol. 1., ch. 2; R.W. Davies, *The Industrialisation of Soviet Russia, vol. 1. The Socialist Offensive. The Collectivisation of Agriculture*, pp. 39–41; A. Nove, *An Economic History of the U.S.S.R*, pp. 139–42.

10. R.W. Davies, *The Industrialisation of Soviet Russia*, vol. 1., p. 41.

11. M. Lewin, 'The Immediate Background of Soviet Collectivization', in *Soviet Studies*, vol. XVII, No. 2, October 1965, p. 166.

12. The title of ch. 11 in M. Lewin's *Russian Peasants and Soviet Power*. Lewin is aware that worthwhile measures in pursuit of the new policy were not undertaken because of the restraints imposed by the debate with the Right. Once the opposition was defeated, a more radical line followed the April 1929 C.C. plenum.

13. M. Lewin, 'The Immediate Background of Soviet Collectivisation', in *Soviet Studies*, vol. XVII, No. 2, October 1965, p. 165.
14. The three types of collective farms (*kolkhoz–kollektivnoe khozyaistvo*) were: (a) the commune (*kommuna*, not to be confused with the *mir*) in which all land, animals and capital were collectivised. Some such farms promoted communal eating facilities and living quarters; (b) the *artel* in which principal animals, capital and land were incorporated into the collective farm; (c) the *toz* (*Tovarishchestvo dlya obshchestvennoi obrabotki zemli*) in which peasants cultivated the land jointly but land, animals and capital not collectivised.
15. *KPSS v rezol . . .* , vol. 3, p., 425.
16. One estimate was that in 1927–8 some 25–30 per cent of poor peasants belonged to agricultural co-operatives, 40 per cent of middle peasants and 50–60 per cent of kulaks; of course in absolute terms this meant that the middle peasant predominated, see V.P. Danilov, '*O kharaktere sotsial'no-ekonomicheskikh otnoshenii sovetskogo krest'yanstva do kollektivizatsii sel'skogo khozyaistva'*, in *Istoriya sovetskogo krest'yanstva i kolkhoznogo stroitel'stva v SSSR*, p. 68.
17. See, for example, R.F. Miller, 'Soviet Agricultural Policy in the Twenties: the Failure of Co-operation', in *Soviet Studies*, vol. XVII, No. 2, April 1975, passim.
18. For a summary of these views, see S.F. Cohen, *Bukharin and the Bolshevik Revolution*, pp. 194–8.
19. On the vitality of the *mir* in this period see D.J. Male, *Russian Peasant Organisation before Collectivisation. A Study of Commune and Gathering 1925–1930*.
20. E.H. Carr, *Socialism in One Country*, vol. 1, p. 214. The *otrub* was a farm holding detached from the mir system where the land was consolidated in one place, but apart from the house. The *khutor* was a fully enclosed farm holding where the land and the house were consolidated on one piece of land. These forms of land holding were supported in the Stolypin reforms after the 1905 revolution.
21. Y. Taniuchi, *The Village Gathering in Russia in the Mid-1920s*, p. 29.
22. V.P. Danilov, '*K kharakteristike obshchestvenno-politicheskoi obstanovki v sovetskoi derevne nakanune kollektivizatsii*', in *Istoricheskie zapiski*, No. 79, 1966, pp. 23–5.
23. G.V. Sharapov, *Razreshenie agrarnogo voprosa v Rossii posle pobedy oktyabr'skoi revolyutsii*, p. 174.
24. T.H. Rigby, *Communist Party Membership in the USSR, 1917–1967*, p. 106.
25. *Sotsial'nyi i natsional'nyi sostav VKP(b): Itogi vsesoyuznoi partiinoi perepisi 1927 goda*, p. 16.
26. T.H. Rigby, *Communist Party Membership in the USSR, 1917–1967*, p. 106.
27. T.P. Bernstein, 'Leadership and Mobilization in the Collectivization of Agriculture in China and Russia: A Comparison', unpublished Ph.D. thesis, Columbia University (1970), p. 203.
28. I. Glazyrin, *Regulirovanie sostava KPSS v period stroitel'stva sotsializma*, p. 28.
29. T.H. Rigby, *Communist Party Membership in the USSR, 1917–1967*, p. 135.
30. E. Smitten, *Sostav Vsesoyuznoi Kommunisticheskoi Partii (bolshevikov), po materialam partiinoi perpisi 1927 goda*, pp. 55 and 58.

31. Ibid.
32. In 1924 peasant-communists actually working in agriculture had represented 'not more than 35 per cent', M. Khataevich, in *Na agrarnom fronte*, No. 2, 1925, p. 106, but with a peasant intake of 95 000 in 1925, 50 800 of whom worked on their own holding, by 1 January 1926 the proportion rose to 45.3 per cent who worked exclusively on their own holding, with a further 12.6 per cent sharing their time between holding and paid administrative work.
33. *Bolshevik*, No. 2, 31 January 1929, p. 88 and *Izvestiya TsK VKP(b)*, No. 10 (269), 12 April 1929, pp. 2–3.
34. Quoted in E.H. Carr, *Foundations of a Planned Economy*, vol. 2, p. 181.
35. *Derevenskii kommunist*, No. 3, 10 February 1929, p. 25.
36. Soviet commentators in the 1920s tended to use the value of the means of production as the measure with which to define the strata in the peasantry: (a) *batraks* and poor peasants were those who owned up to 200 rubles worth of means of production; (b) 'small' middle peasants; 201–400 rubles worth; (c) 'typical' middle peasants 401–800 rubles worth; (d) 'rich' or 'well-to-do' middle peasants 801–800 rubles worth; (e) *kulaks* over 1600 rubles worth.

This type of definition, which as one can judge by the terminology for middle peasants may have been vague and fluid, is used by a leading present-day commentator, V.P. Danilov, in his article '*O kharaktere sotsial'no-ekonomicheskikh otnoshenii sovetskogo krest'yanstva do kollektivizatsii sel'skogo khozyaistva*', in *Istoriya sovetskogo krest'yanstva i kolkhoznogo stroitel'stva v SSSR*, pp. 49–80. On the problems of defining these peasant strata and alternative criteria to that of the value of means of production, see T. Shanin, *The Awkward Class. Political Sociology of Peasantry in a Developing Society: Russia 1910–1925*, ch. 7.
37. V.P. Danilov, '*K kharakteristike obshchestvenno-politicheskoi obstanovki v sovetskoi derevne nakanune kollektivizatsii*', in *Istoricheskie zapiski*, No. 79, 1966, pp. 8 and 12, and E.H. Carr, *Foundations of a Planned Economy*, vol. 2, p. 181.
38. A. Gaister and A. Levin, in *Bolshevik*, No. 9–10, 31 May 1929, pp. 81–2.
39. On this point, see L. Milbraith, *Political Participation*, pp. 53–5 for a summary of the propositions of political participation on the part of different social groups.
40. *Derevenskii kommunist*, No. 5–6 (77–78), 14 March 1928, p. 31.
41. A.S. Bubnov, *VKP(b)*, p. 619 and M.S. Potapenko, *Partiinaya rabota v derevne (1924–1925 gg.)*, p. 29.
42. For the size and population of an average *volost*, see Chapter 4.
43. M. Khataevich, in *Na agrarnom fronte*, p. 106.
44. Smolensk archives, WKP 331, p. 132.
45. M. Khataevich, in *Na agrarnom fronte*, p. 105.
46. For the timing of the measures, see this chapter, pp. 11–12.
47. M.S. Potapenko, *Partiinaya rabota . . .* , p. 22 and *KPSS v rezolyutsiyakh . . .* , vol. 3, p. 184.
48. See M.S. Potapenko, *Partiinaya rabota . . .* , p. 57–9.
49. I. Glazyrin, *Regulirovanie sostava . . .* , p. 32.
50. Ibid.
51. For sources, see Appendix 2.

52. A.S. Bubnov, *VKP (b)*.
53. S.P. Trapeznikov, *Istoricheskii opyt KPSS v osushchestvlenii leninskogo kooperativnogo plana*, p. 226 and I. Glazyrin, *Regulirovanie sostava* ....
54. The 1926 figures are from I. Glazyrin, *Regulirovanie sostava* ..., and those for 1928 from V.P. Danilov, '*K kharakteristike* ...', p. 12.
55. *Izvestiya TsK VKP(b)*, No. 34 (255), 22 November 1928, p. 9, and S.F. Markov, '*Ukreplenie sel'skikh partiinykh organizatsii v period podgotovki massovogo kolkhoznogo dvizheniya*', in *Voprosy istorii KPSS*, No. 3, 1962, p. 114.
56. I. Glazyrin, *Regulirovanie sostava* ... , p. 71. At the beginning of the reconstruction period (1926), there were 73 584 rural Soviets. On average each measured 4–5 kilometres in radius with 7–10 inhabited points and a population of 1 000–3 000, V.P. Danilov, '*K kharakteristike* ...', p. 18.
57. *Shestnadtsataya konferentsiya VKP(b); stenograficheskii otchet* (1962), p. 592.
58. *KPSS v rezolyutsiyakh* ... , vol. 4, p. 148.
59. *Derevenskii kommunist*, No. 1, 12 January 1929, p. 35.
60. *Derevenskii kommunist*, No. 14, 27 July 1929, p. 25.
61. T.P. Bernstein, 'Leadership and Mobilization', pp. 282–3. Bernstein refers here specifically to the period immediately prior to 1930, one which is dealt with in Chapter 3 of this work. Bernstein also is well aware of the rapid growth which took place in the mid-1920s.
62. *Izvestiya TsK VKP(b)*, No. 14 (235), 28 April 1928, p. 20. The sample included 17 857 rural cells.
63. S.F. Markov, '*Ukreplenie sel'skikh* ...', p. 121.
64. *Izvestiya TsK VKP(b)*, No. 14 (235), 28 April 1928, p. 20.
65. Ibid.
66. *Sotsial'nyi i natsional'nyi sostav VKP(b)*, 1928, pp. 79–81.
67. E.H. Carr, *Foundations of a Planned Economy*, Vol. 2, p. 179.
68. S.F. Markov, '*Ukreplenie sel'skikh* ...', p. 118 and S.P. Trapeznikov, *Istoricheskii opyt KPSS v osushchestvlenii leninskogo kooperativnogo plana*, p. 237.
69. *Shestnadtsatya konferentsiya VKP(b): stenograficheskii otchet*, (1962), p. 387. The verb 'to grow into' was associated with Bukharin's idea that the *kulaks* would grow into socialism via the co-operative system.
70. E.H. Carr, *Foundations of a Planned Economy*, vol. 2, p. 188.
71. Soviet historiography depicts NEP and the policies of the mid 1920s as a process leading via the 'Lenin Cooperative Plan' to production co-operatives and collectivisation, see, for example, I.B. Berkin, '*Osnovnye etapy formirovaniya kooperativnogo plana V.I. Lenina*', in *Istoriya sovetskogo krest'yanstva i kolkhoznogo stroitel'stvo v SSSR*, pp. 166–91, and V.P. Danilov and N.A. Ivnitskii, '*Leninskii kooperativnyi plan; ego osushchestvlenie v SSSR*'; in V.P. Danilov (ed.), *Ocherki istorii kollektivizatsii sel'skogo khozyaistva v soyuznykh respublikakh*, p. 4. See also N.W. Heer, 'A Tragedy Revisited; The Story of Collectivization', in N.W. Heer, (ed.), *Politics and History in the Soviet Union*, pp. 220–38.

2 Collectivisation in the Years of the First Five Year Plan

1. See for example E.H. Carr and R.W. Davies, *Foundations of a Planned Economy*, vol. 1; R.W. Davies, *The Industrialisation of Soviet Russia, vol. 1. The Socialist Offensive. The Collectivisation of Soviet Agriculture, 1929– 1930*; N. Jasny, *The Socialized Agriculture of the USSR*.
2. From 286 000 households out of 25 million on 1 October 1927 to 596 000 on 1 October 1928, R.W. Davies, *Industrialisation of Soviet Russia*, pp. 109, 441–2.
3. Ibid., p. 133.
4. Resolution in *Kollektivizatsiya sel'skogo khozyaistva. Vazhneishie postan-ovleniya Kommunisticheskoi partii i sovetskogo pravitel'stva 1927–1935*, p. 258.
5. Amongst many sources on this crucial question, see A.A. Barsov, *Balans stoimostnykh obmenov mezhdu gorodom i derevnei*; M. Ellman, 'Did the Agricultural Surplus Provide the Resources for the Increase in Investment in the USSR during the First Five Year Plan?', in the *Economic Journal*, December 1975, pp. 844–63; J.R. Millar and A. Nove, 'A Debate on Collectivisation. Was Stalin Really Necessary?', in *Problems of Communism*, July–August 1976, p. 55; M. Harrison, 'Why Was NEP Abandoned?', in R.C. Stuart (ed.), *The Soviet Rural Economy*, pp. 63–78; and J.R. Millar, 'Views on the Economics of Soviet Collectivisation of Agriculture: The State of The Revisionist Debate', in ibid., pp. 109–17.
6. R.W. Davies, *Industrialisation of Soviet Russia*, pp. 441–2.
7. Not until 30 July 1930 did the RSFSR enact a law providing for the dissolution of the *mir* when a certain percentage of its members had organised a *kolkhoz, Sobranie uzakonenii i rasporyazhenii RSFSR*, 1930, text 621.
8. *Sdvigi v sel'skom khozyaistve SSSR mezdu XV i XVI partiinymi s''ezdami*, (M., 1931, second edition), p. 30.
9. Between 1928 and 1933, the number of horses declined from 33.5 million to 16.6 million, cattle from 70.5 to 38.4 million and pigs from 26.0 to 12.1 million, *Sotsialisticheskoe stroitel'stvo*, (1936), pp. 342–3 and 354.
10. *Pravda*, 2 March 1930, p. 1.
11. Resolution in *Kollektivizatsiya sel'skogo khozyaistva . . . 1927–1935*, pp. 287–9.
12. R.W. Davies, *Industrialisation of Soviet Russia*, pp. 441–3.
13. See M. Lewin, '"Taking Grain": Soviet Policies of Agricultural Procurements before the War', in C.A. Abramsky and B.J. Williams (eds), *Essays in Honour of E.H. Carr*, pp. 284, 307 and 319, note 8.
14. Resolution in *Sobranie zakonov i rasporyazhenii SSSR*, No. 71, p. 435.
15. For a full discussion, see S.G. Wheatcroft, Grain Production Statistics in the USSR in the 1929s and 1930s, Soviet Industrialisation Project Series, No. 13, Centre for Russian and East European Studies, University of Birmingham, 1977, especially pp. 34–6.
16. E. Zaleski, *Planning for Economic Growth in the Soviet Union, 1918–1932*, (American edition, 1969), p. 338 and M. Lewin, '"Taking Grain"' p. 307.
17. See *Kollektivizatsiya sel'skogo khozyaistava . . . 1927–1935*, pp. 343–4.

18. *Kolkhozy vo vtoroi stalinskoi pyatiletke*, p. 1.
19. E. Zaleski, *Planning for Economic Growth*, p. 339.
20. Yu.A. Moshkov, *Zernovaya problema v gody sploshnoi kollektivizatsii sel'skogo khozyaistva SSSR (1929–1932 gg.)*, pp. 164–5.
21. M. Lewin, '"Taking Grain"', p. 307.
22. Yu.A. Moshkov, *Zernovaya problema . . .*, p. 173.
23. Ibid., pp. 185–6. On page 174 of his book Moshkov puts the figure for Ukrainian *kolkhozy* in 1931 slightly higher at 66.3 per cent and notes that it had been planned at 56.3 per cent, which was a very large proportion any way.
24. M. Lewin, ' "Taking Grain" ', p. 310.
25. *Pravda*, 11 May 1932, p. 2 and *Pravda*, 30 May 1932, p. 2.
26. Yu.A. Moshkov, *Zernovaya Problema . . .*, p. 205. It is hardly surprising that the Kiev *oblast* was in such a mess. Although nationally the grain procurement from the 1931 harvest was 32.9 per cent, in Kiev *oblast* only 20 per cent of the harvest was reported as left in the hands of the *kolkhozniks*, that is 80 per cent procurements, see M. Lewin, '"Taking Grain"', p. 296 and Yu.A. Moshkov, *Zernovaya Problemu . . .*, p. 186.
27. Yu.A. Moshkov, *Zernovaya Problema . . .*, p. 201.
28. *Pravda*, 6 August 1932 and 24 October 1932.
29. *Partiinoe stroitel'stvo*, No. 17–18, September 1932, p. 5.
30. Smolensk archives, WKP 162, p. 102. See also WKP 221, pp. 34–81 for the situation in the Western *oblast* in the summer and autumn 1932.
31. Published in *Pravda*, 8 August 1932, p. 5, and probably for greater prominence on the following day on p. 1.
32. *Pravda*, 21 August 1932, p. 3.
33. Yu.A. Moshkov, *Zernovaya Problema . . .*, p. 215.
34. *Pravda*, 6 December 1932, p. 3.
35. E. Zaleski, *Planning for Economic Growth*, pp. 339 and 384. Other sources cited by him put the harvest at 63.0 and 66.4 million tons.
36. See Chapter 6.

3 The Rural Communist Party 1929–32: Membership, Location and Occupation

1. T.H. Rigby, *Communist Party Membership in the USSR, 1917–1967*, p. 186. Rigby cites a fourth process, that of the 'shifting of the party's rural base from the village to the kolkhoz', ibid. This is indeed a major feature treated fully in ch. 5 on cell organisation.
2. *Derevenskii kommunist*, No. 1, January 1929, p. 25.
3. T.P. Bernstein, 'Leadership and Mobilization in the Collectivization of Agriculture in China and Russia: A Comparison', unpublished Ph.D. thesis, Columbia University 1970, p. 249.
4. *Partiinoe stroitel'stvo*, No. 11–12, June 1930, p. 17. According to *Partiinoe stroitel'stvo*, No. 9, May 1930, p. 21, this refers to only 90 *okrugs*.

5. *KPSS v rezolyutsiyakh i resheniyakh s"ezdov, konferentsii i plenumov TsK,* vol. 4, pp. 142–50.
6. *Izvestiya TsK VKP(b),* No. 4 (263), 15 February 1929, p. 16–17. Yaroslavsky repeated the message with regard to the purge generally when he called for a 'class approach', *Pravda,* 31 March 1929.
7. *Pravda,* 23 March 1929, p. 5.
8. *Derevenskii kommunist,* No. 11–12, 21 June 1930, p. 46.
9. T.H. Rigby, *Communist Party Membership,* pp. 178–9. Rigby gives a very useful explanation of several sources on the purge results in ibid., p. 179, note 33.
10. F.M. Vagonov, '*O regulirovanii sostava partii v 1928–1920 gg.*', in *Voprosy istorii KPSS,* No. 6, 1964, pp. 67–70.
11. E.H. Carr, *Foundations of a Planned Economy,* vol. 2, p. 146.
12. See *Pravda,* 25 August 1929, p. 4.
13. *Pravda,* 20 August 1929, p. 5. Of those processed, 64.5 per cent were expelled who paid more than 150 rubles tax and 47 per cent of those in the tax bracket 100–150 rubles, *Partiinoe stroitel'stvo,* No. 10, May 1930, p. 16. Very comparable information for the Western *oblast* rural cells is in the Smolensk archives, File 116/154 f, p. 76.
14. B.A. Abramov, '*Organizatsionno-massovaya rabota partii v derevne posle XV s"ezda KPSS (1928–1929 gg.)*', in *Partiinaya zhizn',* No. 21, November 1958, p. 59.
15. V. Vlasov, in *Partiinoe stroitel'stvo,* No. 9, May 1930, p. 21.
16. Smolensk archives, WKP 61, pp. 98–168.
17. V. Voronkova, '*Bor'ba kommunisticheskoi partii Sovetskogo soyuza za ukreplenie sovetov v derevne v period kollektivizatsii sel'skogo khozyaistva (1929–1931 gg.)*', in *KPSS v bor'be za sotsialisticheskoe preobrazovanie sel'skogo khozyaistva,* p. 80.
18. *Sovetskoe stroitel'stvo,* No. 7, July 1930, p. 102.
19. P.G. Chernopitskii, *Na velikom perelome: Selskie sovety Dona v period podgotovki i provedeniya massovoi kollektivizatsii (1928–1931 gg.),* p. 110.
20. See *Partiinoe stroitel'stvo,* No. 9, May 1930, p. 21.
21. Ibid., p. 22.
22. Ibid.
23. *Izvestiya TsK VKP (b),* No. 4 (263), 15 February 1929, p. 8.
24. Kaganovich speech in *Pravda,* issues 20, 21, 24 January 1930.
25. *Partiinoe stroitel'stvo,* No. 9, May 1930, p. 19 and N. Jasny, *The Socialized Agriculture of the USSR.,* p. 320.
26. *Pravda,* 11 February 1930 and *Partiinoe stroitel'stvo,* No. 3–4, February 1930, p. 86.
27. Poor peasants who participated in dekulakisation were allotted a share of the goods. This is not to say that all poor peasants, nor even a majority of them, actively supported or condoned the hardships inflicted on their prosperous neighbours, towards whom they may have harboured ambiguous feelings, see examples from M. Fainsod, *Smolensk Under Soviet Rule,* pp. 242–51.
28. *Partiinoe stroitel'stvo,* No. 10, May 1930, p. 10.
29. See Appendix 1.
30. *Partiinoe stroitel'stvo,* No. 21, November 1932, p. 47.
31. See Appendix 1.

32. See note to Table 3.2.
33. T.H. Rigby, *Communist Party Membership*, p. 196.
34. See Chapter 6.
35. This recruitment figure does not include that of employees, which would have only been marginal.
36. There are varying estimates of how large a phenomenon this was in the party as a whole. A. Frenkel estimates that 350 000 members and candidates 'drifted away from or fell out of the party' between 1930 and mid-1932, *Partiinoe stroitel'stvo*, No. 32–23, December 1932, p. 5, whereas another article in this party journal gives a lower total for the two years 1930–31 as 176 000, ibid., No. 9, May 1932, p. 46, and Yaroslavsky supplies an intermediary figure of 223 000 for these two years, T.H. Rigby, *Communist Party Membership*, p. 195, note 75.

  Our seemingly high figures for the rural party are compatible with those for the entire party as these latter do not include intra-party transfers from one party organisation to another which were quite substantial in number. For example, during 1931 there were 507 000 intra-party transfers, that includes all transfers, urban to urban, rural to rural, and rural to urban and vice versa, *Partiinoe stroitel'stvo*, No. 9, May 1932, p. 49.
37. N. Spektor, *Partiya – organisator sheftsva rabochikh nad derevnei*, p. 147.
38. V.M. Selunskaya, *Rabochie-dvadtsatipyatitysyachniki*, p. 43. On the 25 000-ers, see Chapter 6, p. 00.
39. *Partiinoe stroitel'stvo*, No. 11–12, June 1930, p. 18.
40. K. Mezhol', *Partiinoe stroitel'stvo*, No. 10, May 1930, p. 16 puts the proletarian layer in the rural party in the spring of 1930 at 23.2 per cent.
41. Resolution dated 6 March 1930 in *Partiinoe stroitel'stvo*, No. 7, April 1931, p. 68.
42. *Partiinoe stroitel'stvo*, No. 23, December 1931, p. 37.
43. *Partiinoe stroitel'stvo*, No. 7–8, April 1932, p. 54.
44. *Partiinoe stroitel'stvo*, No. 15, August 1932, p. 52 and *Partiinoe stroitel'stvo*, No. 21, November 1932, p. 47.
45. *Partiinoe stroitel'stvo*, No. 9, May 1930, p. 20; *Partiinoe stroitel'stvo*, No. 9, May 1932, p. 49; *Partiinoe stroitel'stvo*, No. 11–12, June 1932, p. 47.
46. *Partiinoe stroitel'stvo*, No. 10, May 1932, p. 43.
47. *Partiinoe stroitel'stvo*, No. 7–8, April 1932, p. 54; *Partiinoe stroitel'stvo*, No. 9, May 1932, p. 49; *Partiinoe stroitel'stvo*, No. 11–12, June 1932, p. 48.
48. See Chapter 6.
49. *Na agrarnom fronte*, No. 10, 1929, p. 113. As the *toz* was the most prevalent form of collective farm before 1930, in those areas with only *tozy* available it was not a matter of choice for local communists.
50. V.P. Danilov, '*K kharakteristike obshchestvenno - politicheskoi obstanovki v sovetskoi derevne nakanune kollektivizatsii*', in *Istoricheskie zapiski*, No. 79, 1966, p. 9.
51. *Derevenskii kommunist*, No. 7, 10 April 1929, p. 41.
52. *Izvestiya TsK VKP(b)*, No. 11–12 (270–1), 24 April 1929, p. 19.
53. After prolonged discussions during 1929 on whether non-party *kulaks* should be allowed within the collective farm system, the November 1929 C.C. plenum pronounced against it. For further details see E.H. Carr and R.W. Davies, *Foundations of a Planned Economy*, vol. 1, pp. 176–9; R.W. Davies, *The Industrialisation of Soviet Russia, vol 1. The Socialist*

Offensive. The Collectivisation of Soviet Agriculture, 1929–1930, pp. 137–46 and 191–4; *Bolshevik*, No. 11, 15 June 1929, pp. 26–35.

54. E.H. Carr states that M. Vareikis was a former Bukharinite, keen to announce his conversion to the official line, E.H. Carr, *Foundations of a Planned Economy*, vol. 2, p. 187, note 2. If this was Vareikis' intention, then to a large extent it back-fired as he was to be sharply criticised as too moderate by more radical commentators.

55. M. Vareikis, in *Izvestiya TsK VKP(b)*, No. 1 (160), 16 January 1929, pp. 6–7.

56. S.P. Trapeznikov, *Istoricheskii opyt KPSS v osushchestvlenii leninskogo kooperativnogo plana*, p. 225 and T.H. Rigby, *Communist Party Membership*, p. 186.

57. V.P. Danilov 'K kharakteristike . . .', pp. 14–5.

58. Ibid. It is a theme of the rural party and the communist party as a whole during the first Five Year Plan to try to excel and outdo others. Here it is party members into *kolkhozy*, later the peasantry and other campaigns.

59. *Izvestiya TsK VKP (b)*, No. 35 (256), 30 November 1928, p. 1.

60. M. Lewin, *Russian Peasants and Soviet Power*, p. 434.

61. T.P. Bernstein makes a very useful comparison with the Chinese communist party on this point. In China after the initial land reform, the party went about a programme of cadre education and training in order to teach them the direction of future change, the nature and content of the future socialist transformation, and especially how to go about implementing policies, T.P. Bernstein, 'Leadership and Mobilization in the Collectivization of Agriculture in China and Russia: A Comparison', unpublished Ph.D. thesis, Columbia University, 1970, pp. 250–68. However, Bernstein draws the wrong conclusion when he states that: 'The data . . . show rather clearly that they [peasant-communists in the Soviet Union] did not in many cases play a vanguard role, but only joined during the most intense phase of all-out collectivisation', ibid., pp. 232–3.

62. My estimates from A. Gaister and A. Levin, in *Bolshevik*, No. 9–10, 31 May 1929, p. 83.

63. *Izvestiya TsK VKP(b)*, No. 4 (263), 15 January 1929, p. 18.

64. *Izvestiya TsK VKP(b)*, No. 7 (266), 20 March 1929, p. 19. As early as autumn 1928, Biisk *okrug* in the Siberian *krai* had 30–50 per cent of its communists in *kolkhozy*, which was an exceptionally high figure, *Izvestiya TsK VKP(b)*, No. 30 (251), 11 October 1928, p. 12.

65. *Izvestiya TsK VKP(b)*, No. 4 (263), 15 February 1929, pp. 16–17.

66. *Pravda*, 17 May 1929, p. 3.

67. *Derevenskii kommunist*, No. 17, 14 September 1929, pp. 24–5 and *Derevenskii kommunist*, No. 11–12, 21 June 1930, p. 46. By summer 1930 a total of 282 586 had been investigated and 47 753 forced to quit the party.

68. *XVI s''ezd Vsesoyuznoi Kommunisticheskoi Partii (b): stenograficheskii otchet*, (1930), p. 340.

69. In fact in areas like Moscow and Leningrad there were larger numbers of *kolkhozy* than in the grain regions: the major difference was that those in the industrial and western *oblasts* were often extremely small 'dwarf kolkhozy', more prone to collapse in time of difficulty.

70. I. Glazyrin, *Regulirovanie sostava KPSS v period stroitel'stva sotsializma*, p. 31. When one takes account of *batraks*, the proportion would be slightly

less than 40 per cent.

71. S.P. Trapeznikov, *Istoricheskii opyt* . . ., p. 222.
72. *Partiinoe stroitel'stvo*, No. 11–12, June 1932, p. 47.
73. T.H. Rigby, *Communist Party Membership*, p. 190; no source is given for this plausible suggestion.
74. *Partiinoe stroitel'stvo*, No. 14, July 1932, p. 28 (Transcaucasus).
75. The figures for 1930 and 1931 are from *Partiinoe stroitel'stvo*, No. 8, April 1931, p. 2, and refer to those 'working directly in agriculture'. The figures for 1932 come from I. Glazyrin, *Regulirovanie sostava KPSS v period stroitel'-stva sotsializma*, p. 88 and *Partiinoe stroitel'stvo*, No. 11–12, June 1932, p. 48.
76. B.A. Abramov, 'Kollektivizatsiya sel'skogo khozyaistva v RSFSR', in V.P. Danilov (ed.), *Ocherki istorii kollektivizatsii sel'skogo khozyaistva v soyuznykh respublikakh*, p. 133; *Partiinoe stroitel'stvo*, No. 9, May 1932, p. 55; *Partiinoe stroitel'stvo*, No. 14, July 1932, p. 21; *Partiinoe stroitel'stvo*, No. 23–4, December 1932, p. 35.
77. *Partiinoe stroitel'stvo*, No. 10, May 1932, pp. 37–9.
78. *Kollektivizatsiya sel'skogo khozyaistva. Vazhneishie postanovleniya Kommunisticheskoi partii i sovetskogo pravitel'stva 1927–1935*, pp. 417–18.
79. *Partiinoe stroitel'stvo*, No. 9, May 1932, p. 11.
80. Once the effects of the 1933–34 purges were felt in the rural party, it tended to concentrate its smaller forces in élite administrative positions.
81. E.I. Lar'kina, *Podgotovka kolkhoznykh kadrov v period massovoi kollektivizatsii*, pp. 90–1. Although the sample for the North Caucasus refers only to 593 *kolkhozy*, Lar'kina goes on to write in terms of the *krai* as a whole, so presumably this is a representative sample.
82. Ibid.
83. Local rural communists were aware of available privileges and keen to preserve them. They were resentful of urban outsiders who stepped into high level *kolkhoz* posts and complained that they were not being allowed to lead the *kolkhozy*, *Partiinoe stroitel'stvo*, No. 6, March 1930, p. 16 (Khoper *okrug*).
84. *Istoriya KPSS*, vol. 4, book 2, p. 256.
85. Some 45–50 per cent of *kolkhoz* party members were heads of production branches (*otrasli*) and a further 20 per cent worked in Soviet institutions, *Partiinoe stroitel'stvo*, No. 11–12, June 1932, p. 48.

4   **The District Party Committee (*raikom*): Organisation, Structure and Personnel 1929–32**

1. For immediate pre-war developments, see J. Harris, 'The Origins of the Conflict Between Malenkov and Zhdanov: 1939–1941', in *Slavic Review*, vol. 35, No. 2, June 1976, pp. 287–303.
2. *XVI s''ezd Vsesoyuznoi Kommunisticheskoi Partii (b): stenograficheskii otchet*, (1930), p. 45 (Stalin) and pp. 82–3 (Kaganovich). Vladimirskii noted that since the previous congress (December 1927) there had been a 20 per cent increase in the number of paid staff at the rural *raikom* and factory cell

levels, with a 66 per cent wage increase for lower apparatus workers, ibid., pp. 92–3.

3. *Partiinoe stroitel'stvo*, No. 16, August 1930, pp. 49–50.
4. D. Gurevich, in *Izvestiya TsK VKP(b)*, No. 22 (243), 24 July 1928, p. 2, states that a 'good half' of existing *raions* in 1928 contained fewer than 100 communists, whereas I. Bogachev, *Izvestiya TsK VKP(b)*, No. 25 (246), 22 August 1928, p. 5 states that the majority of *raions* included 150–300 communists. This discrepancy may be due to regional variation as I. Bogachev was an important party spokesman for the Central Black Earth.
5. *Partiinoe stroitel'stvo*, No. 16, August 1930, pp. 49–50.
6. *Bolshevik*, No. 13, July 1930, p. 17, and for further information see *Partiinoe stroitel'stvo*, No. 17, September 1930, pp. 48, 52 and 57.
7. *Pravda*, 16 July 1930.
8. *XVI s"ezd . . .* , p. 45.
9. *Partiinoe stroitel'stvo*, No. 15, August 1930, p. 15. At the sixteenth party congress Kaganovich mentioned a target figure of only 30 000 *okrug* workers, *XVI s"ezd. . .* , p. 83. It is quite possible that Kaganovich was only referring to communists involved in the transfer.
10. D. Gurevich, in *Derevenskii kommunist*, No. 11, 12 June 1929, p. 30.
11. *Pravda*, 17 July 1930, p. 1.
12. Ibid.
13. *Pravda*, 28 July 1930, p. 3.
14. *Pravda*, 17 July 1930, p. 1.
15. *Pravda*, 21 September 1930, p. 4.
16. *Pravda*, 28 August 1930, p. 3.
17. *Pravda*, 31 August 1930, p. 7 and 26 September 1930, p. 5.
18. *Pravda*, 26 September 1930, p. 5 and *Partiinoe stroitel'stvo*, No. 21, November 1930, p. 35.
19. *Partiinoe stroitel'stvo*, No. 21, November 1930, p. 6.
20. *Pravda*, 26 September 1930, p. 5.
21. *Pravda*, 29 August 1930, p. 3.
22. *Pravda*, 2 September 1930, p. 6 and 10 October 1930, p. 3.
23. *Pravda*, 17 August 1930, p. 3 and 18th September 1930.
24. In the summer of 1930 criticisms were aimed at those who sought to extend the completion date beyond 1 October by as much as one year, and they were labelled quite acrimoniously as 'conservatives' and 'Right opportunists', see *Pravda*, 16 June 1930, p. 1 and *Pravda*, 17 July 1930, p. 1. But there was never any mention or hint that completion ahead of schedule was sought after.
25. *Pravda*, 5 August 1930, p. 3.
26. *Pravda*, 7 August 1930, p. 3.
27. *Pravda*, 24 August 1930, p. 3.
28. It was claimed initially that there was disruption in day-to-day economic campaigns, with not one *okrug* fulfilling its July procurement plan, *Partiinoe stroitel'stvo*, No. 17, September 1930, p. 54. Whether this was wholly attributable to the *okrugs'* abolition is, of course, debatable.
29. *Rabota RKI ot V k VI s"ezdu Sovetov*, (M., 1931), p. 39, cited in M.L. Bogdenko, '*Kolkhoznoe stroitel'stvo vesnoi i letom 1930 g.*', in *Istoricheskie zapiski*, No. 76, 1965, p. 38, note 92, and *Istoriya KPSS*, vol. 4, book 2, p. 103.

30. *Partiinoe stroitel'stvo*, No. 21, November 1930, p. 35 and *Pravda*, 10 October 1930, p. 3.
31. *Partiinoe stroitel'stvo*, No. 11, June 1931, p. 11.
32. S.F. Markov, '*Ukreplenie sel'skikh partiinykh organisatsii v period podgotovki massovogo kolkhoznogo dvizheniya (1928–1929 gg.)*', in *Voprosy istorii KPSS*, No. 3, 1962, p. 115.
33. V.K. Palishko, *Rost i ukreplenie partiinykh ryadov v usloviyakh stroitel'stva i uprocheniya sotsializma*, p. 120.
34. Ibid.
35. For rural *raikom* staff size in later years of the first Five Year Plan, see this chapter, pp. 65–6.
36. *Partiinoe stroitel'stvo*, No. 3–4, February 1931, p. 68.
37. *Partiinoe stroitel'stvo*, No. 16, August 1930, p. 50.
38. Articles which discuss the sectors' defects are *Partiinoe stroitel'stvo*, No. 21, November 1931, pp. 25–40, see especially the speech reported here made by Bravin of the Moscow *obkom*; *Partiinoe stroitel'stvo*, No. 3–4, February 1932, pp. 18–20.
39. *Partiinoe stroitel'stvo*, No. 21, November 1931, p. 35.
40. *Partiinoe stroitel'stvo*, No. 5, March 1931, p. 10. It is worth noting how various forms of organisation later developed from their embryo stage: these groups were an early version of the 1934 instructors (see Chapter 11) and the support points (see Chapter 5) were the forerunners of the political departments (see Chapter 8).
41. *Partiinoe stroitel'stvo*, No. 6, March 1931, p. 6.
42. See for example M. Fainsod, *Smolensk Under Soviet Rule*, pp. 90 and 112.
43. *Bolshevik*, No. 4, February 1933, p. 31.
44. *Partiinoe stroitel'stvo*, No. 16, August 1932, p. 25.
45. *Pravda*, 8 September 1930, p. 3. Much the same occurred when the 25 000-ers arrived in the rural *raions* early in 1930.
46. *Partiinoe stroitel'stvo*, No. 11–12, June 1930, pp. 63–4.
47. *Pravda*, 7 January 1934, p. 3.
48. M. Fainsod, *Smolensk*, p. 112 and V.K. Palishko, *Rost i ukreplenie partiinykh ryadov v usloviyakh stroitel'stva i uprocheniya sotsializma*, p. 144.
49. *XVII s''ezd Vsesoyuznoi Kommunisticheskoi Partii (b): stenograficheskii otchet* (1934), p. 39.
50. *Partiinoe stroitel'stvo*, No. 16, August 1932, p. 25 and *Partiinoe stroitel'stvo*, No. 17–18, September 1932, p. 29.
51. D. Gurevich, in *Izvestiya TsK VKP(b)*, No. 22 (243), 24 July 1928, p. 2.
52. Figures for 198 leading *raion* personnel show that 47.5 per cent were brought in from other *raions*, whilst only 27.2 per cent had risen from middle and lower work in the same *raion*, *Partiinoe stroitel'stvo*, No. 22, November 1932, p. 18.
53. *Partiinoe stroitel'stvo*, No. 11, June 1931, p. 13.
54. *Partiinoe stroitel'stvo*, No. 19, October 1933, p. 43.
55. *Partiinoe stroitel'stvo*, No. 15, August 1932, p. 51.
56. *Partiinoe stroitel'stvo*, No. 14, July 1932, p. 47.
57. *Partiinoe stroitel'stvo*, No. 11, June 1931, p. 14.
58. *Partiinoe stroitel'stvo*, No. 11–12, June 1932, p. 36.
59. Ibid., and *Partiinoe stroitel'stvo*, No. 22, November 1932, p. 28.
60. *Partiinoe stroitel'stvo*, No. 19, October 1933, p. 42.

61. *Partiinoe stroitel'stvo*, No. 11–12, June 1932, p. 46.
62. M. Lewin, 'Society and the Stalinist state in the period of the first Five Year Plans', in *Social History*, No. 2, May 1976, p. 154.
63. *Partiinoe stroitel'stvo*, No. 22, November 1932, p. 23. As early as 1928 there is mention of the desirability to keep *raikom* secretaries, *raion* land department heads and *raion* executive committee chairmen in their posts for a minimum of three years, *Izvestiya TsK VKP(b)*, No. 32 (253), 31 October 1928, p. 16. But, as we have seen, nought came of this. Security of tenure was never a feature of the rural communist party.
64. *Partiinoe stroitel'stvo*, No. 22, November 1932, p. 28.
65. *Partiinoe stroitel'stvo*, No. 11–12, June 1932, p. 48 and *Partiinoe stritel'stvo*, No. 14, July 1932, p. 47.
66. *Pravda*, 20 January 1930, p. 2.
67. But the *raikom* staff were often in a no-win situation, as frequently their duties were beyond them because of quite objective reasons.

5 The Rural Communist Party Cell 1929–32

1. See R.W. Davies, *The Industrialisation of Soviet Russia*, vol. 2. *The Soviet Collective Farm, 1929–1930*, p. 185 and *Partiinoe stroitel'stvo*, No. 7–8, April 1930, p. 10; see also Table 5.1.
2. I. Glazyrin, *Regulirovanie sostava KPSS v period stroitel'stva sotsializma*, p. 71.
3. *Pravda*, 20 January 1930.
4. Among many articles, see Zh. Meerzon, in *Partiinoe stroitel'stvo*, No. 1, November 1929, pp. 17–31; *Partiinoe stroitel'stvo*, No. 3–4, February 1930, pp. 3–9 and *Derevenskii kommunist*, No. 1, 12 January 1930, pp. 25–9.
5. For further information on party organisation in the factories see T. Sadler, 'The Party Organization in the Soviet Enterprise, 1928–1934', unpublished M.Soc.Sci. thesis, University of Birmingham, 1979.
6. V. Ryabokon', in *Partiinoe stroitel'stvo*, No. 7–8, April 1930, p. 9.
7. *Pravda*, 5 February 1930, p. 3.
8. *XVI s''ezd Vsesoyuznoi Kommunisticheskoi Partii (b): stenograficheskii otchet* (1930), p. 66.
9. For one example of the ratio in the Ukraine in 1930, see p. 219, note 28.
10. For statistical purposes the constituent shop cells did not have an independent existence. When most party collectives were broken up in 1933, cell numbers shot up.
11. *Partiinoe stroitel'stvo*, No. 1 January 1930, p. 26 and ibid., No. 3–4, February 1930, p. 23.
12. For example an early debate on the Berezovskii *raion*, Odessa *okrug*, is presented by Ya. Maksimuk, in *Partiinoe stroitel'stvo*, No. 5, March 1930, pp. 29–31.
13. On the support points, see this chapter, pp. 78–82 and for political departments, see Chapter 8.

14. M. Ammosov, in *Partiinoe stroitel'stvo*, No. 9, May 1930, p. 10.
15. A *verst* is equal to 1.1 kilometres.
16. R.W. Davies, *The Industrialisation of Soviet Russia*, Vol. 1. *The Socialist Offensive. The Collectivisation of Soviet Agriculture, 1929–1930*, p. 286.
17. For the *polozhenie*, see *Pravda*, 7 September 1930, p. 4 and *Partiinoe stroitel'stvo*, No. 18, September 1930, pp. 68–72. For the full resolution, see *Kollektivizatsiya sel'skogo khozyaistva*. *Vazhneishie postanovleniya Kommunisticheskoi partii i sovetskogo pravitael'stva 1927–1935*, pp. 363–70.
18. *Pravda*, 7 September 1930, p. 4. The cells could appeal to higher authorities, but only if they were willing to inform the *raikom* of the appeal, thereby incurring its grave displeasure, and if they carried out the *raikom's* order in the first place, which might have had irrevocable consequences before a decision was made on the appeal.
19. M. Ammosov, in *Partiinoe stroitel'stvo*, No. 9, May 1930, p. 11.
20. *Partiinoe stroitel'stvo*, No. 5, March 1931, p. 10.
21. *Partiinoe stroitel'stvo*, No. 12, June 1931, pp. 20–38.
22. *Partiinoe stroitel'stvo*, No. 18, September 1931, p. 39.
23. This is based on information that the number of *kolkhoz* cells in the Central Black Earth in July 1931 was 1 429 at a time when *kolkhoz* cells in the USSR represented 60.7 per cent of all rural cells, see P.N. Sharova, *Kollektivizatsiya sel'skogo khozyaistva Tsentral'no-chernozemnoi oblasti 1928–1932 gg.*, p. 185 and Table 5.1.
24. *Kommunisticheskaya partiya Turkestana i Uzbekistana v tsifrakh 1918–1967*, p. 117. In Uzbekistan 18 MTS and *sovkhozy* had been transformed into support points, whilst 98 had not, ibid.
25. See for example, *Partiinoe stroitel'stvo*, No. 18, September 1931, p. 39 and ibid., No. 21, November 1931, pp. 43–4.
26. Both resolutions are in *Spravochnik partiinogo rabotnika*, vol. 8, pp. 667–8.
27. The political departments' organisational debt to the support points was not recognised, certainly not in the major official pronouncement introducing the departments.
28. Bearing in mind the to and fro in the early months of mass collectivisation, which makes relative changes in different types of cell difficult to gauge – it is probable that in the early stages until the end of 1930 the territorial cells were simply transformed into *kolkhoz* cells as the communists moved in to supervise them, and these provided a substantial proportion of new *kolkhoz* cells. But as time went by, this source dried up, since it was not expedient for territorial cells to disappear entirely, as party supervision was still required over the non-collectivised countryside, and therefore more *kolkhoz* cells were organised from scratch consisting of new recruits. In the Ukraine between April–October 1930, of 966 newly formed *kolkhoz* cells, 493 had been transformed from general rural cells and 473 newly created, *Partiinoe stroitel'stvo*, No. 3–4, February 1931, p. 18.
29. See Appendix 2.
30. The figure for the North Caucasus is from *Partiinoe stroitel'stvo*, No. 6, March 1931, p. 7; for the Mid-Volga and White Russia, see *Kollektivizatsiya sel'skogo khozyaistva v Srednem povol'zhe (1927–1937 gg.)*, p. 285 and *Kommunisticheskaya partiya Belorussii v tsifrakh 1918–1978*, p. 177.
31. See *Partiinoe stroitel'stvo*, No. 3–4, February 1931, p. 18 and Table 5.1.

32. Towards the end of 1930, 6 734 rural Soviets remained without any kind of cell, *Partiinoe stroitel'stvo*, No. 3–4, February 1931, p. 19.
33. *Partiinoe stroitel'stvo*, No. 21, November 1932, p. 46.
34. *Partiinoe stroitel'stvo*, No. 13, July 1932, p. 23.
35. T.H. Rigby, *Communist Party Membership in the USSR, 1917–1967*, p. 333.
36. *Partiinoe stroitel'stvo*, No. 17–18, September 1932, p. 26. Information from 17 *raions*.
37. *Partiinoe stroitel'stvo*, No. 3–4, February 1932, p. 26; *Partiinoe stroitel'stvo*, No. 17–18, September 1932, pp. 26 and 28 and *Partiinoe stroitel'stvo*, November 1932, p. 39.
38. *Partiinoe stroitel'stvo*, No. 17–18, September 1932, p. 26.
39. *Partiinoe stroitel'stvo*, No. 22, November 1931, p. 38.
40. *Kollektivizatsiya sel'skogo khozyaistva. Vazhneishie postanovleniya kommunisticheskoi partii i sovetskogo pravitel'stva 1927–1935*, pp. 409–10.
41. *Spravochnik partiinogo rabotnika*, vol. 8, p. 607.
42. *Saratovskaya partiinaya organizatsiya v period nastupleniya sotsializma po vsemu frontu. Sozdanie kolkhoznogo stroya*, pp. 294–5 and 297.
43. *Partiinoe stroitel'stvo*, No. 9, May 1932, p. 56. These figures refer to 45 *raions* in the *krai*.
44. *Saratovskaya partiinaya organizatsiya ...* , pp. 305–6.
45. *Partiinoe stroitel'stvo*, No. 17–18, September 1932, p. 41 and *Partiinoe stroitel'stvo*, No. 21, November 1932, p. 24.
46. *Partiinoe stroitel'stvo*, No. 9, May 1932, pp. 56–7.
47. *Partiinoe stroitel'stvo*, No. 21, November 1932, p. 34.
48. *Partiinoe stroitel'stvo*, No. 16, August 1933, p. 21. This refers to the Mid-Volga *krai*.
49. *Partiinoe stroitel'stvo*, No. 16, August 1932, p. 20.

6 The Rural Communist Party and Collectivisation 1929–32

1. On this see D.S. Lane, *Politics and Society in the USSR*, ch. 7, and D.S. Lane and F. O'Dell, *The Soviet Industrial Worker*, pp. 22–9.
2. *Kollektivizatsiya sel'skogo khozyaistva. Vazhneishie postanovleniya Kommunisticheskoi partii i sovetskogo pravitel'stva 1927–1935*, pp. 188–9.
3. A description of this technique is available in D.J. Male, *Russian Peasant Organization before Collectivisation: a Study of Commune and Gathering 1925–1930*, pp. 202–3 and in R.W. Davies, *The Industrialisation of Soviet Russia*, vol. 1. *The Socialist Offensive. The Collectivisation of Soviet Agriculture, 1929–1930*, pp. 132–3.
4. See T.P. Bernstein, 'Leadership and Mobilization in the Collectivization of Agriculture in China and Russia: A Comparison', unpublished Ph.D. thesis, Columbia University, 1970, pp. 268–318 for the differences between what he terms 'command mobilisation' and 'participatory mobilisation'.
5. M. Fainsod, *Smolensk Under Soviet Rule*, p. 424.
6. V.M. Selunskaya, *Rabochie-dvadtsatipyatitysyachniki*, p. 107.

7. In our usage not all outsiders were necessarily urban, but could include rural party workers from the *obkoms* and *raikoms* who were not locals of the places to which they were dispatched. Of course, with time, and this applies to those who were mobilised for permanent transfers, 'outsiders' became 'insiders'.

8. Resolution in *Kollektivizatsiya sel'skogo khozyaistva ... 1927–1935*, pp. 228–36, especially p. 232.

9. V.M. Selunskaya, *Rabochie ...*, p. 75.

10. Ibid. This refers to a sample of 19 509.

11. We argue thus because available figures indicate that 140 000 were mobilised during parts of this period in the Central Black Earth and North Caucasus *krai* alone, see B.A. Abramov, '*Kollektivizatsiya sel'skogo khozyaistva v RSFSR*', in V.P. Danilov (ed.), *Ocherki istorii kollektivizatsii sel'skogo khozyaistva v soyuznykh respublikakh*, pp. 94, 103 and 116, and N. Spektor, *Partiya – organizator shefstva rabochikh nad derevnei*, pp. 139– 43, 158, 171–3 and 192.

12. See N. Spektor, *Partiya ...* , and *XVII s''ezd Vsesoyuznoi Kommunisticheskoi Partii (b): stenograficheskii otchet*, (1934), p. 530 for information on 1933.

13. E.I. Lar'kina, *Podgotovka kolkhoznykh kadrov v period massovoi kollektivizatsii*, p. 25.

14. See for example, *Pravda*, 15 March 1930, p. 3; *Partiinoe stroitel'stvo*, No. 11, June 1931, pp. 41–4; *Partiinoe stroitel'stvo*, No. 21, November 1931, pp. 41– 6.

15. See for example, *Pravda*, 3 June 1930.

16. *Derevenskii kommunist*, No. 9–10, 30 May 1930, p. 71

17. *Pravda*, 2 April 1930, p. 3. Similarly the whole Nizhe-Tivinskii *raikom* was dissolved, not just its bureau, ibid.

18. *Pravda*, 21 April 1930, p. 3. For other examples, see *Pravda*, 10 April 1930, p. 4.

19. *Pravda*, 21 April 1930, p. 3. See also *Pravda*, 26 April 1930, p. 3; *Pravda*, 6 May 1930, p. 3 and N.I. Nemakov, *Kommunisticheskaya partiya – organizator massovogo kolkhoznogo dvizheniya (1929–1932 gg.): po materialam nekotorykh oblastei i kraev RSFSR*, pp. 191–9.

20. *Pravda*, 19 January 1930 (Bulat of the Moscow *obkom*).

21. *XVI s''ezd Vsesoyuznoi Kommunisticheskoi Partii (b): stenograficheskii otchet*, (1930), p. 71.

22. Smolensk archives, WKP 218, pp. 209, 344, 372 and 380.

23. *Partiinoe stroitel'stvo*, No. 15, August 1930, pp. 29–30.

24. *Partiinoe stroitel'stvo*, No. 7–8, April 1932, p. 36 (Gubinikhinskii cell, Novo-moshkov *raion*, Ukraine).

25. I. Bogachev, *Partiinoe stroitel'stvo*, No. 2, January 1931, p. 49. Apparently similar priorities were held by Chinese rural communists in the 1950s, see T.P. Bernstein, 'Leadership and Mobilization', p. 287.

26. Vernyi of the C.C. *orginst* department speaking at a C.C. organisational conference reported in *Partiinoe stroitel'stvo*, No. 12, June 1931, p. 20.

27. Zh. Meerzon, *Za perestroiku partiinoi raboty – eshche o voprosakh partiinogo rukovodstva*, p. 14.

28. *Partiinoe stroitel'stvo*, No. 16, August 1930, pp. 5–8.

29. *Partiinoe stroitel'stvo*, No. 5, March 1930, p. 33 (secretary of the Umanskii party collective).
30. *Partiinoe stroitel'stvo*, No. 25, December 1931, pp. 28–9.
31. R.W. Davies, *The Industrialisation of Soviet Russia*, vol. *1*, p. 344. For a detailed discussion of the procurements in 1930 with emphasis on the economic aspects, see Ibid., ch. 8.
32. Smolensk archives, WKP 218.
33. Ibid., p. 352.
34. Ibid., pp. 357 and 360.
35. Ibid., pp. 361 and 365.
36. Ibid., pp. 330 and 383.
37. Ibid., pp. 334 and 382.
38. Ibid., pp. 351 and 384.
39. *Partiinoe stroitel'stvo*, No. 21, November 1931, p. 12.
40. *Partiinoe stroitel'stvo*, No. 18, September 1930, p. 42.
41. Yu.A. Moshkov, *Zernovaya problema v gody sploshnoi kollektivizatsii sel'skogo khozyaistva SSSR (1929–1932 gg.*), p. 150.
42. *Partiinoe stroitel'stvo*, No. 18, September 1930, pp. 42–3. Although our examples are confined to the Central Black Earth, there is no reason to believe that these incidents were peculiar to this region.
43. *Partiinoe stroitel'stvo*, No. 8, April 1931, p. 38.
44. I. Bogachev, in *Partiinoe stroitel'stvo*, No. 6, March 1931, pp. 46–7.
45. Ibid., p. 47.
46. Ibid., p. 48.
47. Resolution in *Kollektivizatsiya sel'skogo khozyaistva. Vazhneishie postanovleniya Kommunisticheskoi partii i sovetskogo pravitel'stva 1927–1935*, pp. 285–90.
48. Yu.A. Moshkov, *Zernovaya problema . . .*, p. 167.
49. Ibid.
50. I.F. Ganzha, I.I. Slin'ko and P.V. Shostak, '*Ukrainskoe selo na puti k sotsializmu*', in V.P. Danilov (ed.), *Ocherki istorii kollektivizatsii sel'skogo khozyaistva v soyuznykh respublikakh*, p. 192, and B.A. Abramov, '*Kollektivizatsiya sel'skogo khozyaistva v RSFSR*', in ibid., pp. 122–3.
51. Cited in Yu.A. Moshkov, *Zernovaya Problema . . .*, p. 213.
52. *Partiinoe stroitel'stvo*, No. 21, November 1931, p. 68.
53. Ibid., p. 67.
54. *Partiinoe stroitel'stvo*, No. 21, November 1931, pp. 15–17.
55. *Partiinoe stroitel'stvo*, No. 24, December 1931, pp. 18–19.
56. *Pravda*, 14 July 1932, pp. 1–2.
57. Ibid.
58. *Smolensk archives*, WKP 221, pp. 23–5.
59. Ibid.
60. Ibid., pp. 53–4.
61. Ibid.
62. Ibid.
63. *Partiinoe stroitel'stvo*, No. 13, July 1932, p. 19. The investigation was specific to the Novobug *raion* party organisation in the Ukraine but its conclusions were general.
64. *Pravda*, 16 October 1932, p. 2. For their pluckiness and integrity, these

raikom cadres may well have suffered later in the year when the *raion* was mentioned as one where party secretaries had assisted the *kulaks* against the party and the state, *Partiinoe stroitel'stvo*, No. 23–24, December 1932, p. 2.

65. *Partiinoe stroitel'stvo*, No. 17–18, September 1932, p. 7.
66. *Partiinoe stroitel'stvo*, No. 5, March 1933, p. 40.
67. I.E. Zelenin, '*Politotdely MTS (1933–1934 gg.)*', in *Istoricheskie zapiski*, No. 76, 1965, p. 57.
68. I.F. Ganzha, I.I. Slin'ko and P.V. Shostak, '*Ukrainskoe selo ...*', p. 145.
69. *Pravda*, 16 October 1932, p. 2.
70. *Pravda*, 5 November 1932, p. 2.
71. Ibid.
72. See B. Sheboldaev, *Stat'i i rechi 1932–1933*, p. 83; *O kolkhoznom stroitel'-stve: sbornik rukovodyashchikh materialov*, p. 273 and *Pravda*, 19 November 1932.
73. *Pravda*, 16 November 1932, p. 1. Several other North Caucasian *raikoms* were accused of 'an opportunist trick' for not meeting their quotas, *Pravda*, 24 November 1932, p. 3.
74. I.F. Ganzha et al., in V.P. Danilov (ed.), *Ocherki istorii ...*, p. 200.
75. *Partiinoe stroitel'stvo*, No. 19, October 1933, p. 43.
76. Ibid.
77. Ibid., p. 42. The chronological period covered was April 1932 – April 1933. Most of the transfers would have involved cadres who were communists.
78. Ibid., p. 43.
79. *O kolkhoznom stroitel'stve: sbornik rukovodyashchikh materialov*, p. 279.
80. R. Medvedev, *Let History Judge*, p. 93.
81. *O kolkhoznom stroitel'stve ...*, p. 281.
82. *Partiinoe stroitel'stvo*, No. 1–2, January 1933, pp. 31–32.
83. Ibid., p. 32.
84. N. Shimotomai, 'The Kuban Affair and the Crisis of Kolkhoz Agriculture (1932–1933) – with Emphasis on the North Caucasus', unpublished paper presented at the S.S.R.C. Conference on Soviet Economic Development in the 1930s, held at the Centre for Russian and East European Studies, University of Birmingham, June 1982, p. 8 mentions a final figure of 10 689 expulsions out of 24 969 checked.
85. A *Pravda* article of 21 November 1932, p. 3, recommended that the purge should be concentrated on the 'leading members of cells', and judging from evidence in the Kuban this was enacted.
86. Yu.A. Moshkov, *Zernovaya Problema ...*, pp. 216–17.
87. See *Partiinoe stroitel'stvo*, No. 10, May 1933, p. 7 and *Partiinoe stroitel'stvo*, No. 1–2, January 1933, p. 27.
88. *Pravda*, 21 December 1932, p. 2.
89. *Partiinoe stroitel'stvo*, No. 22, November 1932, p. 40.
90. *Partiinoe stroitel'stvo*, No. 5, March 1933, p. 39.
91. *Partiinoe stroitel'stvo*, No. 17–18, September 1933, p. 27.
92. Leading article in *Partiinoe stroitel'stvo*, No. 23–4, December 1932, p. 3.
93. *Partiinoe stroitel'stvo*, No. 21, November 1932, pp. 4–5.
94. See for example, *Partiinoe stroitel'stvo*, No. 17–18, September 1932, pp. 22, 70–1 and *Partiinoe stroitel'stvo*, No. 19–20, October 1932, p. 53.
95. *Partiinoe stroitel'stvo*, No. 16, August 1932, p. 9.

7 The Party and Policy Towards the Countryside 1933–39

1. Sovnarkom and C.C. resolution in *Kollektivizatsiya sel'skogo khozyaistva.*
   Vazhneishie postanovleniya Kommunisticheskoi partii i sovetskogo pravitel-
   'stva 1927–35, pp. 441–5.
2. These are high and low variants taken from S.G. Wheatcroft, 'A Re-
   evaluation of Soviet Agricultural Production in the 1920s and 1930s', paper
   presented at the S.S.R.C. Conference on Soviet Economic Development in
   the 1930s held at the Centre for Russian and East European Studies,
   University of Birmingham, June 1982, Appendix 5, pp. 29–30.
3. This is best summarised in M. Lewin, ' "Taking Grain" ': Soviet Policies of
   Agricultural Procurements before the War', in C.A. Abramsky and
   B.J. Williams (eds), *Essays in Honour of E.H. Carr*, p. 307.
4. *Pravda*, 12 November 1935, p. 3. A *pud* is equal to 36 pounds in weight.
5. G.A. Chigrinov, *Bor'ba KPSS za organizatsionno-khozyaistvennoe ukreplenie kolkhozov v dovoennye gody*, p. 113. In the Ukraine *zakupki* were only
   two million *puds* in 1933, but already 11 million *puds* in 1934, Postyshev
   speech to Kiev *obkom* and *oblispolkom* on 17 October 1934, in *Pravda*, 27
   October 1934, p. 2.
6. A.A. Barsov, in *Istoriya SSSR*, No. 6, (1968), p. 19.
7. *Kolkhozy vo vtoroi stalinskoi pyatiletke*, p. 1.
8. Quoted in M. Lewin, ' "Taking Grain": Soviet Policies of Agricultural
   Procurements before the War', in C.A. Abramsky and B.J. Williams (eds),
   Essays in Honour of E.H. Carr, p. 304.
9. I.V. Stalin, speech delivered at the joint C.C. and C.C.C. plenum on 11
   January 1933, in *Problems of Leninism*, pp. 644–5.
10. I.E. Zelenin, '*Politotdely MTS (1933–1934 gg.)*', in *Istoricheskie zapiski*,
    No. 76, 1965, p. 53.
11. Owing to limited sources, one can only conjecture about this fascinating
    prospect. Despite restraints on materials, good work has already been done
    on this, see for example F. Benvenuti, 'Kirov in Soviet Politics', unpublished
    paper in Soviet Industrialisation Project Series, No. 8, Centre for Russian
    and East European Studies, University of Birmingham, 1977; J. Haslam,
    'Political Opposition to Stalin 1932–1936: The Background to the Terror',
    unpublished working paper for Soviet Industrialisation Project, Centre for
    Russian and East European Studies, University of Birmingham, 1983.
12. Smolensk archives, WKP 178, p. 134.
13. See Chapter 8.
14. *KPSS v rezolyutsiyakh i resheniyakh s''ezdov, konferentsi i plenumov TsK*,
    vol. 5, pp. 313–15.

8 The Political Departments 1933–34

1. See the introductory remarks to his speech, in *Partiinoe stroitel'stvo*, No. 1–
   2, January 1933, p. 2.
2. R.F. Miller, '*One Hundred Thousand Tractors*' – the MTS and the Development of Controls in Soviet Agriculture, p. 138.

3. I.E. Zelenin, '*Politotdely MTS (1933–1934)*', in *Istoricheskie zapiski*, No. 76, 1965, p. 45 and note 14.
4. Speech in *Partiinoe stroitel'stvo*, No. 1–2, January 1933, pp. 1–12. This quotation, ibid., p. 12.
5. *KPSS v rezolyutsiyakh i resheniyakh s'''ezdov, konferentsii i plenumov TsK*, vol. 5, p. 81.
6. Ibid.
7. Ibid.
8. V. Markovich, in *Partiinoe stroitel'stvo*, No. 13–14, July 1933, p. 62. The figures presented by Markovich are based on findings of the C.C. statistical department and refer to 7000 of this original consignment.
9. Ibid., p. 63.
10. Ibid., p. 64.
11. Ibid., p. 63.
12. Ibid., p. 64.
13. See S.P. Trapeznikov, *Istoricheskii opyt KPSS v osushchestvlenii leninskogo kooperativnogo plana*, p. 420.
14. I.E. Zelenin, '*Politotdely MTS*', p. 46.
15. S.P. Trapcznikov, *Istoricheskii opyt* . . . , p. 419.
16. I.E. Zelenin, '*Politotdely MTS*', pp. 46–7.
17. See Chapter 6.
18. *Pravda*, 6 February 1933, p. 3.
19. Quoted in I.E. Zelenin, '*Politotdely MTS*', p. 47.
20. Ibid., p. 52.
21. Ibid. It is not difficult to notice the attention paid to accountants and book keepers: at a plenary session of the Ukrainian C.C., S.V. Kosior had spoken of 'kulak arithmetic', *Pravda*, 15 February 1933, p. 3.
22. *Partiinoe stroitel'stvo*, No. 22, November 1933, p. 32.
23. The *raikoms* themselves were frequently headed by secretaries brought in from other *raions*, see Chapter 4.
24. *Partiinoe stroitel'stvo*, No. 1–2, January 1933, p. 21.
25. Ibid., p. 13.
26. *KPSS v rezolyutsiyakh* . . . , vol. 5, p. 88.
27. *Pravda*, 12 June 1933, p. 1. (Tikhoretsk *raion*, North Caucasus).
28. *Pravda*, 6 April 1933, p. 2.
29. J. Hough depicts a similar process of appeals to higher authority to seek alterations at lower levels in different institutions. In his examples the relationship is between party organs on the one hand and factories run by state ministries on the other. This may well make it a constant in Soviet society. See J. Hough, *The Soviet Prefects*, pp. 105–9.
30. *Pravda*, 12 June 1933, p. 1.
31. *Pravda*, 20 June 1933, p. 2.
32. *Pravda*, 12 June 1933, p. 1.
33. *Pravda*, 17 June 1933, p. 1.
34. See Smolensk archives, WKP 315, p. 36 for the example of the Yelnya MTS political department head, who reported that the *raikom* refused to dispatch a previously agreed number of *komsomol* workers who were to assist the department in its work because the *raikom* did not wish to see any improvement in the *kolkhozy* under the supervision of the MTS. This at least was the interpretation of the department head.

35. *KPSS v rezolyutsiyakh* . . ., vol. 5, p. 110.
36. *Pravda*, 22 June 1933, p. 3. The conflict between political departments and *raikoms* was not confined to those at MTS. A resolution introduced them to the railways, see *Pravda*, 11 July 1933, p. 1, but by September there were published complaints of conflict between railway political departments and regular territorial party organisations such as *raikoms*, see *Pravda*, 10 September 1933, p. 2.
37. For a top-secret clarifying circular of 3 February 1933, see M. Fainsod, *Smolensk Under Soviet Rule*, p. 286.
38. Ibid., pp. 286–7.
39. Ibid., p. 287.
40. For an example of the continued high-handed approach of one OGPU deputy, see the report of the political sector of the White Russian SSR, cited in I.E. Zelenin, *'Politotdely MTS'*, p. 54.
41. In September Krinitskii used a familiar technique of comparing one political department which worked well with one that did not, *Pravda*, 16 September 1933, pp. 2–3. The general purpose of such a device was to hint at a more pervasive malaise in the system and to *'encourager les autres'*.
42. R.F. Miller, *'One Hundred Thousand Tractors'*, p. 208.
43. See Chapter 7.
44. R.F. Miller, *'One Hundred Thousand Tractors'*, pp. 239–42.
45. Ibid., p. 239.
46. I.E. Zelenin, *'Politotdely MTS'*, p. 57. An even more convoluted view of this would be that the regional secretaries were smearing the departments from the other extreme with this accusation of leniency.
47. I.F. Ganzha, I.I. Slin'ko and P.V. Shostak, *'Ukrainskoe selo na puti k sotsializmu'*, in V.P. Danilov (ed.), *Ocherki istorii kollektivizatsii sel'skogo khozyaistva v soyuznykh respublikakh*, p. 145.
48. Ibid.
49. Francesco Benvenuti presents a cogent and illuminating paper on S.M. Kirov and his role in the 'thaw' of these years in 'Kirov in Soviet Politics, 1933–1934', Soviet Industrialisation Project Series, No. 8, Centre for Russian and East European Studies, University of Birmingham, 1977. In this study Kirov is depicted as less hawkish a member of the party leadership, who opposed the political departments more vigorously than most, see ibid., pp. 18–19. But Kirov, like his colleagues, was also critical of the departments for their weakness, just as much as for any excesses they may have committed, when, in his speech to an enlarged plenum of the Leningrad *obkom* on 4 July 1934, he complained that some *kolkhozniks*, party workers and political department heads had placed local interests before those of the state, and he favoured a 'decisive struggle against any liberalism in connection with those who did not fulfil the state plan'. Kirov continued more interestingly that the political departments 'had become accustomed to the situation' after having commenced their work well; they had mellowed and 'the voice of the political departments is heard but has become a tone lower', *Pravda*, 19 July 1934, p. 2. Whilst arguing against liberalism, he did believe that plans had to be achieved but without breaking revolutionary legality, ibid. Thus it seems that Kirov represents an amalgam

of attitudes to the situation in the countryside in 1933–34, and in particular to the political departments.

50. I.E. Zelenin, 'Politotdely MTS', p. 56. See also M. Fainsod, Smolensk, p. 291, who cites an example of the Yelnya MTS political department head complaining of a further plan imposed on a kolkhoz. Fainsod concurs with the above drift of argument when he states that: 'Some political department chiefs . . . developed a certain sympathy for the peasants with whom they dealt . . .', ibid.

51. XVII s''ezd Vsesoyuznoi Kommunisticheskoi Partii (b): stenograficheskii otchet (1934), p. 560.

52. See for example article by A. Levin in Pravda, 6 September 1934, p. 3.

53. KPSS v rezolyutsiyakh . . ., vol. 5, pp. 201–2.

54. Ibid.

55. Ibid., p. 202.

56. Ibid.

57. Ibid., p. 199.

58. Pravda, 27 December 1934, pp. 2 and 4.

59. My derivations from S.P. Trapeznikov, Istoricheskii opyt KPSS v osushchestvlenii leninskogo kooperativnogo plana, p. 495.

60. Ibid., p. 497.

61. Pravda, 27 December 1934, pp. 2 and 4.

62. KPSS v rezolyutsiyakh . . ., vol. 5, p. 201.

63. Ibid.

9   The Soviet Rural Communist Party and the Purges 1933–34

1. The resolution was in fact dated 10 December and was later confirmed at the January 1933 joint C.C. and C.C.C. plenum.

2. KPSS v rezolyutsiyakh i resheniyakh s''ezdov, konferentsii i plenumov TsK, vol. 5, pp. 100–1.

3. Ibid., p. 100.

4. Ibid.

5. Ibid., p. 103.

6. XVII s''ezd Vsesoyuznoi Kommunisticheskoi Partii (b): stenograficheskii otchet (1934), p. 287. Later in the year, Em. Yaroslavsky presented a detailed break-down of the purge results with a total number of those undergoing the purge 1 075 943. This article also included Karelia which was not mentioned in the original C.C. resolution on the purge, Em. Yaroslavsky, Bolshevik, No. 15, August 1934, p. 9.

7. Ibid. and Partiinoe stroitel'stvo, No. 14, July 1934, p. 2.

8. Partiinoe stroitel'stvo, No. 17, September 1933, pp. 11–12.

9. These figures do not take into account appeals, which may explain the figure of 182 500 purge expulsions mentioned by Kaganovich at the seventeenth party congress, XVII s''ezd, p. 552.

10. Often what happened to those reduced to sympathiser status in 1933 and 1934 was that, instead of applying for readmission to candidate or full

member status after a one year interval, they ended up expelled completely, drifted away from party life (a sign of poor work with them) or left their original *raions* without trace (a sign of the party's poor accounting system), see *Partiinoe stroitel'stvo*, No. 8, April 1935, p. 26.

11. See J. Arch Getty, *Origins of the Great Purges. The Soviet Communist Party Reconsidered, 1933–1938*, pp. 48–57.
12. Em. Yaroslavsky, *Partiinoe stroitel'stvo*, No. 14, July 1934, p. 2. Both J. Arch Getty, passim and T.H. Rigby, *Communist Party Membership in the USSR, 1917–1967*, passim, fail to distinguish the 1933 and 1934 purges as two separate events.
13. Several sources mention these 17 party organisations outstanding, for example, V. Belyakov and N. Zolotarev, *Partiya ukreplyaet svoi ryady*, p. 133 and V.K. Palishko, *Rost i ukreplenie partiinykh ryadov v usloviyakh stroitel'stva i uprocheniya sotsializma*, p. 60.
14. The figure of 1 916 500 is given in V.K. Palishko, *Rost i ukreplenie . . .*, p. 61.
15. See I.N. Yudin, *Sotsial'naya basa rosta KPSS*, p. 126 and N.A. Zolotarev, *Vazhnyi etap organisatsionnogo ukrepleniya kommunisticheskoi partii (1929–1937 gg.)*, p. 172.
16. This is summarised in Table 9.2.
17. *Partiinoe stroitel'stvo*, No. 7, April 1935, p. 33.
18. N. Shimotomai, 'The Kuban Affair and the Crisis of Kolkhoz Agriculture (1932–1933) – with Emphasis on the North Caucasus', paper presented at the S.S.R.C. Conference on Soviet Economic Development in the 1930s, held at the Centre for Russian and East European Studies, University of Birmingham, England, 16–19 June 1982, p. 14.
19. *KPSS v rezolyutsiyakh.*, vol. 5, pp. 161–2.
20. Passivity is emphasised by T.H. Rigby, *Communist Party Membership*, p. 204 and has been accepted by J.F. Hough and M. Fainsod, *How the Soviet Union is Governed*, p. 172.
21. *Istoriya KPSS*, vol. 4, book 2, p. 283 and *Partiinoe stroitel'stvo*, No. 7, April 1935, p. 32.
22. *Partiinoe stroitel'stvo*, No. 7, April 1935, pp. 33–4.
23. *Istoriya KPSS*, vol. 4, book 2, p. 283.
24. *Partiinoe stroitel'stvo*, No. 17, September 1933, pp. 11–12.
25. Resolution in *Kollektivizatsiya sel'skogo khozyaistva. Vazhneishie postanovleniya kommunisticheskoi partii i sovetskogo pravitel'stva 1927–1935*, p. 458.
26. Many of those expelled were comparatively recent recruits to the party: two-thirds had joined since 1928 and one half since 1929, see *Partiinaya zhizn'*, No. 20, October 1947, p. 79, and *XVII s''ezd Vsesoyuznoi Komunisticheskoi Partii (b) . . .*, p. 552.
27. The most comprehensive Western estimate for the decline in the whole party was made by T.H. Rigby in his pioneering study. On the basis of a statement in a Soviet party journal of 1947 that there were 16.3 per cent expulsions and 5.8 per cent reductions to sympathisers, Rigby concludes: 'While 22% of the CPSU were expelled during the 1933–1934 purge (including those reduced to "sympathiser"), the party membership actually fell in these two years by 33%, or 1.2 million', T.H. Rigby, *Communist Party Membership*, p. 204.

28. N.A. Zolotarev, *Vazhnyi etap organisatsionnogo ukrepleniya kommunisti-cheskoi partii (1929–1937 gg.)*, p. 172, note 95 names the 17 organisations in question. Indeed Rigby himself in one sentence of his book seems aware of the point we are making here, but then fails to appreciate its ramifications, see T.H. Rigby, *Communist Party Membership*, p. 207.

29. N.A. Zolotarev, ibid. The following equation was used, based on Zolotarev's data, to discover what absolute figures were reduced to sympathiser status as presented in Table 9.2:

$$14\% \times A + 22\% \times B = 312\,000$$
$$\text{where } A + B = 1\,916\,500$$

The resulting figures were 556 125 and 1 360 375. Knowing from partial surveys that more full members were investigated than candidates, we can safely assume that 1 360 375 full party members and 556 125 candidates were checked. We can then calculate that 20 405 full party members were reduced to sympathiser (1.5 per cent of full members investigated) and 91 760 candidates (16.5 per cent of candidates investigated). This seems to be the most accurate breakdown of purge results and coincides quite closely with the *Partiinaya zhizn'* figure of 111 157 reduced to sympathiser, *Partiinaya zhizn'*, No. 20, October 1947, pp. 77–80.

30. For example, it is known that the Western *oblast* was one of those 17 organisations not included in either of the official purges, and yet communists were being expelled here prior to the 1935 verification of party cards. Expulsion levels of 50 per cent were noted in some *raions* of the *oblast*, *Partiinoe stroitel'stvo*, No. 7, April 1935, p. 34.

31. J. Arch Getty lists the expulsion levels of party members during non-purge years, see J. Arch Getty, 'Party and Purge in Smolensk: 1933–1937', in *Slavic Review*, vol. 42, No. 1, spring 1983, p. 69, Table A, but this is not the same as ordinary disciplinary expulsions alongside major, simultaneous official purges.

32. We therefore have doubts that one can seek the precision aimed for in calculations on party membership for 1933–34 in S.G. Wheatcroft, 'Towards a Thorough Analysis of Soviet Forced Labour Statistics', in *Soviet Studies*, vol. XXXV, No. 2, April 1983, Appendix 1, pp. 235–6.

33. *KPSS v rezolyutsiyakh . . .*, vol. 5, p. 245.

34. *Partiinoe stroitel'stvo*, No. 2, January 1936, p. 12.

35. See comments by Shil'man of the Western *obkom* in *Partiinoe stroitel'stvo*, No. 19–20, October 1935, p. 49.

36. See for example the Smolensk archives, File 116/154e, pp. 69–79 for a most savage indictment signed in the summer of 1935 by Ezhov and Malenkov (Ezhov's deputy at the C.C.'s Department of leading party organs), in which dozens of communists were listed in a catalogue of 'spies', 'White Guards', 'kulaks', 'Trotskyites' and 'Zinovievites'.

37. *KPSS v rezolyutsiyakh . . .*, vol. 5, pp. 248–50.

38. All this decline need not be attributable to the exchange of party cards.

39. The revised interpretation is made by J. Arch Getty, *Origins of the Great Purges. The Soviet Communist Party Reconsidered, 1933–1938*, pp. 90–1. The standard view has been expressed by M. Fainsod, *How Russia is Ruled*, and R. Conquest, *The Great Terror*, among others.

40. That is the January 1937 base figure of 1 981 697 plus 40 000 recruits in the period November 1936–December 1937 equals 2 021 697 minus the January 1938 base figure of 1 920 002.
41. *Bolshevik*, No. 10, May 1937, p. 16. In some regions the removal rate of ppo committees was even higher: 66 per cent in Chernigov *oblast*, 64 per cent in the Crimea, 57.2 per cent in Kiev *oblast* and 57.0 per cent in Donets *oblast*, ibid.
42. *Kommunisticheskaya partiya Belorussii v tsifrakh, 1918–1978*, pp. 34, 117 and 121.
43. 252 714 (100 per cent) in January 1983 and 149 930 (59 per cent) in January 1938, *Leningradskaya organizatsiya KPSS v tsifrakh, 1917–1973*, pp. 60–70.
44. *Ocherki istorii Stavropol'skoi organisatii KPSS*, pp. 258–306.
45. See remarks made by Kaganovich and Stalin at the seventeenth and eighteenth party congresses respectively, *XVII s''ezd* . . . (1934), p. 558 and *XVIII s''ezd Vsesouyuznoi Kommunisticheskoi Partii (b): stenograficheskii otchet* (1939), p. 28.
46. *XVII s''ezd* . . . (1934), p. 558.
47. Quoted in I.E. Zelenin, '*Politotdely MTS (1933–1934 gg.)*', in *Istoricheskie zapiski*, No. 76, 1965, p. 50.
48. Letter from the C.C. to all party organisations, dated 29 September 1936, in *Partiinoe stroitel'stvo*, No. 19, October 1936, pp. 3–5. As early as the seventeenth party congress (January–February 1934), it had been resolved to renew recruitment from the second half of 1934, *KPSS v rezolyutsiyakh*, vol. 5, p. 155. This had been postponed until the C.C. plenum of December 1935 declared that the enrolments would recommence of 1 June 1936, ibid., p. 250, and finally recruitment only began on 1 November 1936.
49. *XVIII s''ezd Vsesoyuznoi Kommunisticheskoi Partii (b): stenograficheskii otchet* (1939), p. 109.

10 The Rural Party Cell 1933–39: Structure, Numbers and Deployment

1. A. Sadler, 'The Party Organisation in the Soviet Enterprise, 1928–1934', unpublished M.Soc.Sci. thesis, University of Birmingham, 1979, p. 79.
2. Ya. Druzhinin, in *Partiinoe stroitel'stvo*, No. 9, May 1932, p. 55.
3. *Partiinoe stroitel'stvo*, No. 22, November 1932, p. 42.
4. I. Bannayan, in *Partiinoe stroitel'stvo*, No. 17–18, September 1932, p. 67.
5. T. Sadler, 'The Party Organisation', p. 124.
6. See Chapter 5.
7. *KPSS v rezolyutsiyakh i resheniyakh konferentsii, s''ezdov i plenumov TsK*, vol. 5, pp. 109–10.
8. I. Mar'yanskii, in *Partiinoe stroitel'stvo*, No. 10, May 1932, p. 36.
9. *Partiinoe stroitel'stvo*, No. 21, November 1932, p. 19.
10. For the example of Luninskii *raion*, Mid-Volga, see *Partiinoe stroitel'stvo*, No. 21, November 1932, p. 9.
11. *KPSS v rezolyutsiyakh* . . . , vol. 5, pp. 109–10.
12. Ibid., p. 110.

13. See Table 10.1.
14. V.K. Palishko, *Rost i ukreplenie partiinykh ryadov v usloviyakh stroitel'stva i uprocheniya sotsializma*, p. 126.
15. *Partiinoe stroitel'stvo*, No. 12, June 1933, p. 39.
16. *Ocherki istorii kommunisticheskoi partii Ukrainy* (1964), p. 443.
17. *Partiinoe stroitel'stvo*, No. 17, September 1933, p. 37.
18. *Pravda*, 5 December 1933, p. 1.
19. *XVII s''ezd . . .* (1934), p. 557. For the transformation of cells into ppos, see ibid., p. 678. The introduction of the ppos affected mostly large cells with over 100 communists and therefore hardly concerned most rural cells.
20. See ibid and F. Chivirev, in *Partiinoe stroitel'stvo*, No. 14, July 1935, pp. 30–4.
21. See Table 10.1.
22. *Kommunisticheskaya partiya Belorussii v tsifrakh 1918–1978*, pp. 172–3.
23. See *VIII s''ezd Vsesoyuznoi Kommunisticheskoi Partii (b): stenograficheskii otchet* (1939), p. 109.
24. This applies less to Kazakhstan (a relatively important grain region) than to the other national republics.
25. *Kommunisticheskaya partiya Belorussii v tsifrakh 1918–1978*, pp. 172–3.
26. *Kommunisticheskaya partiya Turkestana i Uzbekistana v tsifrakh 1918–1967*, pp. 117 and 121.
27. *Partiinoe stroitel'stvo*, No. 15, August 1933, p. 26.
28. See Table 10.1.
29. *Partiinoe stroitel'stvo*, No. 1–2, January 1935, p.45.
30. This would seem to be the case in the Kukmorskii *raion*, Tartariya, where of 59 single communists, 27 of whom were candidates, 15 were *kolkhoz* chairmen, 12 brigade leaders, 12 Soviet chairmen and six accountants, *Partiinoe stroitel'stvo*, No. 14, July 1935, p. 34.
31. See Chapter 12.
32. M. Volin, in *Partiinoe stroitel'stvo*, No.12, June 1933, p. 5. This article was a commentary on the C.C. resolution of 15 June 1933.
33. M. Meksina, in *Partiinoe stroitel'stvo*, No. 11, June 1935, pp. 19–20.
34. F. Chivirev, in *Partiinoe stroitel'stvo*, No. 14, July 1935, p. 32.
35. *XVIII s''ezd Vsesoyuznoi Kommunisticheskoi Partii (b); stenograficheskii otchet* (1939), p. 109; D. Bakhshiev, *Partiinoe stroitel'stvo v usloviyakh pobedy sotsializma v SSSR*, p. 87; and derived from V.K. Palishko, *Rost i ukreplenie partiinykh ryadvov usloviyakh stroitel'stva i uprocheniya sotsializma*, p. 162.
36. G.A. Chigrinov, *Bor'ba KPSS za organizatsionno-khozyaistvennoe ukreplenie kolkhozov v dovoennye gody*, p. 163.

11 The *raikom* 1933–39: Adapting to Change

1. *Partiinoe stroitel'stvo*, No. 19, October 1933, p. 44. Other examples refer to Azerbaidjan and the Mid-Volga, see *Partiinoe stroitel'stvo*, No. 21, November 1933, pp. 42–3 and *Partiinoe stroitel'stvo*, No. 22, November 1933, pp. 34–5.

2. *KPSS v rezolyutsiyakh i resheniyakh s''ezdov, konferentsii i plenumov TsK*, vol. 5, p. 156.
3. *Partiinoe stroitel'stvo*, No. 10, May 1934, p. 13.
4. *Partiinoe stroitel'stvo*, No. 11, June 1934, p. 10.
5. *Partiinoe stroitel'stvo*, No. 10, May 1934, p. 14.
6. Ibid.
7. *Partiinoe stroitel'stvo*, No. 8, April 1934, p. 23 and *Partiinoe stroitel'stvo*, No. 9, May 1934, p.30.
8. The ORPOs are discussed further in this chapter, see pp. 177–9.
9. *KPSS v rezolyutsiyakh* . . . , vol. 5, p. 202.
10. In modified forms this had happened with the mobilisation of rural communists into *kolkhozy* and the transfer of the *okrug* personnel to the *raions* in 1930, see Chapters 3 and 4.
11. *Partiinoe stroitel'stvo*, No. 6, March 1935, p. 6.
12. Ibid., p. 7.
13. *Partiinoe stroitel'stvo*, No. 7, April 1935, p. 2.
14. Ibid.
15. V.K. Palishko, *Rost i ukreplenie partiinykh ryadov v usloviyakh stroitel'stva i uprocheniya sotsializma*, p. 148 and *Istoriya KPSS*, vol. 4, book 2, p. 279.
16. *Pravda*, 28 April 1936, p. 2.
17. *Partiinoe stroitel'stvo*, No. 20, October 1934, p. 11.
18. See Chapter 4.
19. *KPSS v rezolyutiyakh* . . . , vol. 5, p. 201.
20. Ibid., p. 169. At the eighteenth party congress in March 1939 the effects of the intervening purges were manifest and the need to promote relatively raw party personnel became apparent. Changes in the party statutes admitted as much. 'In order to create the necessary conditions for the promotion into leading party work of new cadres . . . ' the required *stazh* of the following was reduced: *obkom* and *kraikom* secretaries from a minimum of 12 to 5 years, *gorkom* secretaries from a minimum of ten years to 3 and *raikom* secretaries from seven to three years, ibid., p. 379.
21. For the relevant information on the first Five Year Plan, see Chapter 4; for 1934, see *Partiinoe stroitel'stvo*, No. 24, December 1934, p. 4.
22. See for example *Sovnarkom* and C.C. resolution of 19 April 1938 in *KPSS v rezolyutsiyakh* . . . , vol. 5, pp. 313–15.
23. *Pravda*, 28 July 1936, p. 3 and *Partiinoe stroitel'stvo*, No. 19, October 1936, p. 19.
24. *KPSS v rezolyutiyakh* . . . , vol. 5, pp. 155–6.
25. KPKs were not established in the *raions* to replace the former *raion* control commissions, the staff of which were redeployed to other duties. Some *raion* control commission chairmen became *raikom* instructors. The type of work formerly performed by the *raion* control commissions was entrusted to the *raikoms* themselves, *Partiinoe stroitel'stvo*, No. 7, April 1934, p. 7.
26. Smolensk archives, File 116/154e, p. 88.
27. J. Arch Getty, 'The "Great Purges" Reconsidered. The Soviet Communist Party, 1933–1939', unpublished Ph.D. thesis, Boston College, Mass., 1979, p. 89.
28. *XVII s''ezd Vsesoyuznoi Kommunisticheskoi Partii (b): stenograficheskii otchet* (1934), p. 562.

29. *Partiinoe stroitel'stvo*, No. 19, October 1934, pp. 4–5.
30. D. Bulatov, in *Partiinoe stroitel'stvo*, No. 18, September 1934, p. 11.

12 The Role of the Rural Communist Party 1933–39 and in Perspective

1. In *Kollektivizatsiya sel'skogo khozyaistva. Vazhneishie postanovleniya Kommunisticheskoi partii i sovetskogo pravitel'stva 1927–1935*, pp. 455–59.
2. Ibid., p. 458.
3. Ibid.
4. This was asked of organisational-instruction departments (orginst) in the Ukraine, M. Meksina, in *Partiinoe stroitel'stvo*, No. 12, June 1933, p. 39, and of the *orginst* in Bashkiriya, A. Lyapunov, in *Partiinoe stroitel'stvo*, No. 12, p. 42.
5. I. Karpov, a close colleague of P.P. Postyshev in the Ukraine, in *Partiinoe stroitel'stvo*, No. 22, November 1933, pp. 35–6.
6. *XVII s''ezd Vsesoyuznoi Kommunisticheskoi Partii (b): stenograficheskii otchet* (1934), pp. 539, 542, 552–4.
7. *Pravda*, 24 November 1934, p. 3.
8. *Pravda*, 7 March 1935, p. 3. Similar authoritative views were expressed in the resolution of the Saratov *kraikom* plenum held 5–7 July 1935 and chaired by Zhdanov, the Leningrad *obkom* first secretary since Kirov's assassination, *Pravda*, 12 July 1935, pp. 6 7.
9. *Pravda*, 6 February 1937, p. 1.
10. R.F. Miller, 'One Hundred Thousand Tractors': the MTS and the Development of Controls in Soviet Agriculture, p. 145.
11. *Pravda*, 8 June 1936, p. 2.
12. *Partiinoe stroitel'stvo*, No. 15, August 1936, p. 23.
13. *Pravda*, 8 March 1937, p. 3.
14. *Pravda*, 31 March 1937, p. 1. The regions in question were the Azov-Black Sea *krai* and the Ordzhonikidze, Odessa and Dnepropetrovsk *oblasts*.
15. *Pravda*, 9 March 1937, p. 1.
16. *Partiinoe stroitel'stvo*, No. 11, June 1939, p. 25.
17. See Chapters 9 and 10.
18. We are speaking generally here. There were of course exceptions, as in the 1928 grain crisis.
19. N.S. Khrushchev, *O merakh dal'neishego razvitiya sel'skogo khozyaistva SSSR*, pp. 4 and 72.
20. *Pravda*, 13 March 1947, p. 1. Editorial entitled 'The fighting tasks of kolkhoz party organisations!'.
21. See for example recommendations by Lazar Slepar in *Bolshevik*, No. 2, January 1951, p. 49, in which his advice consists of how to lead by following a middle course of not meddling in detail but without neglecting economic affairs.

Bibliography

Newspapers, Journals and Periodical Publications

Annali dell' Instituto Italiano per gli Studi Storici
Bolshevik
Derevenskii kommunist
The Economic Journal
Istochnikovedenie istorii sovetskogo obshchestva
Istoricheskie zapiski
Istoriya SSSR
Izvestiya
Izvestiya Tsentral'nogo Komiteta Vsesoyuznoi Kommunisticheskoi Partii (b)
Kolkhoznik
Kommunist
Krasnaya zvezda
Krest'yanskaya gazeta
Materialy po istorii SSSR
Na agrarnom fronte
Na fronte kollektivizatsii
Na fronte sel'sko-khozyaistvennykh zagotovok
Partiinoe stroitel'stvo
Partiinaya zhizn'
Pravda
Problems of Communism
Proletarii
Slavic Review
Social History
Sotsialisticheskoe zemledelie
Sovetskoe stroitel'stvo
Soviet Studies
Spravochnik partiinogo rabotnika
Sputnik kommunista v derevne
Vlast' sovetov
Voprosy istorii
Voprosy istorii KPSS

Works in Russian

Place of publication is Moscow or Moscow-Leningrad, unless otherwise stated.

Administrativno-territorial'noe delenie Soyuza SSR i spisok vazhneishikh naselen-nykh punktov, 8th edn (1929).

Bakhshiev, D., *Partiinoe stroitel'stvo v usloviyakh pobedy sotsializma v SSSR (1934–1941 gg.)* (1954).

Barsov, A.A., *Balans stoimostnykh obmenov mezhdu gorodom i derevnei* (1969).

Belyakov, V.K., and Zolotarev, N.A., *Partiya ukreplyaet svoi ryady* (1970).

Belyakov, V.K., and Zolotarev, N.A., *Organizatsiya udesyateryaet sily: razvitie organisatsionnoi struktury KPSS 1917–1974 gg.* (1975).

Chernopitskii, P.G., *Na velikom perelome: sel'skie sovety Dona v period podgotovki i provedeniya massovoi kollektivizatsii (1928–1931 gg.)* (Rostov, 1965).

Chigrinov, G.A., *Bor'ba KPSS za organizatsionno-khozyaistvennoe ukreplenie kolkhozov v dovoennye gody* (1970).

Danilov, V.P., *Sozdanie material'no-tekhnicheskikh predposylok kollektivizatsii sel'skogo khozyaistva v SSSR* (1957).

Danilov, V.P., *Sovetskaya dokolkhoznaya derevnya: naselenie, zemlepol'zovanie, khozyaistvo* (1977).

Danilov, V.P., (ed.), *Ocherki istorii sel'skogo khozyaistva v soyuznykh respublikakh* (1963).

Danilov, V.P., Kim, M.P., and Trokina, N.V., (eds), *Sovetskoe krestyanstvo: Kratkii ocherk istorii (1917–1969)* (1970).

Direktivy KPSS i sovetskogo pravitel'stva po khozyaistvennym voprosam: sbornik dokumentov (1957–58).

Dvenadtsatyi s"ezd Rossiskoi Kommunisticheskoi partii (bol'shevikov): stenograficheskii otchet, 17–25 aprelya 1923 g. (1923).

Gladkov, I., *Sovetskoe narodnoe khozyaistvo (1921–1925)* (1960).

Glazyrin, I., *Regulirovanie sostava KPSS v period stroitel'stva sotsializma* (1957).

Istoriya Kommunisticheskoi partii Sovetskogo Soyuza, 2nd edn (1962).

Istoriya Kommunisticheskoi partii Sovetskogo Soyuza, vols 4 and 5 (1971).

Istoriya sovetskogo krest'yanstva i kolkhoznogo stroitel'stva v SSSR: materialy nauchnoi sessii, sostoyavsheisya 18–21 aprelya 1961 v Moskve (1963).

Ivnitskii, N.A., *Klassovaya bor'ba v derevne i likvidatsiya kulachestva kak klassa (1929–1932 gg.)* (1972).

Izmeneniya sotsial'noi struktury sovetskogo obshchestva 1921-seredina 30-x godov (1979).

Khrushchev, N.S., *O merakh dal'neishnogo razvitiya sel'skogo khozyaistva SSSR* (1953).

Kolkhozy vo vtoroi stalinskoi pyatiletke (1939).

Kollektivizatsiya sel'skogo khozyaistva na Severnom kavkaze (1927–1937 gg.) (Krasnodar, 1972).

Kollektivizatsiya sel'skogo khozyaistva. Vazhneishie postanovleniya Kommunisticheskoi partii i Sovetskogo pravitel'stva, 1927–1935 (1957).

Kollektivizatsiya sel'skogo khozyaistva v Srednem povol'zhe (1927–1937 gg.) (Kuibyshev, 1970).

Kollektivizatsiya sel'skogo khozyaistva zapadnoi sibiri (1927–1937 gg.) (Tomsk, 1972).

Kommunisticheskaya partiya Belorussii v tsifrakh 1918–1978 (Minsk, 1978).

Kommunisticheskaya partiya Sovetskogo soyuza v rezolyutsiyakh i resheniyakh s"ezdov, konferentsii i plenumov TsK, vols 3, 4 and 5 (1971).

Kommunisticheskaya partiya Turkestana i Uzbekistana v tsifrakh 1918–1967 (Tashkent, 1968).

Kommunisticheskaya partiya Ukrainy v rezolyutsiyakh i resheniyakh s''ezdov, konferentsii i plenumov TsK, vol. 1, (1918–1941) (Kiev, 1976).

Konyukhov, G.A., *KPSS v bor'be s khlebnymi zatrudneniyami v strane 1928– 1929* (1960).

Kozlova, L., *K pobede kolkhoznogo stroya: bor'ba moskovskoi partiinoi organizatsii za podgotovku i provedenie kollektivizatsii* (1971).

KPSS. *Smolenskii oblastnoi komitet. Partiinyi arkhiv.* (The Smolensk archives).

KPSS v bor'be za sotsialisticheskoe preobrazovanie sel'skogo khozyaistva. Sbornik statei (1961).

Kritsman, L., *Klassovoe rassloenie sovetskoi derevni* (1926).

Kuibyshevskaya oblastnaya partiinaya organizatsiya v dokumentakh i tsifrakh (1902–1977 gg.) (Kuibyshev, 1978).

Lar'kina, E.I., *Podgotovka kolkhoznykh kadrov v period massovoi kollektivizatsii* (1960).

Leningradskaya organizatsiya KPSS v tsifrakh 1917–1973 (Leningrad, 1974).

Levykhin, K.G., *KPSS – organizator kolkhoznogo proisvodstva v gody vtoroi pyatiletki (1933–1937)* (1969).

Meerzon, Zh., *Za perestroiku partiinoi raboty – eshche o voprosakh partiinogo rukovodstva* (1929).

Mitrofanov, A.Kh., *Kolkhoznoe dvizhenie* (1928).

Mordovskaya partiinaya organizatsiya v dokumentakh i tsifrakh, 1918–1972 gg. (Saransk, 1975).

Moshkov, Yu.A., *Zernovaya problema v gody sploshnoi kollektivizatsii sel'skogo khozyaistva SSSR (1929–1932 gg.)* (1966).

Nemakov, N.I., *Kommunisticheskaya partiya – organizator massovogo kolkhoznogo dvizheniya (1929–1932 gg.): po materialam nekotorykh oblastei i kraev RSFSR* (1966).

Neznanov, S.V., (ed.), *Partiya – organizator kolkhoznogo stroya* (1958).

O kolkhoznom stroitel'stve: sbornik rukovodyashchikh materialov (Rostov on Don, 1932).

Ocherki istorii Kommunisticheskoi partii Belorussii, chast' 2, 1921–1966 (Minsk, 1967).

Ocherki istorii Kommunisticheskoi partii Gruzii 1883–1970 (Tbilisi, 1971).

Ocherki istorii Kommunisticheskoi partii Ukrainy (Kiev, 1961 and 1964).

Ocherki istorii Kurskoi organizatsii KPSS (Voronezh, 1980).

Ocherki istorii Moskovskoi organizatsii KPSS, 1883–1965 (1966).

Ocherki istorii Stavropolskoi organizatsii KPSS (Stavropol', 1970).

Palishko, V.K., *Rost i ukreplenie partiinykh ryadov v usloviyakh stroitel'stva i uprocheniya sotsializma* (Kiev, 1979).

Partiya v period nastupleniya sotsializma po vsemu frontu. Sozdanie kolkhoznogo stroya (1929–1932 gg.) (1961).

Penzenskaya partiinaya organizatsiya v tsifrakh i faktakh, 1918–1978 gg. (Saratov, 1979).

Pervichnaya partiinaya organizatsiya. Dokumenty KPSS (1970).

Podgotovka sploshnoi kollektivizatsii Belorusskoi SSR (1927–1929 gg.): sbornik dokumentov i materialov (Minsk, 1976).

Potapenko, M.S., *Partiinaya rabota v derevne (1924–1925 gg.)* (1972).

Programmy i ustavy KPSS (1969).

Pyatnadtsatyi s''ezd VKP(b) Dekabr' 1927 goda: stenograficheskii otchet, two vols (1962).
Rabota RKI ot V k VI s''ezdu Sovetov (1931).
Resheniya partii i pravitel'stva po khozyaistvennym voprosam. Sbornik dokumentov za 50 let, vols 2 and 3 (1967).
Rol' partiinogo kontrolya v rukovodyashchei deyatel'nosti KPSS (1978).
Rostovskaya oblastnaya organizatsiya KPSS v tsifrakh, 1917–1975 (Rostov, 1976).
Saratovskaya partiinaya organizatsiya v period nastupleniya sotsializma po vsemu frontu. Sozdanie kolkhoznogo stroya: dokumenty i materialy 1930–1932 gg. (Saratov, 1961).
Sdvigi v sel'skom khozyaistve SSSR mezhdu XV i XVI partiinymi s''ezdami: statisticheskie svedeniya po sel'skomu khozyaistvu za 1927–1930 gg. (1st edn 1930 and 2nd edn 1931).
Sel'skoe khozyaistvo SSSR: ezhegodnik 1935 g. (1936).
Selunskaya, V.M., *Rabochie-dvadtsatipyatitysyachniki* (1964).
XVII (semnadtsatyi) s''ezd Vsesoyuznoi Kommunisticheskoi Partii (b) 26 yanvarya-10 fevralya 1934 g.: stenograficheskii otchet (1934).
Set' sel'skokhozyaistvennoi kooperatsii SSSR (1929).
Sharapov, G., *Razreshenie agrarnogo voprosa v Rossii posle pobedy oktyabr'skoi revolyutsii* (1961).
Sharova, P.N., *Kollektivizatsiya sel'skogo khozyaistva v Tsentral'no-chernozemnoi oblasti 1928–1932 gg.* (1963).
Sheboldaev, B.P., *Stat'i i rechi 1932–1933* (Rostov on Don, 1934).
Shestnadtsataya konferentsiya VKP (b): aprel' 1929 goda: stenograficheskii otchet (1962).
XVI (shestnadtsatyi) s''ezd Vsesoyuznoi Kommunisticheskoi Partii (b): stenograficheskii otchet (1930).
Smitten, E., *Sostav Vsesoyuznoi Kommunisticheskoi Partii (bolshevikov), po materialam partiinoi perepisi* (1927).
Spektor, N., *Partiya – organizator shefstva rabochikh nad derevnei* (1957).
Sobranie uzakonenii i rasporyazhenii RSFSR 1917–1949 (1920–50).
Sobranie zakonov i rasporyazhenii Raboche-Krest'yanskogo Pravitel'stva SSSR, 1934–1935 (1934–35).
Sobranie zakonov i rasporyashenii SSSR 1924–1929 (1925–50).
Sotsialisticheskoe stroitel'stvo SSSR: statisticheskii ezhegodnik (1934).
Sotsialisticheskoe stroitel'stvo SSSR: statisticheskii ezhegodnik (1935).
Sotsialisticheskoe stroitel'stvo SSSR: statisticheskii ezhegodnik (1936).
Sotsial'nyi i natsional'nyi sostav VKP (b): Itogi vsesoyuznoi partiinoi perepisi 1927 goda (1928).
Stalin, I.V., *Sochineniya*, vols 11 and 12 (1949).
Tomskaya oblastnaya partiinaya organizatsiya v tsifrakh, 1920–1975 gg. (Tomsk, 1975).
Trapeznikov, S.P., *Kommunisticheskaya partiya v period nastupleniya sotsializma po vsemu frontu. Pobeda kolkhoznogo stroya (1929–1932)* (1961).
Trapeznikov, S.P., *Istoricheskii opyt KPSS v osushchestvlenii leninskogo kooperativnogo plana* (1965).
Trinadtsatyi s''ezd RKP (b): Mai 1924 goda: stenograficheskii otchet (1963).

Vaganov, F.M., *Pravyi uklon v VKP (b) i ego razgrom, 1928–1930 gg.* (1970).
Volgogradskaya oblastnaya organizatsiya KPSS v tsifrakh, 1917–1978 (Volgograd, 1979).
XVIII (vosemnadtsatyi) s''ezd Vsesoyuznoi Kommunisticheskoi Partii (b) 10–21 marta 1939 g.: stenograficheskii otchet (1939).
Vsesoyuznaya Kommunisticheskaya Partiya (bolshevikov) v rezolyutsiyakh i resheniyakh s''ezdov, konferentsii i plenumov TsK, chast' 2, 1925–1939 (1941).
Vsesoyuznaya perepis' naseleniya 1926 goda, vol. 17 (1927).
Yakovlev, Ya. A., *Voprosy oganizatsii sotsialisticheskogo sel'skogo khozyaistva* (1933).
Yudachev, S.A., *Bor'ba KPSS za organisatsionno-khozyaistvennoe ukreplenie kolkhozov (1933–1934 gg.)* (1962).
Yudin, I.N., *Sotsial'naya baza rosta KPSS* (1973).
Zolotarev, N.A., *Vazhnyi etap organizatsionnogo ukrepleniya kommunisticheskoi partii (1929–1937 gg.)* (1979).

Works in English

Abramsky, C.A., and Williams, B.J., (eds), *Essays in Honour of E.H. Carr* (London, 1974).
Belov, F., *History of a Soviet Collective Farm* (London, 1956).
Benvenuti, F., 'Kirov in Soviet Politics, 1933–1934', unpublished discussion paper, Soviet Industrialisation Project Series No. 8, Centre for Russian and East European Studies, University of Birmingham, 1977.
Bernstein, T.P., 'Leadership and Mobilization in the Collectivization of Agriculture in China and Russia: A Comparison', unpublished Ph.D. thesis, Columbia University, 1970.
Carr, E.H., *The Bolshevik Revolution 1917–1923,* vol. 1 (London, 1950) and vol. 2 (London, 1951).
Carr, E.H., *The Interregnum 1923–1924* (London, 1954).
Carr, E.H., *Socialism in One Country,* vol. 1 (London, 1958) and vol. 2 (London, 1959).
Carr, E.H., *Foundations of a Planned Economy 1926–1929,* vol. 2 (London, 1971).
Carr, E.H., and Davies, R.W., *Foundations of a Planned Economy 1926–1929,* vol. 1 (London, 1969).
Chayanov, A.V., *The Theory of Peasant Economy* (Homeward, Illinois, 1966).
Cohen, S.F., *Bukharin and the Bolshevik Revolution: a Political Biography 1888–1938* (Oxford University Press, 1980).
Comparisons of the United States and Soviet Economies. Joint Economic Committee, Congress of the United States, Part 1 (Washington, 1959).
Conquest, R., *The Great Terror, Stalin's Purge of the Thirties* (London, 1968).
Cooper, J.M., Davies, R.W., and Wheatcroft, S.G., 'Contradictions in Soviet Industrialisation', unpublished discussion paper, Centre for Russian and East European Studies, University of Birmingham, 1977.
Dale, P., 'The "Landed Proletariat": Soviet Industrial Workers' Connections

with the Land 1929–1932', unpublished discussion paper presented at the West European Conference on Soviet Industry and the Working Class in the Inter-War Years, University of Birmingham, 1981.

Daniels, R.V., *The Conscience of the Revolution: Communist Opposition in Soviet Russia* (Cambridge, Mass., 1960).

Davies, R.W., 'The Soviet Economic Crisis of 1931–1933', unpublished discussion paper, Soviet Industrialisation Project Series No. 4, Centre for Russian and East European Studies, University of Birmingham, 1976.

Davies, R.W., *The Industrialisation of Soviet Russia, vol. 1. The Socialist Offensive. The Collectivisation of Soviet Agriculture, 1929–1930* (London, 1980).

Davies, R.W., *The Industrialisation of Soviet Russia, vol. 2. The Soviet Collective Farm, 1929–1930* (London, 1980).

Day, R.B., *Leon Trotsky and the Politics of Economic Isolation* (Cambridge, 1973).

Deutscher, I., *The Prophet Armed. Trotsky: 1879–1921* (Oxford, 1970).

Erlich, A., *The Soviet Industrialization Debate, 1924–1928* (Cambridge, Mass., 1960).

Fainsod, M., *How Russia is Ruled* (Cambridge, Mass., 1st ed. 1953 and 1970 revised ed.).

Fainsod, M., *Smolensk Under Soviet Rule* (London, 1958).

Fitzpatrick, S., (ed.), *Cultural Revolution in Russia, 1928–1931* (Bloomington and London, 1978).

Getty, J. Arch, 'The "Great Purges" Reconsidered. The Soviet Communist Party 1933–1939', unpublished Ph.D. thesis, Boston College, Mass., 1979.

Getty, J. Arch, *Origins of the Great Purges. The Soviet Communist Party Reconsidered, 1933–1938* (Cambridge, 1985).

Halpern, I.P., 'Stalin's Revolution: the Struggle to Collectivize Rural Russia, 1927–1933', unpublished Ph.D. thesis, Columbia University, 1965.

Haslam, J., 'Political Opposition to Stalin 1932–1936; the Background to the Terror', unpublished working paper, Soviet Industrialisation Project, Centre for Russian and East European Studies, University of Birmingham, 1983.

Heer, N.W., (ed.), *Politics and History in the Soviet Union* (Cambridge, Mass., 1971).

Hough, J.F., *The Soviet Prefects: The Local Party Organs in Industrial Decision-Making* (Cambridge, Mass., 1969).

Hough, J.F., and Fainsod, M., *How the Soviet Union is Governed* (Cambridge, Mass. and London, 1980).

Jasny, N., *The Socialized Agriculture of the U.S.S.R.: Plans and Performance* (Stanford, 1949).

Knei-Paz, B., *The Social and Political Thought of Leon Trotsky* (Oxford, 1979).

Lane, D.S., *Politics and Society in the USSR*, 2nd ed (London, 1978).

Lane, D.S., and O'Dell, F., *The Soviet Industrial Worker: Social Class, Education and Control* (Oxford, 1978).

Lewin, M., *Russian Peasants and Soviet Power: a Study of Collectivization* (London, 1968).

Male, D.J., *Russian Peasant Organization before Collectivization: a Study of Commune and Gathering, 1925–1930* (Cambridge, 1971).

Medvedev, R., *Let History Judge: The Origins and Consequences of Stalinism* (London, 1976).

Milbraith, L.W., *Political Participation. How and Why do People Get Involved in Politics?* (Chicago, 1965).

Miller, R., *'One Hundred Thousand Tractors': the MTS and the Development of Controls in Soviet Agriculture* (Cambridge, Mass., 1970).

Nove, A., *An Economic History of the USSR* (Penguin Books, London, 1976).

Nove, A., *Was Stalin Really Necessary? Some Problems of Soviet Political Economy* (London, 1964).

Pethybridge, R., *The Social Prelude to Stalinism* (London, 1977).

Ploss, S.I. *Conflict and Decision-Making in Soviet Russia: A Case-Study of Agricultural Policy, 1953–1963* (Princeton, 1965).

Rigby, T.H. *Communist Party Membership in the U.S.S.R., 1917–1967* (Princeton, 1968).

Sadler, A., 'The Party Organisation in the Soviet Enterprise, 1928–1934', unpublished M.Soc.Sci. thesis, Centre for Russian and East European Studies, University of Birmingham, 1979.

Service, R., *The Bolshevik Party in Revolution, 1917–1923. A Study in Organisational Change* (London, 1979).

Schapiro, L., *The Communist Party of the Soviet Union*, 1st edn (London, 1960).

Scott, D.J.R., *Russian Political Institutions* (London, 1969).

Shanin, T., *The Awkward Class: Political Sociology of Peasantry in a Developing Society: Russia, 1910–1925* (Oxford, 1972).

Shimotomai, N., 'The Kuban Affair and the Crisis of Kolkhoz Agriculture (1932–1933) – with Emphasis on the North Caucasus', unpublished paper presented at the SSRC, Conference on Soviet Economic Development in the 1930s, Centre for Russian and East European Studies, University of Birmingham, 1982.

Sholokov, M., *Virgin Soil Upturned* (Penguin Books, London, 1978).

Stalin, I.V., *Problems of Leninism* (Peking, 1976).

Stuart, R.C., (ed.), *The Soviet Rural Economy* (Totowa, New Jersey, 1984).

Taniuchi, Y., *The Village Gathering in Russia in Mid-1920s* (Centre for Russian and East European Studies, University of Birmingham, 1968).

Taniuchi, Y., 'A Note on the Urals-Siberian Method', unpublished discussion paper, Soviet Industrialisation Project Series No. 17, Centre for Russian and East European Studies, University of Birmingham, 1979.

Trotsky, L.D., *1905* (Penguin Books, London, 1971).

Tucker, R.C., (ed.), *Stalinism: Essays in Historical Perspective* (New York, 1977).

Vucinich, W.S., (ed.), *The Peasant in Nineteenth Century Russia* (Stanford, 1968).

Wheatcroft, S.G. 'Soviet Grain Production Statistics for the 1920s and the 1930s', unpublished discussion paper, Soviet Industrialisation Project Series No. 13, Centre for Russian and East European Studies, University of Birmingham, 1977.

Wheatcroft, S.G., 'Famine and Factors Affecting Mortality in the USSR: The Demographic Crisis of 1914–1922 and 1930–1933', Appendices, unpublished discussion paper, Soviet Industrialisation Project Series No. 21, Centre for Russian and East European Studies, University of Birmingham, 1982.

Wheatcroft, S.G., 'A Re-evaluation of Soviet Agricultural Production in the 1920s and 1930s', unpublished discussion paper presented at the SSRC Conference on Soviet Economic Development in the 1930s, Centre for Russian and East European Studies, University of Birmingham, 1982.

Wheatcroft, S.G., Davies, R.W., and Cooper, J.M., 'Soviet Industrialisation Reconsidered: Some Preliminary Conclusions about Economic Development between 1926 and 1941', unpublished discussion paper presented at the SSRC Conference on Soviet Economic Development in the 1930s, Centre for Russian and East European Studies, University of Birmingham, 1982.

Zagoria, J.D., (ed.), *Power and the Soviet Elite. 'The Letter of an Old Bolshevik' and Other Essays by Boris I. Nicolaevsky* (Michigan, 1975).

Zaleski, E., *Planning for Economic Growth in the Soviet Union, 1918–1932* (American ed., Chapel Hill, 1969).

Glossary

This glossary is presented in addition to a number of definitions and explanations provided in the text and footnotes.

Aktiv Activists in the communist party. During the 1920s this category included those who read party literature and attended meetings; during the first Five Year Plan emphasis was focused on the need to participate in production work.

Artel See *Kolkhoz*.

Batrak Landless agricultural labourer. See Chapter 1, note 36.

Guberniya Largest unit of local administration in pre-revolutionary Russia, retained to the mid-1920s, when gradually replaced by the *oblast* and *krai*. See Figure 4.1 and Table 4.1.

Gubkom Party committee at the *guberniya* level.

Hectare Unit of area – 2.47 acres.

Khlebotsentr All Russian Union of Agricultural Cooperatives for the Production, Processing and Sale of Grains and Oil Feeds.

Khutor A fully enclosed farm holding where the land and the house were consolidated on one piece of land.

Kolkhoz A collective farm. There were three types of collective farm: (a) the commune (*kommuna*) in which all land, animals and capital were collectivised; (b) the *artel* in which principal animals, capital and land were incorporated into the collective farm; (c) the *toz* (*Tovarishchestvo dlya obshchestvennoi obrabotki zemli*) in which peasants cultivated the land jointly but land, animals and capital not collectivised. See Chapter 1, note 14.

Kolkhoznik Member of a collective farm.

Kolkhoztsentr All Russian (from November 1929 All Union) Union of Agricultural Collectives.

Kommuna See *Kolkhoz*.

Komsomol Young Communist League.

Komvuz Party institution of higher education.

Krai Unit of local administration which together with the *oblast* replaced the *guberniya*. See Figure 4.1 and Table 4.1.

Kraikom Party committee at the *krai* level.

Kulak A rich peasant. See Chapter 1, note 36.

Mir A traditional peasant institution to control the land and redistribute it periodically among its member households. See Chapter 1, note 3.

Narkomtorg People's Commissariat of Trade.

Narkomzem People's Commissariat of Agriculture.

Nomenklatura Posts and appointments which require the approval of a relevant party committee.

Oblast Unit of local administration which replaced the *guberniya*. See Figure 4.1 and Table 4.1.

Obkom Party committee at the *oblast* level.

Oblispolkom *Oblast* executive committee. Local government committee at the *oblast* level.

242

Okrug Middle-level unit of local government between the *raion* and *oblast* which replaced the uezd, but was abolished in 1930. See Figure 4.1 and Table 4.1.

Okruzhkom Party committee at the *okrug* level.

Orginst Organisational-instruction department within party committees.

Otkhodnik Peasant who undertook seasonal work in a town.

Otrub A farm holding detached from the *mir* system where the land was consolidated in one place, but apart from the house. See Chapter 1, note 20.

Otdel Rukovodyashchikh Partiinykh Organov Department of leading party organs. Departments which existed from 1934 to 1939 and dealt with the selection and deployment of party cadres in the *obkoms* and *raikoms*.

Po Sovmestitel'stvu To work in a party post whilst receiving remuneration from other, generally part-time, employment.

Prodrazverstka Term used to describe a system of expropriation of agricultural surpluses from the peasants, employed during the period of War Communism in the Civil War.

Raikom Party committee at the *raion* level. See Figure 4.2.

Raion Unit of local administration immediately superior to the rural Soviet area and, until its abolition, below the *okrug*. Replaced the former *volost*. See Figure 4.1.

Raizo *Raion* land department.

Razukrupnenie Term used to refer to the breaking down in size of party units.

Skhod Gathering of heads of households in the *mir*.

Smychka Term used to refer to the link between workers and peasants based on association of their political and economic interests.

Sovkhoz A state farm.

Sovnarkom Council of People's Commissars.

Soyuzkhleb All Union Association (*Ob"edinenie*) of *Narkomtorg*.

Stazh Length of party membership.

Toz See *Kolkhoz*.

Traktorotsentr All Union Centre of Machine Tractor Stations.

Uezd Middle level of local government in pre-revolutionary Russia, retained until the mid-1920s when superseded by the larger *okrug*. See Figure 4.1.

Ukom Party committee at the *uezd* level.

Volkom Party committee at the *volost* level.

Volost Lowest level of local administration in pre-revolutionary times, below the *uezd*. See Figure 4.1.

Zavorg The head of the organisation-instruction department in party committees. Often the deputy first secretary in the party committee.

Index